Computerized Accounting Methods and Controls

COMPUTERIZED ACCOUNTING METHODS AND CONTROLS

Michael R. Tyran

PRENTICE-HALL, INC.

Englewood Cliffs, New Jersey

PRENTICE-HALL INTERNATIONAL, INC., *London*
PRENTICE-HALL OF AUSTRALIA, PTY. LTD., *Sydney*
PRENTICE-HALL OF CANADA, LTD., *Toronto*
PRENTICE-HALL OF INDIA PRIVATE LTD., *New Delhi*
PRENTICE-HALL OF JAPAN, INC., *Tokyo*

LIBRARY OF CONGRESS
CATALOG CARD NUMBER: 74–174631

Ninth Printing . . . . . February, 1978

PRINTED IN THE UNITED STATES OF AMERICA
ISBN–0–13–166090–X
B & P

To my wife, Betty M. Tyran,
for her tremendous patience during the
many hours devoted to writing this book
and
Messrs J. D. Eiland and T. L. McPherson,
General Dynamics Controllers, for their
continued support and for providing me
the opportunity to pursue the state-of-
the-art techniques for the computerization
and advancement of accounting, budgeting
and simulation model practices.

The Author

Michael R. Tyran is Assistant to the Controller, Pomona Division of the General Dynamics Corporation. He has designed, developed and supervised a wide variety of computerized financial information systems, including the STAR-FIRE Program at Lockheed Missiles and General Dynamics.

He is a popular speaker and has written articles for *Management Accounting, Management Services* and budgeting publications. A graduate of Rider College with an M.B.A. from the University of Southern California, the author is the only two-time winner of the National Association of Accountants' Lybrand Gold Medal for outstanding contribution to accounting literature. The Association has also presented him with three Certificates of Merit and a Certificate of Recognition. He is presently Vice President of the National Association's Pomona Chapter and Director of Manuscripts.

The Benefits This Book Offers

This book will assist Directors of Financial Operations, Controllers, Project Financial Officers, Accounting and Budgeting Organization Managers as well as their pertinent Sectional Supervision in the following processes:

- The approach to a systematic review of their Accounting functions and the techniques used in designing, developing and installing a completely automated Accounting System which is a prerequisite to introducing sophisticated managerial techniques.

- The "how to" in constructing financial data banks, their utilization and benefits in information processing.

- The procedures involved in integrating financial data mechanically in order to achieve multifile updating and reporting.

- The ultimate in improvement of informal as well as external controls in the recording, processing and reporting of financial data in the computerized environment.

- The acceleration and improvement in the decision-making process resulting from timely and succinct display of relevant and pertinent information associated with that activity. This will be achieved through resident preconceived parameter applications by the computer program.

- The decrease in financial document flow and associated detailed clerical activities thus increasing the organization's analysis and planning capabilities.

- The step-by-step approach to mechanizing an important Management control tool —budgets and forecasts. The financial direction will be developed by the computer based on operating plans and predetermined application factors. Mechanization will provide the capability for a flexible budgeting system for making varied changes. Mechanically, the financial implications and feasibility of a plan can be simulated in advance, thus providing Management with more visibility into future anticipated results before action is taken.

9

- This book will describe the requirements for obtaining more meaningful financial data at various levels of responsibility in order to meet different needs of the Accounting line supervision.

- Improvement of an organization's cash position by more rapid and thorough mechanical billing resulting from more timely and detailed cost collection with less operating supervision (performance criteria), the planners, financial management, clerical effort.

- The approach to monitor mechanically an organization's travel expenses and at the same time maintain a detailed reconciliation of each traveler's status with respect to the return of unused travel advances, justification of expenditures and evaluation of trip results.

- The establishment of controls for monitoring computer utilization and costs and the requirements concerned with equitable distribution of computer costs to the concerned users.

- The mechanical comparison of actuals to the financial plan will provide Management an advantageous basis for making intelligent decisions and/or taking appropriate actions.

- Automated Accounting will provide Management with the results of their operations on the day following the closing of the books rather than two to four weeks later which is the current situation in most all organizations.

- The procedures presented utilize mechanical statistical techniques such as correlation, scattergraphs, econometrics, etc. in the development of budgets and analyzing the results of operations.

- Mechanical procedures will provide a dynamic approach to an organization's recordkeeping process in that the computerized system will manipulate the data mechanically and output summary and report requirements—further, the records will be "on call" as needed.

- This book covers the mechanical means for monitoring and recording employee attendance as well as distributing the costs to the appropriate product, contract and organization.

- This book arms the reader with the ideas, the guidelines, the pertinent requirements for preparing himself to meet the challenge. It will detail direct comunication processing and its prerequisites.

MICHAEL R. TYRAN

Contents

CONTENTS

14. THE EFFECTIVE MANAGEMENT BUDGET AND FORECASTING PROGRAM (Continued)

1

Gathering the Data for the
Automated Accounting System

Dynamic management reporting is achieved by planning the ultimate objectives and then establishing the means to attain them. An automated accounting system can accomplish these objectives but effort must be initiated at the basic data source; that is, the lowest level of transaction in terms of cost, commitment and/or other document information.

TYPES OF ACCOUNTING DATA

All accounting information and reporting can be divided into three categories which provide different summaries of data that are significant to meet varying user requirements.

Exhibit A displays the type of information at the three levels of reporting which result in an end data product peculiar to satisfying specific needs.

Operating Data

The lowest information level on this chart indicates that transactions occurring from an organization's activities provide reporting at the detailed level and functionally represent the basic record of "what happened."

This information is used primarily by operating organizations to monitor detailed performance and schedule and provide the basic data for the hierarchy summary reporting.

The reporting at this level is concerned with data associated with design, engineering, production, inspection, etc. of products and performance. It would also include the initiation and placement of purchase orders resulting in vendor commitments, customer invoicing, acquiring fixed assets, paying vendors and employes—all of which represent operating transaction data. Appropriate compilation of this information results in reports such as labor distribution, payroll, expense and cost ledgers and other operating transaction records.

Tactical Information

In order to control an organization's operations, a summary of the operating information must be made to provide higher level management with appropriate data summaries which can portray an organization's activity and progress in terms of plan, action and control performance.

As noted in Exhibit A, data is summarized into the general ledger account structure

ESTIMATE OF THE SITUATION

SIMULATION MODELS
CRITICAL DATA

ACTION DIRECTION
DECISIONS

STRATEGIC (PLANNING)

SUMMARY
SELECTIVE DATA

OPERATION
MANAGEMENT
CONTROLS

TACTICAL (CONTROL)

ACTIVITY
TRANSACTIONS

REPORTS

OPERATING (FUNCTIONAL)

LABOR DISTRIBUTION / PAYROLL
ACCOUNTS PAYABLE / INVENTORY
COST / EXPENSE LEDGER

GENERAL LEDGER / TRIAL BALANCE / FIXED ASSET
DEPRECIATION / NEW ORDERS BOOKED / BACKLOG
CONTRACT PROFIT & LOSS / ESTIMATING CRITERIA

FINANCIAL SCHEDULES / ASSET MANAGEMENT / MANAGEMENT
BUDGETS / FORECASTS / SELECTIVE "GAMING DETAIL"

Exhibit A

and trial balance which provides account detail for analysis and overview of financial operations' status. New orders and profit or losses are assessed and reported by contract, product line, customer, type contract and backlog effects. Tactical information highlights problem areas in those and other specific financial reporting. The data is accumulated and reported in formats that are readily understood and/or actually designated by management. Through review and analysis of this data, management is able to monitor the actual versus planned effort and take action for correcting inadequacies by redirecting effort.

Strategic Data

The next level of information is summarized to satisfy top level management requirements. Strategic data is used in simulating alternate courses of action and is a tool which allows management the capability of viewing their overall financial operations in terms of required and/or critical needs.

Overview financial schedules are prepared which incorporate such statistics as working capital position, inventory balances, ratio of current assets to liabilities, net investment, profit and its associated detail. Meaningful, selective and exception reporting requires minimal management review and analysis in assessing a situation and making the appropriate decisions.

The above information differentiation, therefore, reflects the building of a precise accountng model or system which will fulfill dynamic management reporting needs at the appropriate level of information.

ANALYSIS OF MANUAL OPERATIONS

The first prerequisite to the development of an overall automated accounting system is to prepare a plan for the complete analysis of the manual operations and semi-mechanical programs (if they exist). This is necessary in order to establish a systematic approach in the review of source documentation, its processing, recording, summation and reporting.

After the plan, objectives and/or requirements have been prepared and approved, the next determination involves the level of manpower effort and the type of personnel required. Depending upon the size and complexity of the organization, analysts should be assigned to each functional area to work with the user organizations with two or three analysts assuming the task for more detailed overall planning of data integration and top management reporting needs.

Exhibit B displays the general procedure for assessing manual accounting operations to establish the basis for the mechanization process. If an organization is semi-automated, the same type of analysis is necessary in order to resolve all of the input that is available, its processing, integration and reporting.

AUTOMATED ACCOUNTING SYSTEMS

After the detailed investigation of the manual operations has been completed, evaluated and resolved with the user organizations as to validity of input records, processing and reporting involved, then the procedures are initiated for the mechanization of the accounting requirements.

Exhibit C illustrates the type of tasks to be performed for the development of an automated system. An analysis of the manual process is made to determine adequacy of

INITIATING THE MANUAL OPERATION ASSESSMENT ACTION

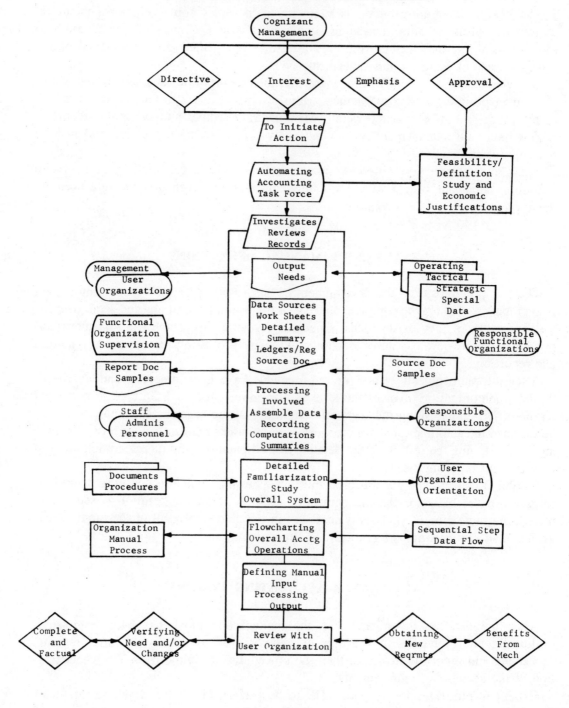

EXHIBIT B

DEVELOPING THE AUTOMATED SYSTEM

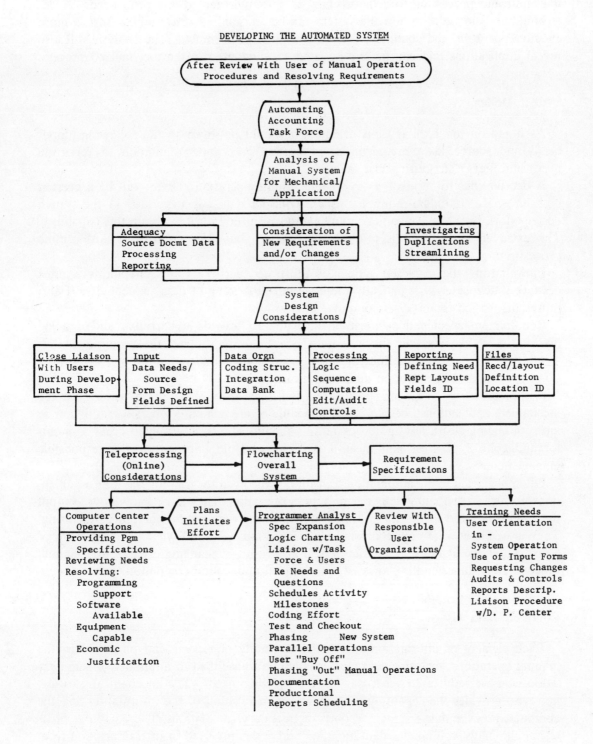

EXHIBIT C

the input and processing to achieve changed or supplemented reporting needs. A determination is made as to how the system can be reorganized or streamlined for a more effective operation and conducive for the computer environment. The analysis will also reveal duplications that can be consolidated or eliminated in the mechanized process.

System Design

As noted on the Exhibit C, consideration should be given to the following: input needs and source, data organization, processing procedures, definition of reporting needs and file(s) structuring and layout.

A decision has to be made as to whether online operation activity will be a current or future need. If online requirements are considered and incorporated in the system design effort, it will save countless hours and costs in the future to obtain this capability. The extra effort involved is minimal in making data files compatible with online processing.

Flowcharting the proposed system as illustrated earlier in this chapter is a must because it delineates systematically the flow and processing of data sequentially. It also represents the jobstream(s) of computer processing.

Requirement specifications must be prepared to provide a narrative and detailed description of all facets of the automated system proposal and the requirements. It should be reviewed with the user organizations for their understanding of the automation approach and the effect on their operations.

As noted in Exhibit C, the specification will have to be generally expanded for the mechanical application process. A time schedule of the computer operation activities in terms of coding effort, test and checkout, paralleling, etc. is necessary in order to monitor and control progress and meet a possible schedule imposed by the responsible management.

Often neglected in the automation transition is the need for training the user organizations in their participating activities of system operation. They must know how to input the appropriate and significant information in the form required for computer processing. They must know what data controls have been established and what type and form of reporting will be available. Automation will also result in changing organization manual procedures of data handling to satisfy mechanical application compatibility.

Common Data Usage

Each element of information is used for a variety of reports and purposes. In the manual operations, the same data element may be transcribed to a number of summary worksheets or ledgers to meet particular reporting needs. The mechanical process, however, provides the capability for a one-time acquisition of the information and the computer uses the data for many reports or necessary calculations. The computer processing eliminates voluminous data handling and errors involved in its transcription from one record to another.

Exhibit D illustrates the usage of labor data for various purposes.

As noted in the exhibit, labor data is associated or used in practically every functional organization for one reason or another. It is required for product costing, identified to

COMMON DATA USAGE

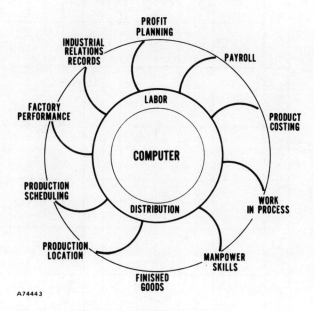

EXHIBIT D

location of effort involved, workload scheduling, performance measurement, payroll, personnel records, etc.

Every detail concerned with labor cost or manpower is closely monitored, interpreted, controlled and reported. Data is collected by individual organization, task and contract as shown in Exhibit E.

DATA FLOW AND USAGE
(LABOR)

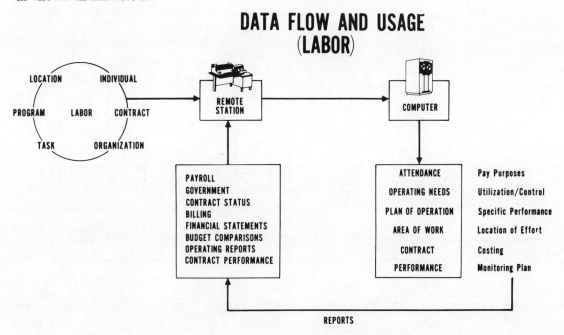

EXHIBIT E

PROFIT AND LOSS DATA FLOW

| INPUT FROM | | | | DATA | INPUT TO | | | | | | | |
Devel-oped	Cost Led	Exp Led	Blng		JV	Gen Led	Accts Rec	Accts Pay	Cash Recpts	Cash Disburs	Bklog Syst	WIP TB
			O	Sales	O	O	O		O		O	
	O	O		Cost of Sales	O	O		O		O		O
O				Gross Profit								
	O	O		General/Admin. Expense	O	O		O		O		O
	O	O		Proposal/Bidding "	O	O		O		O		O
	O	O		Independent Developmt	O	O		O		O		O
	O	O		Selling Expense	O	O		O		O		O
O				Profit fr Operations								
				Other Income/Expense								
			O	Interest Income	O	O	O		O			
			O	Royalty Income	O	O	O		O			
		O		Interest Expense	O	O		O		O		
			O	Sale of Fixed Assets	O	O	O		O			
O				Profit Before Taxes	O	O						
O				Provision for Taxes				O		O		
O				Net Income	O	O						

EXHIBIT F

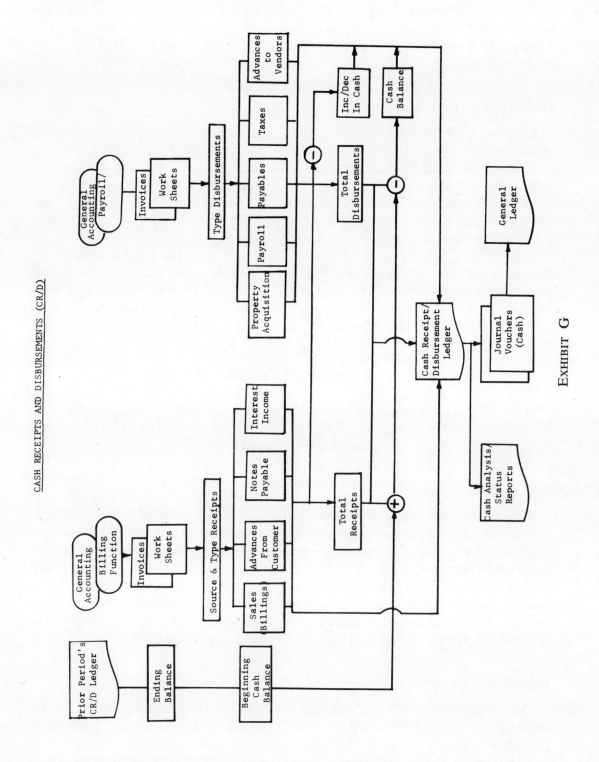

EXHIBIT G

The computer processes this data for various reports as shown in this exhibit. The same type of illustration can be prepared for all elements of cost to illustrate its usage. The data developed from this type of research is necessary for integration planning and storage file banks.

Charting Data Requirements

There are a number of means to determine data requirements and its flow, but two of the more effective and conducive for understanding are illustrated in Exhibits F and G.

Exhibit F illustrates in a columnar chart form the source of data and its input into various records and report summaries. For example, sales derived from the billing invoice process are recorded as a journal voucher, entered into the general ledger, and subsequently affects the accounts receivable in your balance sheet, the cash receipts in your cash schedule and the backlog balance.

Exhibit G, on the other hand, provides in flowchart form the input and its source, processing and the output reporting. In this exhibit, it is shown that there are various sources for cash receipts and types of disbursements which will provide data as to increases or decreases in the cash balance. This information is journalized, enters the general ledger and is further reported in detail in the cash schedule and status reports.

DATA BANK DEVELOPMENT

In the planning and development of the automated accounting system, consideration and effort should be devoted to the effective storage of data. This can be accomplished through the means and use of the data bank concept.

Role of Data Banks

A data bank is defined as predetermined file record locations which serve as a depository for information. There are various levels of data banks, dependent upon their need and usage. For example, a detailed or incremental labor bank would contain current data such as hours and dollars relative to an employee, organization, contract, product line, etc., and associated possibly to similar budget and/or forecast data.

The data banks can be constructed in terms of individual or collective elements (as in the case of data integration) in order to achieve minimal extraction requirements. The banks must contain sufficient flexibility so that changes to the data can be readily made.

Organization of Data

The information in the files must be organized to meet varying needs both for online processing and batch reporting. An example of a detailed file is shown in Exhibit H.

There are five record files in a mechanical backlog system. Depending upon organization needs, there could be more or less.

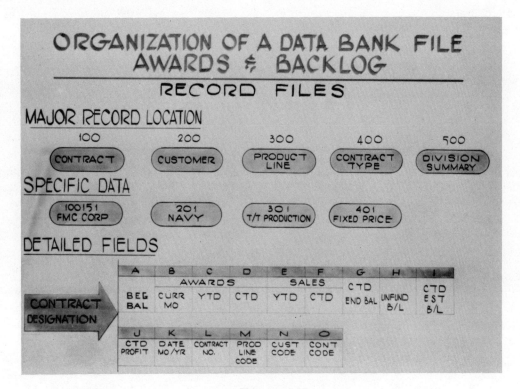

EXHIBIT H

When an award or sales order is inputted into the system, it is identified to a contract code, customer, product line and contract type. The identification inputted is by code assignment numbers which are recognized by the table file which contains descriptions and locations of specific data. For example, the "100" identifies the input to the contract file location and with the addition of the contract code as shown under the specific data illustration of "151", a specific contract is identified. The coding of the other files is a little different. The "200" identifies the input for the customer file but the last character in that number identification (201) refers to a specific customer—in this case, "Navy". A "2" could be for Army, "3" for Foreign, etc. The same coding technique applies to the product line, contract type and division summary.

Each major location is also linked to its detailed fields. The letter designation identifies the location of specific items. This allows for a capability to retrieve online specific information. For example, if a person wanted to know the "year-to-date sales" for contract code "151", he would query the file with the following message:

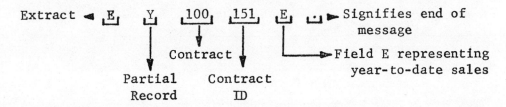

If the complete record for the customer "Navy" was required, the message would be as follows:

Extract ◄ E X 201 ⸱⸱ ► Signifies end of
                                message

Complete
Record ──────► Complete record for the Navy
                            as a customer

File organization is very important for rapid access to any desired location for specific items of data or the complete record itself.

Master Summary Files

When data enters into the mechanical process, it is directed by the computer program monitor or controller for processing in accordance with the program instructions. The data is then used to update the appropriate disk files. For example, Exhibit I displays subsystem banks (travel, property, expense, etc.) which are used for updating summary file banks.

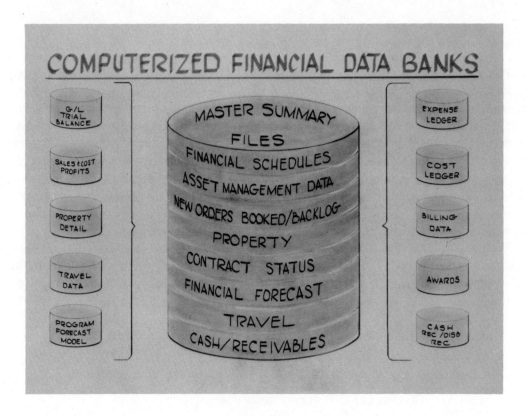

Exhibit I

The subsystem banks are collection files which are used for reporting detailed information. For example, the "general ledger/trial balance" file contains data by account number. The identification is lost, however, when the data is summarized for the classification contained on the financial schedules. The subsystem banks preclude the need for manual maintenance of registers, ledgers and worksheets.

Online retrieval needs are easily met through the use of data banks. Each file has an exact location and data within it is specifically identified.

File Updating

Update process. The data banks are updated through the sort processing of the detailed input. The value of the incoming record is added to each data bank level signified in its identity. Some records do not contain all levels of activity (contract, work order, class, function, segment, etc.). The values are also added to control totals for summary reporting.

The time span accumulations are also considered in the update process. Totals would be derived for the week (in the case of daily activity), month, year-to-date and inception-to-date.

Multifile process. A number of files can be updated simultaneously. Referring back to Exhibit F, when new business or sales activity are inputted to a contract, its complete record is adjusted. The input data is reflected in year-to-date and cumulative-to-date totals as well as changes the backlog balances. These changes are then reflected automatically and simultaneously in the customer, product line, contract type and division summary files. All of the file-recorded data can be updated in seconds using the online update process.

Output Determination

Output needs are predicated on the type of information required to monitor performance, accumulate costs, bill a customer, pay a vendor or assess the financial position of an organization as a result of its operations. The users of the information whether operational, accountants or management naturally are the best source in determining the data reporting requirements. The output must reflect the ultimate specific usage. Exhibit J illustrates the type of data, its usage and required reports which represents the basic output common to most organizations.

EDIT AND AUDIT CONTROLS

In the ever-changing environment of increasing mechanical processes, the computer has become the major source for financial and management reports. In order to entrust the validity of cost data input and manipulation to a computerized process, it is mandatory that a capability be established to control and reject within the various involved processes data which is extraneous, irrelevant and/or inaccurate. The system must be

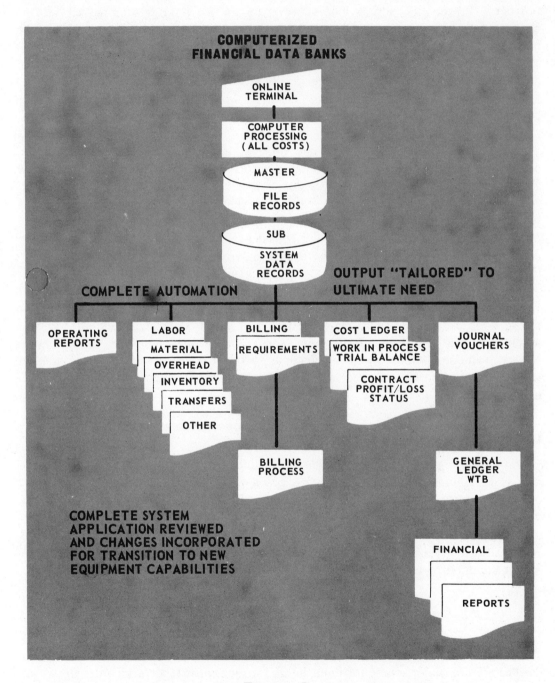

EXHIBIT J

able to properly identify and eliminate the information before it is processed, finalized and reflected in the ultimate reporting.

Edit Controls

These controls are defined as "internal" program type which initially police such data as follows before the audit control check is made:

- Program identifiers
- Data location in the files
- Table or description files
- Numeric/alpha fields
- Length of fields in a record
- Codes
- Blank or filler acceptance
- Transaction designator

These controls are built into the system and rejection is made if the input data does not meet the criteria specified in the program.

Audit Controls

These controls are concerned primarily with monitoring the validity of data being inputted into the system such as the master audit file usage for the cost accumulation system. A specific example of the controls possible with respect to the general ledger is noted as follows.

General Ledger Account Audit

- Journal Voucher Association—In order to restrict the transaction from the account file, it is necessary that each journal voucher be associated with a general ledger account. This will preclude the entrance of an invalid entry into the account bank.

- Subaccount—This sub number is assigned in order to further define the reporting of detail within the control account. It should be associated with the control account in order that invalid sub data does not gain entrance into the control account file.

- Submitting Organization—The organization associated to general ledger account will prohibit data entrance if that organization does not have responsibility to submit this type of input.

- Reporting Schedule—Each general ledger account must be identified to a reporting schedule in order that its output can be properly included in the appropriate financial schedule. This will preclude the entrance of account data into financial schedules where they do not belong.

Different functional areas, of course, have their own varying control numbers that can be inputted into the system for auditing their data—for example, procurement and purchase orders; accounts payable and vendor invoices; travel and travel order and expense documents.

Benefits

There are a number of benefits to be derived from the data bank implementation, and these are summarized on Exhibit K. The banks are the source for multi-reporting purposes and should be tailored to reflect the needs of reporting. Periodically, a "purging" process is required to delete from the file records that information which has served its current reporting needs and is transferred to history files.

BENEFITS FROM IMPLEMENTATION OF DATA BANKS

- ACCELERATED MONTHLY CLOSING
- AVAILABILITY OF DETAILED & SUMMARY DATA
- FLEXIBILITY IN REPORTING
- GREATER ACCURACY IN DATA COLLECTION & REPORTING
- CENTRALIZED FILES
- DATA INTEGRATION
- MORE EFFECTIVE UTILIZATION OF COMPUTERS
- HISTORICAL DATA AVAILABILITY
- OPERATING IN THE ONLINE ENVIRONMENT
- DECREASED CLERICAL EFFORT

EXHIBIT K

2

Organizing the Cost Accumulation
and Control Structure

The primary objective of the Cost Accumulation System is to satisfy management requirements with respect to properly identifying costs to their elements (labor, overhead, material, etc.) to the contract and/or product, to the organization performing or benefiting (budget authorization) and accurate and timely information to all levels of reporting.

INITIAL PROCESSING PROCEDURE

After a contract or sales order is negotiated, certain steps have to be taken in order to accumulate, record and report costs against a contract (product or service). When the sales order or contract is received, it is analyzed as to who or what organization will actually perform certain functions of that contract.

Generally, an expenditure authorization is prepared which allows certain organizations the authority to expend time, material and other costs to accomplish the requirements of the contract or sales order. An identification is placed on this authorization which relates it specifically to the items specified in the agreement. In addition, there is a work authorization and accounting work order assignment made to further identify costs that are accumulated against the order/contract. As work progresses and labor time is spent or material is utilized, these costs are recorded against the contract, work order, work authorization number and the information forwarded to the accounting area where it is recorded in ledgers and reported in contract or sales status reports. The general procedure followed in the action process and the built-in controls are displayed in Exhibit A.

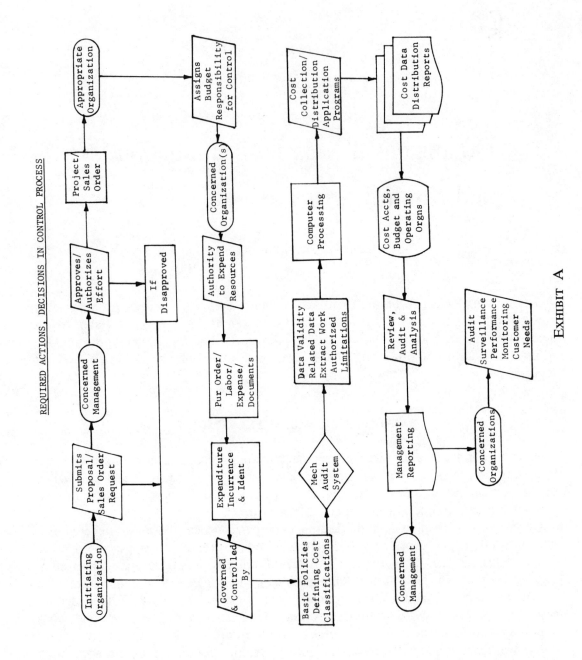

REQUIRED ACTIONS, DECISIONS IN CONTROL PROCESS

EXHIBIT A

COST ACCUMULATION STRUCTURE

No cost collection system can be efficient, flexible and successful without a sophisticated and detailed cost accumulation structure that will provide and consider all aspects of data identification needs. As noted in Exhibit B, there are four inventory identifications in the record files which allow for storage and reporting capability by the indicated classifications.

COST ACCUMULATION BREAKDOWN STRUCTURE

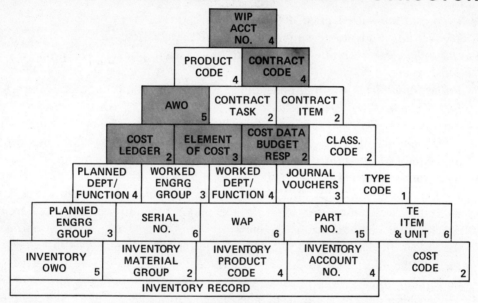

Exhibit B

With respect to the work in process accounts, there are 21 levels of data segregation. The levels of data for work in process information are summarized from the cost code classification up through contracts and general ledger (WIP) account as shown on the exhibit. Cost data is maintained and updated in the files for satisfying retrieval and reporting needs. The breakdown structure displayed in one organization was expanded considerably from the original needs as represented by the shady areas on the exhibit resulting from customer and internal reporting requirements.

Costs are collected and related to requirements involved with the basic product, product line, contract, task, performance and financial reporting which result from the needs of operations, management, customer and legal.

Direct Versus Indirect Costs

Direct costs are those that can be specifically identified to an organization's product or service. Work is performed through work order assignment or other classifications consistent with effort identification. These costs consist of direct labor, direct material or inventory, work in process and pertinent overhead expenses.

Indirect costs—support type expenditures which do not contribute directly or are unidentifiable to an end product—represent costs for administration, management, control, selling or reporting functions.

Structure Descriptions

A definition of some of the identifiers in the work order structure is noted below to satisfy reporting needs.

1. *Cost code*—Army, Navy, Air Force, etc.
2. *Type contract*—fixed price, CPFF, commercial, etc.
3. *Product line*—missile development, product, support, etc.
4. *General ledger account*—cost type contract, fixed price, WIP, property, inter-division, etc.
5. *Project identifier*—a 2-digit code which will identify the cost to the contract.
6. *Identification work order*—this is a 4-digit number of which the first 2 digits identify the project and the last 2 digits indicate the major function of the contract.
7. *Functional activity*—this is a 4-digit number which further breaks down the identity of the task performed and the cost incurred; or it may also signify specialized type work performed.
8. *Organization*—the work breakdown structure should include the detail for organization association; for example, the major function would be research and development, manufacturing, engineering, etc. The next two digits would identify the task to the second level which could be the department. The last digit could identify the effort to a section or control center which could be a specific group performing the task.
9. *Task*—this would be a 4-digit number which further refines and identifies the cost or effort to a lower level of reporting. This reporting would be primarily used by an operating organization in measuring the performance, costing the operation, establishing standards of operation, etc.

In order to distribute cost properly, the identifiers should be inputted into the system from basic source documents (vendor invoices, shop orders, time cards, material requisitions, etc.) and accumulated in various data banks. Each transaction performed, whether it be a liability generated, a payment, billing to the customer, paying the employe, or charging a contract must be associated with a journal voucher in order to achieve its proper flow to a general ledger account.

Work in Process Breakdown

Exhibit C displays the structure of elements of cost identified and summarized to project budget centers, accounting work orders, contract items and their total and work in process account.

WORK-IN-PROCESS BREAKDOWN

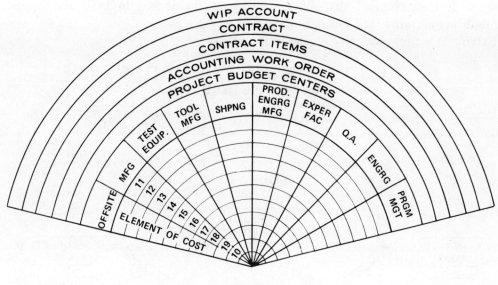

EXHIBIT C

The elements of cost considered include direct labor hours and amount, overtime, overhead, material, other direct costs, interdivision activity and corporate office expense.

As further noted in Exhibit C, there are ten project budget centers for which costs are accumulated by element. Budget centers are established to fulfill certain reporting needs for control and measuring performance. Organizations may have different requirements, but the processing would be approximately the same for a greater or lesser number of budget or cost centers.

The costs are summarized into accounting work orders which is the next hierarchy of cost accumulation and totaled to the contract or sales item level. The more than one items of a contract are then summarized to the contract total and the value of groups of contracts are reflected in the work in process account totals.

This system reflects two basic WIP account classifications, particularly in the aerospace industry—one for cost type contracts and the other for fixed price. Commercial endeavors also have various summaries of data in order to accommodate their summation processes.

Accounting Work Order (AWO)

There are many detailed functions falling within contract tasks which necessitate cost collection for performance review, detailed level control purposes and future contract estimating. Tasks are covered by a basic authority to perform work and an AWO is designated to which the effort and cost will be charged. A minimum of one AWO is required for each contract or other work authorization to support generation of direct charges. The number of AWOs assigned to a contract is dependent upon reporting needs. The four-digit alpha-numeric AWO, therefore, contains complete reference data to the work authority, basic work requirements and a guide to departments that incur charges. It is emphasized that all contract costs distributed to WIP and inventory accounts are accomplished through the use of AWO identifiers.

Exhibit D reflects the AWO master file record.

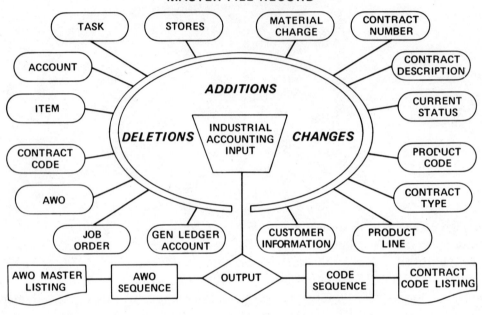

ACCOUNTING WORK ORDER
MASTER FILE RECORD

EXHIBIT D

As displayed, the record consists of various identifying data to serve a number of requirements. Additions, deletions and changes are a function of industrial accounting. Weekly reports by AWO and contract sequence identification are issued to concerned organizations for reference and utilization for proper cost assignments.

Cost Accumulation System

Exhibit E indicates the elements of cost and adjustments which are inputted into the system for generating the necessary files for the reporting requirements.

The source for the elements of cost data into this system is noted as follows:

- Labor hours and amounts in the detailed identifications discussed above are obtained from the labor distribution system which is generated from mechanical device and time card input.

- Overhead dollars are mechanically calculated on a basis of the overhead percent times direct labor dollars. The overhead percent is derived by mechanical computation using the expense ledger system and appropriate direct labor dollars base.

COST ACCUMULATION REPORTING

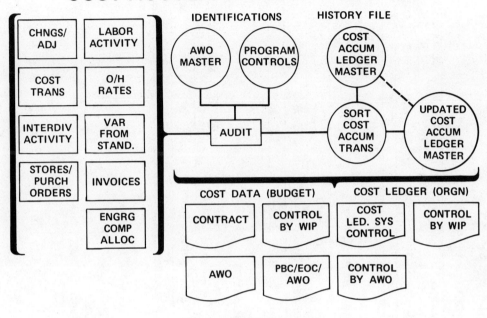

EXHIBIT E

- Material, other than from inventory requisition, and other direct costs are obtained from the mechanical accounts payable program.

- Adjustments and cost transfers are the result of manual entries prepared by various organizations and entered into the system through journal vouchers.

All of this data is identified, sorted and summarized to produce the cost collection file.

Cost Accumulation File Reporting

There are basically seven reports that emanate from the cost accumulation system. In Exhibit F will be noted the columnar headings for each of these reports.

As noted, they are quite similar with the exception of the control report by Work in Process in that it reflects data by journal voucher identification. Summary totals are shown by WIP account, product code, contract (code, item and task), element of cost, project budget center, classification code, AWO and journal voucher. The data is by month, year-to-date and cumulative-to-date.

The significant difference between the data maintained in the *project cost ledger* as versus the *cost data ledger* is in the distribution of labor and overhead costs. The costs shown in the project cost ledger for each burden center are those incurred by the center in which the work was performed. The cost data ledger reflects for each burden center those costs incurred for the benefit of a center regardless of where the work was performed. The cost ledger is maintained, primarily, for external and financial management

COST ACCUMULATION REPORTS

Cost Data/Ledger by Contract

WIP ACCT	PRODUCT CODE	CONTRACT			ELEMENT OF COST	PROJECT BUDGET CENTER	CLASS. CODE	JOURNAL VOUCHER NUMBER	CURRENT		YEAR-TO-DATE		CUMULATIVE-TO-DATE	
		CODE	ITEM	TASK					HRS	AMT	HRS	AMT	HRS	AMT
*	*	*			*	*	*							

Cost Data/Ledger by Accounting Work Order

WIP ACCT	PRODUCT CODE	CONTRACT			ELEMENT OF COST	PROJECT BUDGET CENTER	AWO	JOURNAL VOUCHER NUMBER	CURRENT		YEAR-TO-DATE		CUMULATIVE-TO-DATE	
		CODE	ITEM	TASK					HRS	AMT	HRS	AMT	HRS	AMT
*	*	*			*	*	*							

Cost Data by PBC/EOC/AWO

WIP ACCT	PRODUCT CODE	CONTRACT			ELEMENT OF COST	PROJECT BUDGET CENTER	AWO	JOURNAL VOUCHER NUMBER	CURRENT		YEAR-TO-DATE		CUMULATIVE-TO-DATE	
		CODE	ITEM	TASK					HRS	AMT	HRS	AMT	HRS	AMT
*	*	*			*	*	*							

Cost Data/Ledger Control by Work in Process

WIP ACCT	PROJECT BUDGET CENTER	ELEMENT OF COST	JOURNAL VOUCHER NUMBER	CURRENT		YEAR-TO-DATE		CUMULATIVE-TO-DATE	
				HRS	AMT	HRS	AMT	HRS	AMT
*	*	*	*						

*TOTALS SHOWN BY COLUMNAR HEADING

EXHIBIT F

requirements and provides a basis for billing completed WIP costs, allocation of overhead to direct dollars, work in process, trial balance and source of costs by contract totals. The cost data ledger provides a basis for budget performance reporting, contract redetermination schedules and general internal control totals for product hours, test equipment and tooling costs, assist work and management reporting.

Cost Accumulation Interface with Materials and Purchased Parts

Exhibit G displays the flow of data in the direct procurement system to the work in process cost collection program.

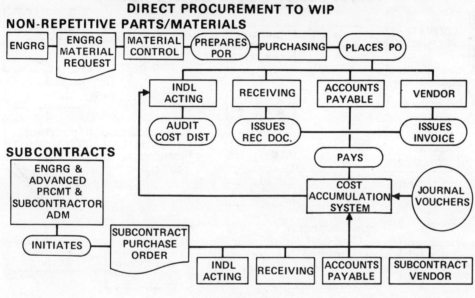

COST ACCUMULATION INTERFACE
Materials & Purchased Parts
DIRECT PROCUREMENT TO WIP

EXHIBIT G

Formal requests for material are prepared by engineering and forwarded to material control where they are screened for contract budget authorization and checked against internal inventory availability. If requirement is valid, then a purchase order request is placed on the purchasing organization who initiates the purchase order and negotiates the requirement with the vendor.

As shown in the exhibit, various organizations receive copies of the purchase order and industrial accounting performs an audit as to description and budget authorization and provides the cost distribution account identification.

When the items are received, a receiving document is issued and forwarded to accounts payable and purchasing for reconciliation purposes. The vendor's invoice is also forwarded to accounts payable who screen and compare it with the other related documents on file. This information flows mechanically into the cost accumulation system along with pertinent journal voucher data. Subcontract purchase order requirements are handled in almost the same manner as reflected on Exhibit G.

Cost System Compatibility with Proposal Data Flow

In developing the basic mechanical cost accumulation system, it is mandatory that its compatibility be achieved with the new business bids, sales orders, proposals and the negotiated budget. This is absolutely necessary for proper comparisons and reconciliation of the data throughout the cost recording and reporting cycle. Exhibit H indicates that the proposal estimates are generally prepared by the "grass roots" or operating level.

COST ACCUMULATION SYSTEM COMPATIBILITY WITH PROPOSAL DATA FLOW

EXHIBIT H

The data is forwarded to the estimating department where it is audited for proposal guidelines, consistency and reasonableness based on past performance and then consolidated into a complete formal overall proposal.

The contract organization negotiates the proposal with the customer and the approved document or contract is forwarded to the budget department where the budget is developed in detail and control responsibility assigned. The actual results are compared and evaluated against the original proposal estimate.

This interfaced process represents the capability required to monitor data from the point of plan development through the actual cost collection and reporting process. Management is able, in this environment, to effectively review and control detailed progress and performance of the effort planned and contracted in the proposal against actual costs incurred.

Interface with Financial Management Reporting

In addition to the interface relationship with procurement, proposals, budget and other activities, the cost collection system is the major source of information for management reporting. The detailed cost data is entered through journal vouchers into the cost accumulation file. This file is used for various purposes as shown in Exhibit I.

COST ACCUMULATION SYSTEM
INTERFACE WITH FINANCIAL MANAGEMENT REPORTING

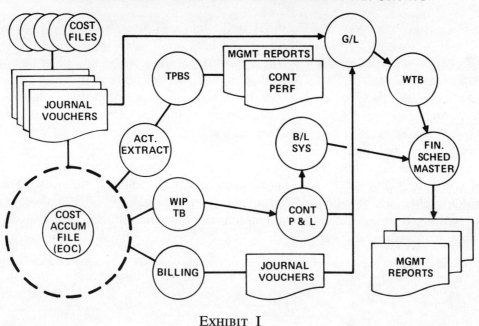

EXHIBIT I

Actual costs are extracted from the file at the appropriate level for utilization in the time-phased budget system where a comparison is made to ascertain performance status and variances. Selective reporting is achieved by establishing criteria that necessitates output of only that data requiring attention as, for example, over and underruns, schedule delays, etc.

WORK IN PROCESS TRIAL BALANCE

Actual information is also used for the work in process trial balance which includes total costs incurred, bid and proposal, independent development and research and development expenses, transfers to other divisions, cost of sales and work in process balance. The format of this report is shown below:

WIP Trial Balance

Contract Code or Sales Order ID	Contract Number or Descrip	Total Incurred Costs	Cost of Sales	Trans to O. Div.	Corp Office Expense	Admin Exp	Bal WIP	Closed to Cost Sales	Balance WIP

Cost of sales and expense information is extracted for the profit and loss schedule requirements by contract.

DATA BANK AND ONLINE OPERATIONS

The type of data required for a cost accumulation data bank and online operations is displayed on Exhibit J. This exhibit displays the types of detailed identifiers and sub-system cost collection file data which permit the flow of information data to the appropriate major files for reporting purposes. This type of data file organization provides the maximum flexibility for accommodating changes, updating and instant retrieval of selective information.

The cost accumulation area is the basic source of pricing and other statistics required in the reporting process. Its mechanization will afford capturing information at its lowest level. It would provide multi-file updating and data bases to fulfill multi-organization reporting requirements. It is the building block to the ultimate data required for dynamic management reporting.

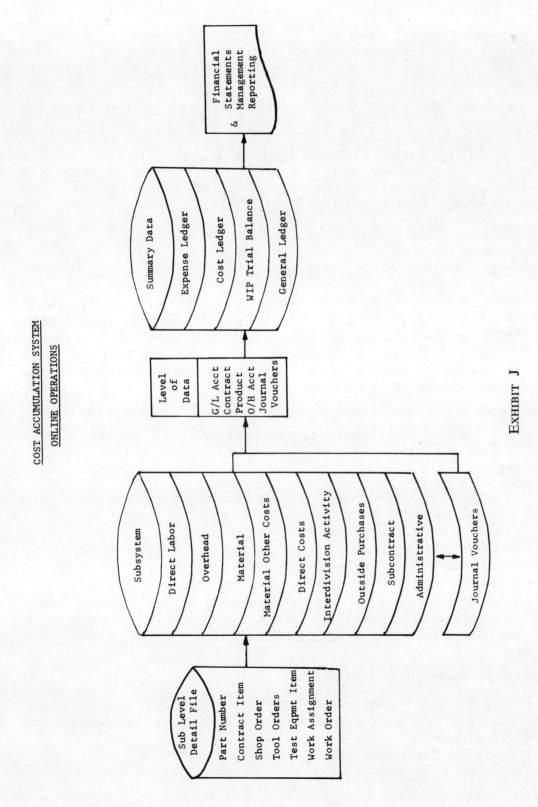

COST ACCUMULATION SYSTEM
ONLINE OPERATIONS

EXHIBIT J

3

Managing Direct Labor Cost, Distribution and Control

Salaries and wages of employes are the major expenditures in any organization whether it be a product-producing or service-rendering entity. They are subject to audit for compliance with federal and state laws, customer policies (particularly in government business) and the organization's own internal policy and procedures. It is, therefore, essential that the recording and distribution of these costs be accomplished with a maximum degree of efficiency and accuracy.

COMPUTERIZED SYSTEM

Objectives

- All employes (direct and indirect) would be included in this system.
- Timecards/timeclocks to be eliminated.
- Attendance would be reported on an exception basis.
- All records and transactions will be inputted into the system only once for payroll and organization statistics and reporting.
- Progressive "state of the art" input/output devices would be used.
- A plastic card badge would be available for all employes which would include their name, employe number, organization, job classification and whether they were classified as a direct or indirect employe.

Recording Employes' Time (Attendance)

The computer assumes a normal eight-hour day for attendance purposes based upon the employe's shift. An electronic input device would be used to collect attendance and labor data at its source.

The procedure of attendance recording would be as follows:

46

Input/Output Device

One or more devices, depending upon the size of the organization, would be physically located in the employe's work station area. The device would accommodate two separate plastic token badge slots and space for the insertion of an eighty-column work traveler card as shown below:

Employe Token Badge

```
A. A. Amose
     35482
1000    I    5100
Jones Corporation
Smithville, N. Y.
```

Punched on this card would be slots

for identifying:

35482	Employe Number	(5 columns)
1000	Organization	(4 columns)
5100	Job Classification	(4 columns)
D/I	Direct or Indirect	(1 column)

Authorizing
Supervision Badge

```
101-07-2701-120
Plant Engineering
Jones Corporation
Smithville, N. Y.
```

On this card, slots would be punched

the following:

101	Group Leader Designation
07	Foreman or Supervisor
2701	Organization
120	Cost Control or Burden Center Number

Work Traveler Card

Shop Order Number	Resp Orgn No	Serial Number	Part Number	Lot/ Quantity	Accounting Work Order or Account Number	Task Number	Engrng Section	Cost Code	Work Week
			Test Equipmt Item / Tool Order / Mfg Work Ord / Plant Engrng / Engineering Work Order			Work Author / Engrng Release / Test No			

Only the employe and supervisory token badges would be used for attendance recording and the traveler card would be utilized for direct labor identification and distribution to projects, tasks, etc. as shown on the above card format. The above items can be changed to reflect the pertinent data requirements for any organization.

The input device would contain keys or buttons which would designate the attendance criteria, transaction selectors and labor distribution quantities and unassigned codes.

Attendance and Status (employe and supervisory badge inserted)

01—All employes present
02—Absent
03—Unexcused tardiness
04—Jury duty
05—Medical
06—Authorized company business
07—Authorized overtime (direct effort would also include the work traveler card)
08—Short time
09—Authorized exception time
10—Excessive lunch period time

Attendance Transaction Selectors

A—Enter record
B—Display serialized employe attendance and exception records
C—Delete record
D—Substitute Record

Labor Distribution Recording (all three cards are inserted)

A0—Quantity being entered and amount
B0—Indirect labor authorized (unassigned time) for *reason codes*
    10—Machine breakdown
    11—Employe services
    12—Waiting for tools
    13—Waiting for material
    14—Waiting for inspection
    15—Blood donation
    16—Union business
    17—Jury duty

Attendance Data Processing

The procedure of data flow operations is displayed in Exhibit A and is described as follows:

- All employes should be at their work station at the beginning of the shift or advise supervision otherwise.

- Appropriate supervision will visually check for physical presence of the employe.

- If all present and accounted for, he will advise his time clerk to enter the transaction (A) and record (01) into the transactor device. Only supervision's token card is necessary with the transaction code if all employes are present.

ATTENDANCE DATA PROCESSING

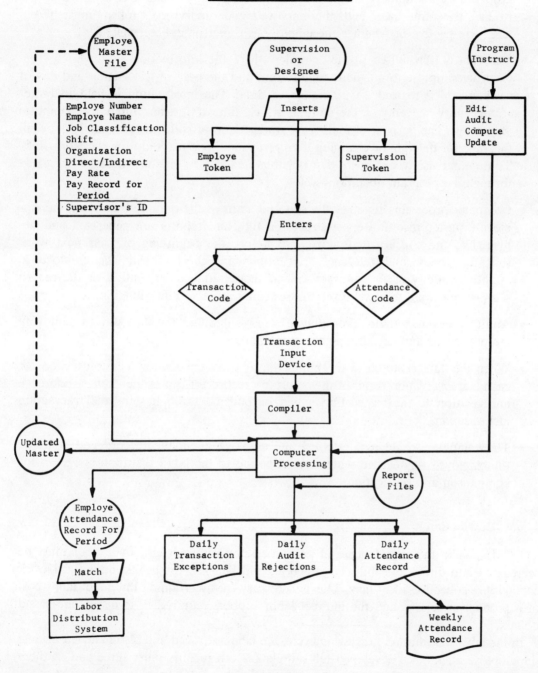

EXHIBIT A

- If there are exceptions at the beginning, during or at the end of the shift, the appropriate transaction and attendance status codes will be entered as outlined above. In each exception case, both the employe's and supervision's tokens must be entered irrespective of whether the employe is direct or indirect classified.

- The data is transmitted to the compiler where the information is converted from electronic impulse to magnetic tape format and the time of transaction and day of week is added to each set of incoming data. The information is held in buffer storage until the end of the shift at which time it is transmitted for computer processing. The purpose of temporary storage is to provide an opportunity to recall this data for deleting or changing if an error had been made during the work shift. To do otherwise would mean that possible invalid information would be processed through the program operation cycle.

- Computer processing involves the edit and audit of the data and updating the employe's master record. Report structured files and reports are generated and delivered to the concerned organizations before the beginning of their next work shift for review and reference. Exceptions are checked with the employe to establish validity of the transaction and their initialed verification of the record if a problem were to arise in the future relative to a specific situation.

- Audit rejections and/or other changes are resubmitted the next day by removing the old record and substituting the new input.

- When the data is stored in the buffer file, it is assigned a number transaction for each employe. Upon recall of the employe's record for a possible change, reference and revision to the transaction would be effected through serialized transaction identification.

- The computer would also establish the employe attendance record and compute the employe's pay earned which would be fed to the labor distribution system for comparison and verification.

Labor Distribution

In addition to the attendance and pay processing for each employe, labor must be segregated into direct and indirect categories and charged to specific authorized work expenditure collection identifiers. This is necessary for ascertaining the direct labor cost of a product or service and the indirect labor support required in terms of hours and dollars.

In the labor distribution processing cycle, the labor is priced and also matched against the employe attendance developed labor dollars. Both records must agree and, if there is a difference, an exception report is outputted for investigation.

Direct labor distribution reporting is required by functional work order within an organization as well as accounting work order or task within contract or product indicating total time expended for each activity.

A report of the unassigned time usage by employe and organization is necessary for analysis and corrective action if a problem exists.

Performance reporting is necessary to measure standard versus actual hours by accounting work order and functional organization. This establishes the percent realization from the effort expended.

Indirect labor distribution is identified to an overhead account and organization which is necessary for the expense collection system and functional organization reporting.

Labor distribution data is used in billing the customer, estimating statistics, overall cost accumulation system, pricing the product, etc. The indirect effort is an expenditure for recording as part of the total overhead pool.

A sample format of the data entered into and reported in the labor distribution and attendance records is noted below:

Oper No.	Orgn No.	Cost Center	Cost Code	Tvlr Ord No.	Part No.	AWO A/C #	Transactor Punch		Time on Activity				Var. From Attend
							In	Out	S.T.	O.T.	D.T.	Tot	

Where there is a variance from the attendance records, the time auditor investigates the difference and makes an adjustment input from his transactor. The format of the input is as follows:

Dr/ Cr	Employe No.	Oper No.	Work Day	Group Supvsr	Orgn	Cost Center	Cost Code	Part No.	AWO A/c #	Tvlr Card	Time		
											S.T.	O.T.	D.T.

The adjustment is reflected throughout the files thus making the data compatible including the online disk files.

LABOR DATA BANK

Labor data in terms of headcount, attendance, cost accumulation and distribution as well as pay records are established in disk storage files as well as on magnetic tape. The latter files are used for updating, processing and batch reporting. The disk files are used for online inquiry and real time reporting. Information in these files is segregated into specific locations for ease of access in satisfying various reporting retrieval needs.

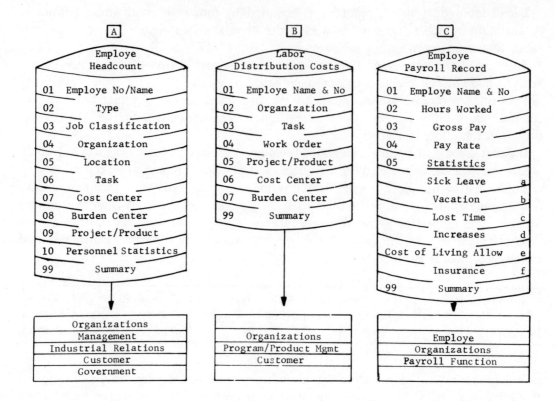

As noted above, any input relative to an employe is captured only once and placed into the affected file(s).

Online Inquiries/Response

Codes would have to be assigned to the file for each record or sets of data that was to be retrieved. File A data retrieval will be discussed and the B and C files would work quite similarly. The procedure follows:

Requirement — Extract complete headcount file data for Employe 12345.

	File Location	Record Extent (Complete)	Employe Number	Identifier Location
Message —	A	X	12345	01

The response to this message would include the following:
. Employe Number and Name
. Type—Direct or Indirect

. Job Classification Code
. Organization Number to Which Assigned
. Building and Area Code Location
. Name of Task Assigned
. Cost Center Assignment Number
. Burden Center Assignment
. Project or Product Association
. Personnel Statistics (Age, Male or Female,
      Education, Shift, Gross Pay Rate, etc..

<u>Requirement</u> — Retrieve organization number for Employe 12345.

	File Location	Record Extent (Partial)	Employe Number	Identifier Location	Organization Secondary Location
<u>Message</u> —	A	Y	12345	01	04

<u>Response</u> — Employe 12345 organization number is 2710.

Overview of Data Bank Flow

Exhibit B indicates information flow and control of data at end of shift for assurance that the files have been properly updated.

As is noted in this exhibit, if there is no labor distribution activity reported, the computer checks the exception report and, if it reveals no absenteeism or other related entry, the computer makes the assumption that the employe was present and credits him with full time of work. An exception might indicate "short time" which would then be reflected as a reduction to the total hours of assumed activity effort. If the employe had more than one activity during the work shift, the program computes the time between the two activities for proper apportionment of the labor effort to specific charge numbers.

Data Bank Interface and Usage

The information that is generated within an organization relative to labor attendance and distribution is used in a number of satellite systems/reporting and eventually becomes a part of data used in management online or batch reporting. As shown in Exhibit C, the basic costs flow through the systems indicated—attendance, distribution and payroll.

Performance Reporting

Valid information is sorted and formatted for a master labor file which, in turn, is structured into reporting files for major systems and the various reports as shown in Exhibit C. Some of the major performance reports are as shown on p. 56.

OVERVIEW OF DATA BANK FLOW

End of Day

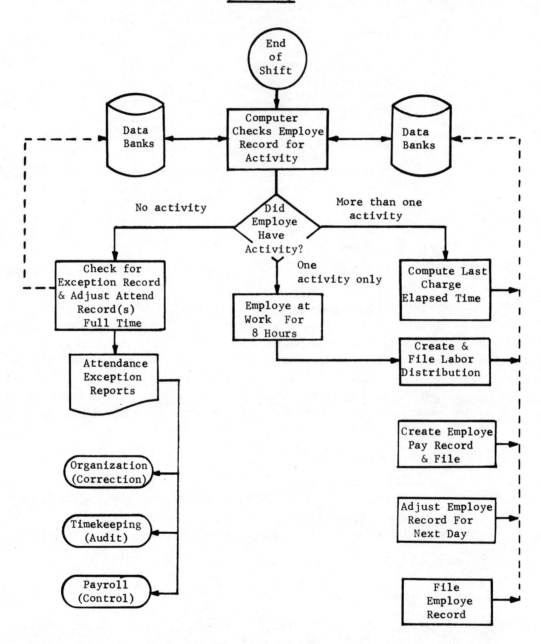

EXHIBIT B

DATA BANK INTERFACE AND USAGE

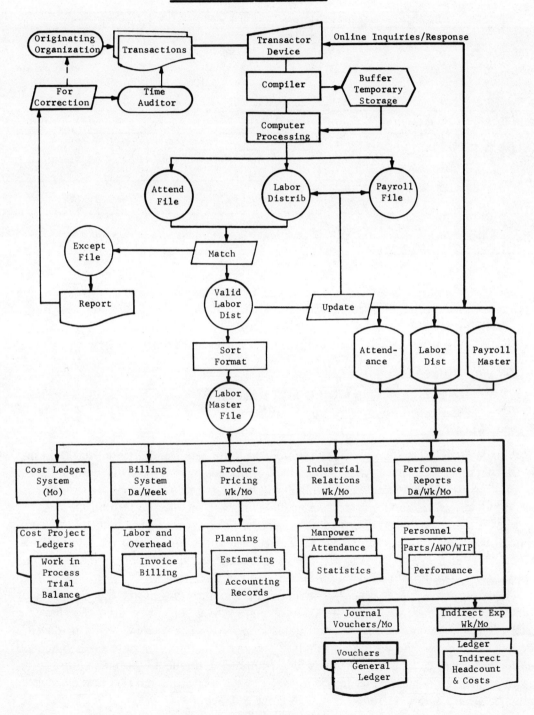

EXHIBIT C

Accounting Work Order Performance

AWO	Program No.	Direct Labor Hours						
		Standard	Actual	Effect %	Off Std	Realization %	Target	Variance

| | | Standard Hrs ÷ by Actuals x 100 | | | | Standard Hrs ÷ by Actuals + "off" Stndrd x 100 | Optimum | Difference between Act. + Std Compared to Target |

Factory Parts Performance

Dept_____Group_____Cost Center_____Program_____												
Part No.	AWO No.	Oper No.	Qty	Std Hrs	Act Hrs	% Effect	Off Std Hrs	Scrap Std Hrs	% Realiz.	Target Realiz.	Total Hrs	% Task Completed

Weekly Performance by Group

Part No.	Group	Std Hours	Actual Hours	Engrg	Rework Vendor	Inspect	% Realiz.

There are many advantages to an effective performance reporting system which includes identification of specific problem areas, estimating requirements for future contracts, identifying areas of exceptional performance and interface reporting for AWOs, groups, parts, tooling, test equipment, employes and programs.

PAYROLL MECHANIZATION

Payroll Master

A major statellite system that is closely related to the labor and attendance processing is the payroll processing activity. Accurate recordkeeping provides the basic data for computing payroll costs and its attendant withholdings and deductions. Basic statistics are inputted for creating a payroll master file which is structured in Exhibit D.

File locations A, B and C indicate the type of information that is available and updated on a weekly cycle. Access is readily achievable through record filed designators. Codes "CD" are also assigned to provide specific compressed input, but at the same time serve as the identity to the various data contained in this master.

There are two general processes involved in updating the master file. The first or preliminary is concerned with rate table changes, status and deductions, accruals for sick leave and vacations, prior period adjustments, etc. The second step is to develop priced earnings for the period and update the gross amount, compute taxes based on earnings, collect deductions for bonds, contributions, retirement, allotments, insurance, etc. Payroll checks must be written with the voucher supporting data. A payroll register must be generated for reference, controlling and balancing.

PAYROLL MASTER FILE

Basic Statistics

A	Status	Employe Number	Employe Name	Date of Birth			Date of Hire			Orgn	Engr Grp	Occup Grp Code	Rate Per Hour	Monthly Pay	Social Security Number
1	7	2-6	8-26	27-9	30-1	32-3	34-5	36-7	38-9	40-4	45-7	48-51	52-6	57-62	63-70

A	Sex	Payroll Code H or S	Payroll Exempt	Labor/Salary Grade	Marital Status	Shift	Vacation Date
	71	72	73	74-5	76	77	78-80

Withholding & Other

B	Gross Pay YTD	Income Tax	Taxable Amounts				Year-to-date Paid				Retirement		
			FICA	SDI	SUI	FUI	FICA	SDI	SUI	FUI	Hourly Sal (Hrs)	Gross	Sick Leave $
1	2-8	9-14	15-20	21-6	27-32	33-8	39-43	44-7	48-52	53-7	58-62	63-8	69-75

Deductions

C	Bonds					Contrib		Retrmt		Allot		Insurns		Purch		Cash Advance		Travel		Savings	
	Cost	$	Dedn	Pur	Bal	$	Amt	$	Amt	$	Amt	$	Amt	$	Amt	$	Amt	$	Amt	$	Amt
1	2-6	7	8-12	13-17	18-21	22	23-26	27	28-31	32	33-36	37	38-42	43	44-47	48	49-52	53	54-58	59	60-64

C	Dues		Misc Deducs		Total Deducs	
	$	Amt	$	Amt	$	Amt
	65	66-69	70	71-73	74	75-79

EXHIBIT D

PAYROLL AUDIT AND CONTROL FLOW

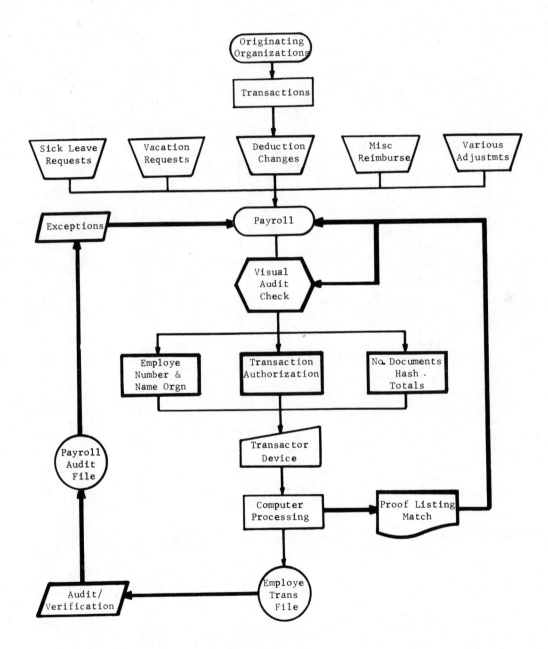

EXHIBIT E

AUDIT TRAILS AND CONTROLS

The audit trail in the payroll system is provided through the reference to an employe number which appears on every source document, accompanies every input transaction and basic reference point in the master file. Audit, control and verification of data is provided by predetermined "hash" totals of input amounts and a check of the output proof listings. Program controls and edit tables reject obvious and, determinable in advance, input errors. Transactor usage provides a capability for input audit at the source of its entry—the originating organization. A simplified version of payroll audit trail and control is shown in Exhibit E and the heavy lines indicate the flow of input and output data control and action points.

For the direct and indirect labor system, some of the audits and controls have been discussed above but, in summary, the major verification criteria are noted as follows:

Labor attendance audit for all employes—time reconciliation—authorized work time plus exceptions equals 40 hours/week.

Direct labor attendance plus exceptions equals the labor distribution time.

Accounting work order master file check for validity of organizations, tasks, programs, products, contracts, sales orders.

Visual audit of transaction listing output.

Employe and supervision time audit and verification of exceptions.

Work Task authorization and proper work department identification.

A computerized labor and attendance system designed to capture basic data at its source, edit, audit, manipulate and store, it can eliminate one of the most necessary, but costly functions in any organization. It places the responsibility for accurate input upon supervision. Adjustments are also accomplished by either supervision or time auditors who are the most experienced in this type of effort.

4

Effectively Handling the
Accounts Payable Function

The main role of the accounts payable function is to accrue and record liability payment transactions for material and services purchased outside the organization as well as to satisfy the internal payment requirements resulting from employe travel, awards and other miscellaneous incurred expense. This function is responsible for the appropriate accounting distribution of costs to organizations, products and individuals as applicable. Vendor records must be maintained. Payments must be supported by proper documentation which includes the authorization for purchase, receipt, acceptance and validity of the vendor invoice data.

DATA COLLECTION FROM SOURCE DOCUMENTATION

Purchase Order Commitment Cycle

The effort commences with an approved authorizing document which indicates that certain items or services are required in order to perform assigned tasks. The responsible originating organization initiates a request for purchase to procurement or material planning for a specific item(s).

The requirement is reviewed, the need established and a determination is made as to whether there is a budget assigned for the requisitioned item or service. The processing and reporting procedure is displayed in Exhibit A.

Purchase Order Generation

The procurement organization prepares the purchase order, locates the suppliers, negotiates terms and price, places the order and monitors supplier performance. The purchase orders are keypunched and entered into the outstanding commitment reporting system. This source document is then the initial action in the invoicing cycle.

PURCHASE ORDER COMMITMENT CYCLE

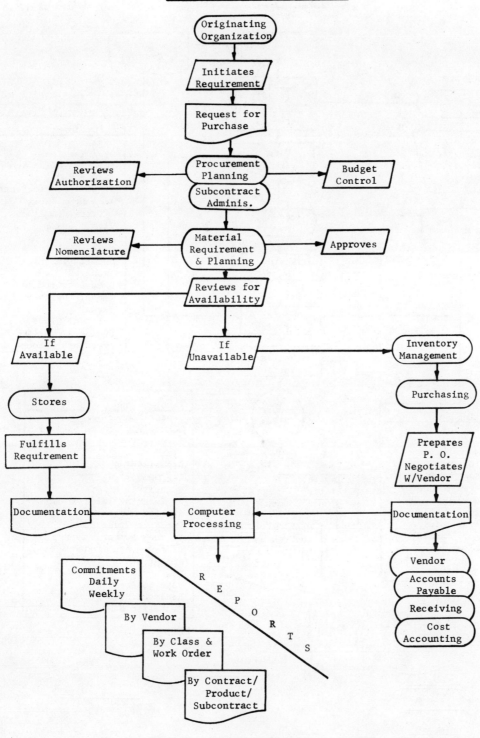

EXHIBIT A

COMMITMENT RELIEF CYCLE

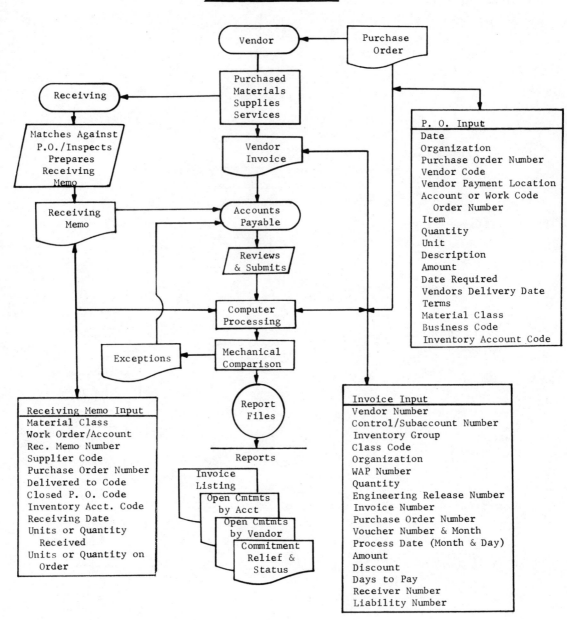

EXHIBIT B

Commitment Relief Cycle

When the delivery of purchased materials has been made to the receiving organization, they match the shipping document and the receipt against the purchase order. They also prepare a receiving memo which indicates any exceptions that were noted from the above comparison. The receiving memos are forwarded to purchasing, the originating organization and accounts payable. The information as shown in Exhibit B is inputted into the system and merged with the open commitment files.

Mechanical Comparisons and Reconcilement

Upon receipt of the invoice, accounts payable enters the accounting distribution and other appropriate, but possibly missing information on the invoice. This data is then directly inputted from the invoice to the computer via a terminal device. The data is edited and audited and merged with the purchase order and receiving memo files. The common matching criteria on all documents is the purchase order number. Quantity, dollar values, due dates, terms and unit price are matched and variations are outputted in an exception report for investigation and correction. The exception report will be formatted as follows and will only be generated if there are differences:

Document	Purchase Order Number	Quan.	Unit Price	Total Amount	Disc.	Due Date	Terms
Purchase Order	x	x	x	x	x	x	x
Receiving Memo	x	x	?	?	?	?	?
Invoice	x	x	x	x	x	x	x

The purchase order and invoice data above should match on every item. In the case of the receiving document, however, unless there is a standard or regular purchase order involved, the "?" indicates that receiving would not have that designated data for matching. The regular purchase order contains the receiving information at the bottom of the purchase order with all of the other matching data above. A purchase authorization document, for example, forwarded to receiving would not contain the "?" information.

Although displayed in Exhibit B as input from receiving, the only information that they actually input is receiving memo number, receiving date and units or quantity received. The other data would have been prepunched on a card for them out of the purchase order commitment system.

Mechanical Due Date Comparisons

Based on the terms specified in the purchase order, a due date will be established mechanically for each purchase receipt. The receipt date on the receiving memo will be the basis for establishing this due date. The processing will be as follows:

- A julian date conversion will be made in the computer system from the calendar receipt date submission by receiving.

- From the purchase order, the number of days in the terms will be added to the julian receipt date and this date will be converted back to calendar date for reporting and paying purposes. If no date settlement is specified in the terms, it will be assumed in the program that payment will be made thirty days after receipt of the material.

- On a daily cycle, an output report will be produced showing the unpaid invoice for 10 work days in advance with their amounts and due dates in the following format:

Invoice	Disc.	Report	Unpaid Net Invoice Amounts										
	X - Yes	Day of	+										
No Date	0 - No	Month	01	02	03	04	05	06	07	08	09	10	Total

In other words, if the report was produced on January 2 of a given year, then January 3 data would be entered in Column "01", and so on excluding weekends and holidays, for the following next nine working days. This provides an excellent means of knowing and planning the cash outflow for two weeks in advance. The discount information should be known as an incentive to meet the invoice payment schedule.

- If invoices were unpaid, on the scheduled date, they would be dropped from the above reporting and shown on a "past due report" which format would be as follows:

Invoice		Date		Unpaid Invoice	No. Days
No.	Date	Due	Report	Amount	Past Due

This report would be extremely useful in analyzing the past due unpaid balances for action in contacting the vendor and/or planning cash requirements.

- The above information would also be included in a composite report of all of the unpaid balances by due date sequence and totaled. It would contain the detail as shown in the following format:

Due Date	Vendor	Curr Date	Invoice		P.O. No.	Unpaid Invoice Amount			No. Days Before Due Date
			No.	Date		Gross	Disc	Net	

- This type of report would include all unpaid invoices and provide the number of days remaining before payment is due. The julian due date would be compared with the julian current date in order for the computer to calculate the "number of days remaining" before payment is due.

The above information reporting mechanically relative to unpaid invoices and due dates is a planning, controlling and decision-making tool. Through a code input into the system, any invoice could be delayed indefinitely for payment or accelerated dependent upon the requirement or management instruction.

MECHANICAL INVOICE PROCESSING

When invoice data is entered into the system, it is edited and audited to verify the validity of account, contract, product and organization numbers. Also, the purchase order number on the invoice is matched against the commitment purchase orders to determine if such an order exists; if it does not, the data is rejected for investigation.

A vendor invoice transaction file as shown in Exhibit C is created which is used to update the master files and also to create registers and vendor payment checks.

The vendor master is entered into the processing activity in order to obtain the vendor name and address. The monthly cost distribution is prepared and it, in turn, provides data for the cost accumulation systems as well as the general ledger. A new master is created which contains information for other reporting relative to paid and unpaid cost distribution, tool and equipment material costs, etc. The outstanding commitment reports are also produced which, in essence, provide the status of undelivered purchases.

INVENTORY TRANSACTION AND SUPPLY STATUS FILES

All inventory designated items are catalogued by commodity or material group and identified within the group by a serial number. Transaction data is forwarded to computer operations for processing and file updates as displayed in Exhibit D.

A daily transaction report is produced and forwarded to stores, inventory management and material planning and control. Cumulative weekly and monthly transaction reports are also issued. The material cost file is updated and provides data for the material cost control system. The inventory control and allocation system is also updated and it provides inventory management reports relative to inventory stock usage and trends and produces the supply status data. The inventory record reflects the net position (total requirements less total inventory status) from which intelligent procurement or internal action adjustments may be decided and initiated.

VENDOR LOCATOR FILE

To establish the initial records, accounts payable inputs all of the pertinent detail such as vendor name, paying address (the vendor purchase file contains the order address), county, state, vendor code, etc., as shown in Exhibit E. Financial accounting investigates the vendor's financial rating and enters this data.

The file record is maintained on magnetic tape and also on disk for online inquiries.

MECHANICAL INVOICE PROCESSING

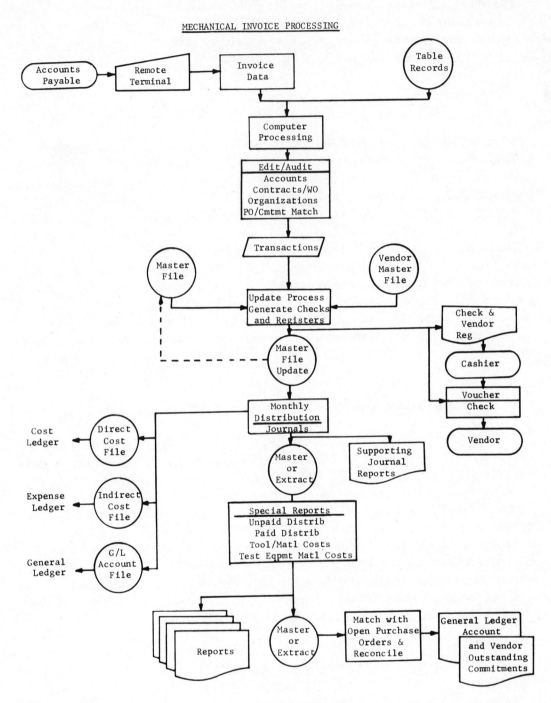

EXHIBIT C

INVENTORY TRANSACTION AND STATUS FILES

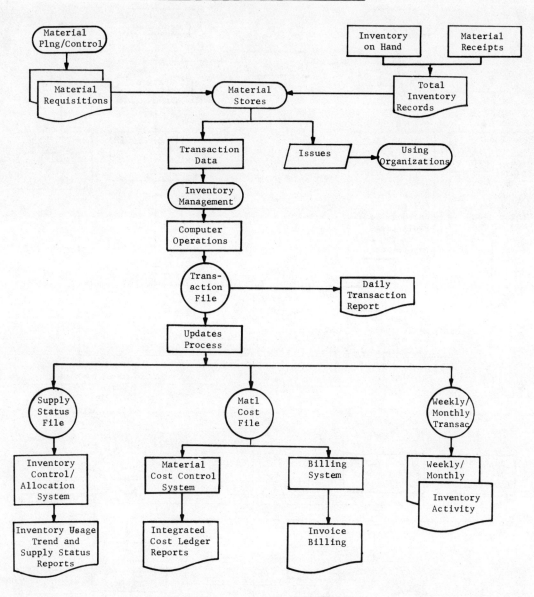

EXHIBIT D

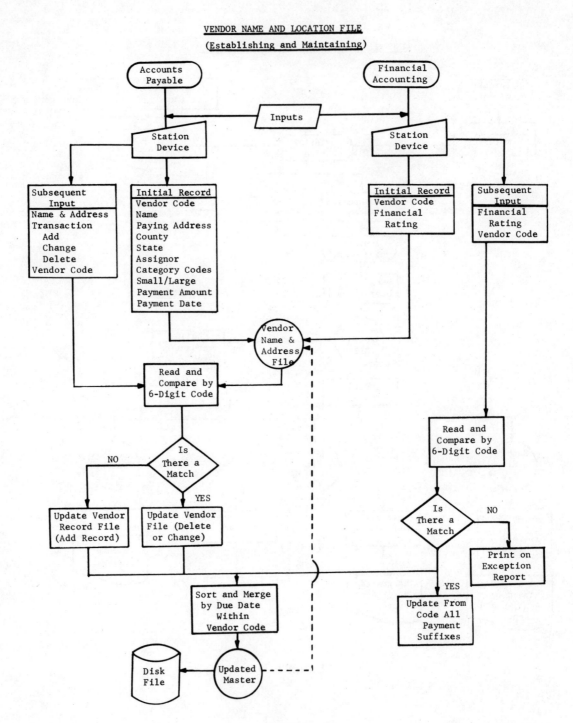

VENDOR NAME AND LOCATION FILE
(Establishing and Maintaining)

EXHIBIT E

For inquiry purposes, only the vendor code is necessary to obtain specific or all of the other pertinent vendor information.

In subsequent additions, changes or deletions to the file, only the vendor code identifier is used unless a new vendor is being added.

The vendor file record layout is noted below:

Vendor Code	Name		Paying Address			
			Street	Building	P.O. Box	City

County	State	Withhold Code	Assignor	Financial Rating	Material Category Codes	Small or Large

Activity Date	Payment Amount	Payment Due Date

The contents of the file record can be expanded or contracted depending upon the needs of the organization relative to vendor data.

CASH DISBURSEMENTS

Upon receipt of invoices or credit memos, accounts payable will assign a vendor code number, liability number and due date.

Documented Disbursement Records

On a daily basis, invoices, debit and credit memos that have been processed, audited and ready for payment will be forwarded to computer operations for processing and reporting. Each day accounts payable will receive the following reports relative to the payment process:

- Invoices Eligible for Payment
- Vendor Debit Balance Listing
- Mechanically Generated Checks and Their Attendant Voucher Data
- Disbursement Register
- Unpaid Invoices Beyond Due Date

Based on due dates assigned, the computer will generate the invoices eligible for payment by using julian date comparisons and conversion to calendar date. It will match vendor invoice to the debit balance file and provide the net amount for payment. Accounts payable will review, daily, the listing and indicate the invoices to be paid or held. An unpaid listing report will be outputted for those invoices where the report date is greater than the due date.

When computer operations receives the "to pay" list, they will process those invoices for payment and mechanically the check and voucher and the disbursement register will be produced. Accounts payable will audit the checks to the list they submitted for payment and also the disbursement register. Variances will be resubmitted to computer operations in the form of adjustments to the files. The approved checks will be processed through a check signer device for signature imprint and an address device which will "stuff" the check and print the vendor address on the envelope.

Cash Disbursement Register

An example format of a cash disbursement register is noted as follows:

Check No. Date	Vendor Code	Invoice No. Date	P.O. No.	R.M. No.	Tax Code	Gross Amount	Discount Amount	Check Amount

Undocumented Disbursements

In situations where no purchase order and/or receiving memo is required, a payment document must be used such as a check request, special invoice, mileage expense report, etc. These "pay" documents will be forwarded to computer operations. The information will be processed and entered on a cash disbursement register. It is accounts payable function to audit the submitted input on a daily basis to the disbursement register.

Computer Generated Statistics

Due to the amount of reporting involved for the accounts payable function, many and varied statistics can be generated to predict cash disbursements for short and long range forecasting.

Short Range Projections

The "due date" file, for example, summarizes by vendor within date scheduled for payment the amount of cash outflow that is anticipated. As discussed earlier, the computer will generate a report which will show for ten working days in advance the amount of dollars scheduled to be paid based on due dates. Of course, this type of disbursement projection has to be tempered by management policy, cash availability and judgment. The method should be fairly accurate for short range projections.

By week and month, particularly, it is known historically the value of the total invoices forwarded to computer operations during a given period. Also, it is known what the paid and unpaid amounts are for a particular time span. Analysis of the data should reveal a relationship which can be translated into a mathematical formula. Based on a predicted flow of invoices by periods, a cash disbursement forecast can be made by formula application mechanically.

There may also be a management edict that specifies the amount of cash that will be paid out during a given period of time or establishes a percent of the total value dollars outstanding that can be paid based on anticipated cash receipts.

Long Range Projections

Cash outflow for a six-month period, year, or a greater period of time is more difficult to achieve. However, there are a number of techniques that could be used.

Mechanically, the computer could segregate the inhouse commitments by date and total the amounts. To these values by date could be added the anticipated major purchases as planned by both material planning and control and procurement groups. Based on a five-day lag for invoice receipt and processing, this data now represents anticipated invoice liability. The next step would be to determine an average lag between liability setup and payment. The computer would then apply the lag factor to obtain projected cash disbursements.

Another approach would be to analyze the different types of costs and their payment cycle in order to determine the average time between *cost accrual and cash disbursement*. For example, in the aerospace industry, the following lag periods were developed based on the analysis of past performance:

- Purchased Material — 3 weeks
- Subcontract — 6 weeks
- Labor and Overhead — 2 weeks
- Employee Deductions — 1 week
- State Disability Insurance — 3 months plus one week

A thorough evaluation of an oganization's pertinent performance will reveal the appropriate lags that can be used. Next, the projected costs must be determined for lag factor application. The two principal considerations in the lagging process are the establishment of the length of the lag period and the number of weeks in the accounting period. An example of a lag factor chart that can be used for mechanical application is as follows:

Lag Factors			
Periods	Accounting Periods		
	Months		Quarters
	5 Wks	4 Wks	13 Wks
1	.20	.25	7.69
2	.40	.50	15.38
3	.60	.75	23.08
4	.80	1.00	30.77
5	1.00	1.25	38.46

An example of a projected disbursement calculation is as follows:

Material Purchases in 000$_s$ (2-Week Period Lag)					
	Jan*	Feb	Mar	Apr*	Jan-April
Accrual	50	42	44	73	209
Lag In	39	20	21	22	102
Lag Out	(20)	(21)	(22)	(29)	(92)
Payment	69	41	43	66	219

*Five-week accounting periods.

The best approach to projecting cash disbursements can only be determined by a detailed analysis of historical data. It could be that a combination of the above approaches would be the solution for some organizations.

RECORDS FOR ANALYSIS, PLANNING AND REPORTING

Various records are generated in the computerized system which provide the capability for analysis, planning and reporting. An analysis of the reported data serves as a basis for planning and measuring the effect of accounts payable operations on other organizations. Illustrated below are examples of the effects and/or interfaces:

- Certain open commitments may mean delays in engineering and/or production tasks.

- Excessive unpaid invoice balances may mean that borrowing is in order due to limited cash resources. There may be a cash receipt problem or unanticipated high delivery rate.

- Loss of discounts may be attributed to inefficient payment practices or inadequate cash resources.

- Large vendor debit balances would indicate action was necessary to make collections or undetected errors in vendor payments.

- Low vendor financial ratings might be an indicator to poor or delayed vendor performance.

- Excessive purchases might be a forerunner to budget overruns, inefficient procurement practices or depleted inventories.

The above represents some of the general type deficiencies or problems that can be revealed by report record analyses. As indicated above, cash disbursement planning can be more effective through record analysis.

Reporting

Examples of report formats that would be derived from Accounts Payable records are as follows:

Daily Liability Report

Vendor	Numbers			Date	Gross Amount	Sales Tax	Freight	Disc.	Net Amount
	Liab	P.O.	Inv.						

Daily Invoice Distribution

Vendor	Charge/ Account Number	Numbers		Dates		Extraneous Charges	Sales Tax	Freight	Payment Amount
		Liab	Inv	Inv	Due				

Debit Balance Vendors

Vendor	Numbers			Dates			Gross Amount	Discount	Net Amount
	P.O.	Liab	Inv	P.O	Inv	Due			

Open Invoice Report

Vendor	Numbers			Invoice Date	Gross Amount	Extended Value	Sales Tax	Freight
	P.O.	Liab	Inv					

Discount	Net Amount

Weekly Distribution

P.O. No.	Charge No			Amount	RM		Invoice		Liab No	Seller	Descrip
	Cl	WO	CC		No	Date	No	Date			

Commitment Report

Contract		WIP Acct	Commitments		Current Month Invoices	Curr Mo Cmtmt Balance	Curr Mo Pd	Curr Mo Unpd
No	Code		Prior Mo Balance	Current Month				

Subcontractors Analysis Report

Line 1	Contract Number	Prod Line	Contract Description	Vendor Name	Vendor Code

Line 2	P.O. No.	W.O. No.	Acct No.	Commitments		Invoices		Adjustmts	Balance Open
				Curr Mo	Cum Author	Curr Mo Pd	Cum Pd		

Every organization, whether small or large, is involved in the accounts payable function. Every purchase of direct or indirect material or services creates a liability that must be paid. Computerization of the processes involved is the most effective means to collect, record, plan, control and report the mass of data that is associated with this function.

Indirect Expense,

Allocation and Control

that expense incurred in an organization's activity identified or assigned to the cost of designing, engineering, inspecting or producing a product or performing a service. It is representative of administrative, management, clerical or control function expenses.

EXPENSE COLLECTION FROM SOURCE DOCUMENTS

Indirect expense is accumulated by organizations and identified to burden centers such as manufacturing, engineering, field services and administrative. There can be many more burden centers such as procurement and material, remote sites and plant services dependent upon organization objectives and need. Indirect expense is redistributed from one burden center to another when organizations perform services or incur expenses which are identifiable to organizations in other burden centers.

The expense data required is developed in various other mechanized systems from which information is extracted and merged into one composite file to meet the expense ledger reporting requirements. Exhibit A displays a generalized flow of data to meet these requirements.

A description of the procedure and processing is as follows:

Timecard and adjustment data from timekeeping is keypunched in the prescribed input format and enters the mechanical labor processing system for rate application and distribution to accounts.

In the payroll mechanical system, new rates or adjustments are entered for indirect labor expense changes.

Property accounting inputs the pertinent data for a fixed asset acquisition and this information is merged with the property ledger master. Depreciation expense is mechanically developed, and the file master updated for cumulative depreciation.

Accounts payable submits its vendor invoices and added expense distribution and

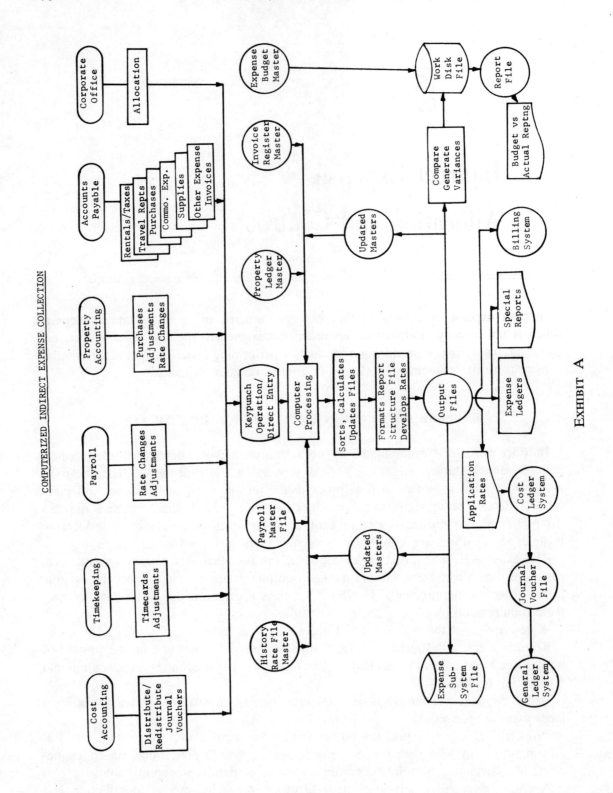

COMPUTERIZED INDIRECT EXPENSE COLLECTION

EXHIBIT A

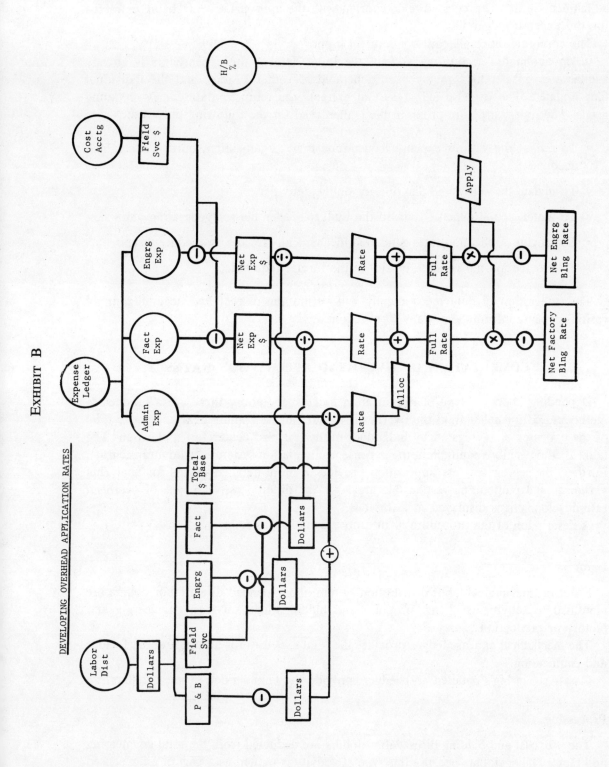

ExHIBIT B

DEVELOPING OVERHEAD APPLICATION RATES

adjustments which is processed and reported with the appropriate data being extracted for the expense ledger file.

The corporate office allocation is a direct input.

In an automated accounting system, the input data to the expense file is already available on master files having been generated for other systems and the individual files updated. The expense ledger system extracts the required data for its updating needs. The report structure program file is then used for the following purposes:

- To output the various expense ledger reports by organization, burden center and account.

- To update the subsystem disk file for online activities.

- To match actual expense data to the budget master file for generating variances.

- To provide application rates generated mechanically for the cost ledger system.

- To provide journal voucher entries in the format required.

The integration of data mechanically will permit the extract and accumulation of various expense information in any form required.

COMPUTATION OF OVERHEAD APPLICATION RATES

Depending upon the type of organization and its operation, there are a number of methods used for calculating the overhead rate. It can be applied as a composite total of the expenses or segregated by individual burden or cost center for application. The latter method is more equitable if the expense accumulation system is valid and accurate. Further, the segregated rate application provides a more detailed means for analyzing variances and pinpointing responsible areas for the differences. One type of overhead rate development is displayed in Exhibit B.

A description of the procedure in the above exhibit is as follows:

Input

From the mechanical labor distribution system, the expended direct labor dollars are identified to activities such as: proposal and bidding, field services, engineering and factory or production.

The mechanical expense ledger provides the total expenses for administration, factory and engineering.

Cost Accounting's detailed cost ledgers provide the field service expense dollars.

Processing

The proposal and bidding direct labor dollars are deducted from the total engineering and factory labor dollars because this type of activity is treated as a part of an expensed period cost in the reporting system and has its own burden rate.

Field service direct dollars are deducted from the engineering and factory labor dollars because a separate overhead rate is used for this activity. The net engineering and factory dollars are combined and the resultant total of the hours is divided into the total administrative expense to obtain the administrative overhead percent.

Output

The field services expense dollars are deducted from the factory and engineering overhead to obtain the net above expense.

The net total expense for factory and engineering is divided by their direct labor dollars to obtain their individual overhead rates.

The administrative rate is allocated to the factory and engineering rates to obtain the overhead application rate for booking costs in the cost ledger accumulation system.

In most commercial organizations, there is generally only one overhead rate which is calculated by taking the sum of the expenses and dividing by the total direct labor hours or dollars.

DISTRIBUTION OF EXPENSE TO BURDEN CENTERS

All organizational indirect expenses are identified to and collected in several basic expense pools that can be classified as cost or burden centers. These centers have their own identifying number designation and are further associated to department organizations. This association provides a control in the mechanical process input in that if the wrong department number is entered with a valid burden center or vice versa, the input is rejected.

Distribution journals accumulate final distribution expense from source data collected by the expense accounts. These expenses are summarized by overhead account. Examples of distribution journal postings to the expense ledger are as follows: sales and use tax accrual, accrued and prepaid insurance, distribution of nonproductive material, etc.

The organization generally sets forth the policy for distribution of expenses to burden centers in their accounting practice directives.

EXPENSE LEDGER REPORTING

Actual expenditures are reported weekly, monthly and year to date. The expense can be reported in varying sorts as required and some typical expense ledger formats are organized as follows:

Expense Ledger Detailed Transactions

(and Overhead Account Summary)

Date			Ref Source	O/H Acct No	Orgn	Item Description	Amounts					
							Curr	Wk	MTD		YTD	
Wk	Mo	Yr					DR	CR	DR	CR	DR	CR

The same type of summary is desirable by organization for analysis of their detailed expense transactions by period.

A summary of this report's information would be organization within burden center

<u>Expense Ledger by G/L Account</u>

(Organization Summary)

Date	Orgn	B.C.	J.V. No.	G/L Account	Amounts					
					Curr		Wk		MTD	YTD
Wk Mo Yr				No. Description	DR	CR	DR	CR	DR CR	

and its totals. This type of report provides the burden center with distribution of expenses by organization.

BUDGET VERSUS ACTUAL COMPARISONS

In order to assist management in managing, planning and controlling its operations, it must have a capability to assess expense performance. An expense budget is a tool that reflects a plan against which to measure actual results. Significant variances from the plan generally indicate problems or other criteria for investigation and action.

There are a number of reports that can be utilized in order to analyze the overhead expense performance from the summary level to the detail. A typical format example is displayed below:

<u>Overhead Budget Vs Actuals</u>
(Division Summary)

Major Expense Categories	Current Period				Year-to-date			
	Act	Bud	Var	% Var	Act	Bud	Var	% Var
Indirect Labor								
Fringe Benefits								
Supplies/Services								
Communication								
Other Expense								
Corporate Allocation								
Total Expense								
Personnel								
Direct								
Indirect								
Direct Hours								
Direct Dollars								
Rate								
Per Direct Hour								
Per Direct Dollar								

Provided with the above summary level of data, management can readily locate the areas which show significant variances from the planned objectives. Variances can be assessed not only in terms of the expenses, but also for personnel, direct hours, dollars and rates. The problem would be obvious if direct effort were to decrease and expenses remained unchanged, then the overhead rates would naturally increase.

If a particular expense required further investigation, then a detailed expense report would be the source for the analysis. The format would be the same as above except that the detailed accounts would be substituted for the major expense categories.

Similar type reporting as indicated above is also necessary by individual organization and burden center.

Mechanization of indirect expense collection, distribution and reporting is ideal for exception reporting. Analysis parameters or factors could be entered into the program which would serve as a guide for generating output automatically. For example, if actuals exceeded budget, either by account, burden center or organization, by a predetermined percent, plus or minus, the specific problem output would be "flagged" on the report. This would save countless hours of analysis effort to pinpoint a problem area.

PROJECTING INDIRECT EXPENSE

The natural follow-up to a mechanical indirect expense system is the automation of the overhead budgeting or forecasting process. Computerization would provide the necessary capability to accomplish the following: development of overhead application rates, reporting data in various sorts and summaries, ease in time-phasing the information for any number of periods, flexibility in making changes, providing an actual vs. budget comparison file, and generating variances and testing the results of various changes.

There are a number of methods that can be used in generating projected indirect expenses dependent upon the degree of detail and/or refinement required. Whichever approach is employed, the first and basic task is to review all of the pertinent historical data in detail and establish independent and dependent variables.

In the development of indirect expense projections, consideration should be given to the following:

Fixed expense represents account values which vary with time and management decision generally rather than being dependent upon changes or fluctuations of an organization's level of activity.

Variable expense represents account values which fluctuate directly with changing levels of activity.

Semi-variable expense are those account values which fluctuate with the level of activity but not in direct proportion such as indirect labor.

The projection processes to be discussed below are primarily concerned with the fixed and variable expenses.

Scattergraph Approach

In this method, the total overhead expense is plotted against direct labor volume (hours or dollars). Although at least two years of historical data should be used to develop a correlation line, only eight months of statistical data were used for illustration purposes as shown below.

SCATTERGRAPH STATISTICS

(In Thousands of Dollars)

	DL	OH	DLX Formula Developed
January	374.0	650.0	696.0
February	451.0	812.0	801.0
March	536.0	916.0	916.0
April	539.0	922.0	920.0
May	617.0	1076.0	1025.0
June	651.0	1153.0	1071.0
July	700.0	1125.0	1137.0
August	813.0	1203.0	1290.0
Total	4681.0	7857.0	
September	722.7	1029.5	1168.0
November	870.4	1233.8	1368.0

Exhibit C illustrates the plotting of the overhead and labor statistics above.

A correlation line was drawn and at the point of intersection on the vertical axis, it was determined by "inspection" that the indicated monthly fixed expenses were approximately $191,000.

The next step was to determine the variable expense value which is calculated by subtracting the predetermined fixed expense dollars of $1,528.0 ($191.0 x 8 months) from the total expense ($7856.0) to obtain the variable expense amount of $6,328.0 as shown on the exhibit. The variable expense divided by the direct labor provided an expense rate of 135.2%.

The procedure described above is a rapid means of developing a projected fixed expense and a variable rate, but for greater accuracy, the fixed expense should be statistically generated as shown in Exhibit C. In this process, a formula is used wherein the fixed expense is equal to the minimum expense less the difference between the maximum and minimum expenses. The resulting value is then divided by the result from maximum direct labor divided by the minimum labor less the whole number "1".

As noted in the exhibit, $1203.0 was the maximum expense for a month in the eight-month period and $650.0 was the minimum—the difference then was $553.0. The maximum labor dollars for any one month was $813.0 and this value divided by the

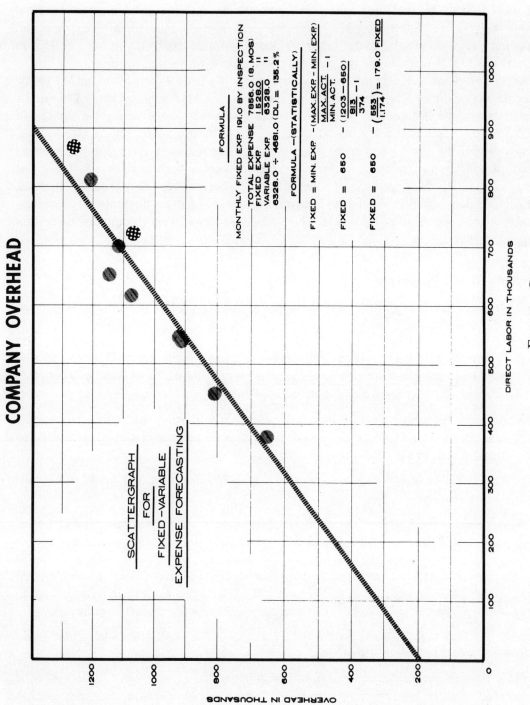

EXHIBIT C

minimum labor dollars of $374.0 resulted in a value of 2.174. Subtracting "1.0" from this value produced the "1.174" amount. $553.0 divided by 1.174 resulted in a value of $471.0. This amount then subtracted from the $650.0 produced a statistical fixed expense of $179.0. Subtracting the computed fixed expense from the total expense and dividing the result by the direct labor yielded a variable expense rate of 137.3% as versus the 135.2% developed through the above initial inspection process.

As a test of the accuracy of the data developed, the fixed expense was added to the calculation of direct labor multiplied by the above variable expense rate. The results are shown in the last column of the scattergraph statistics above under the caption of "DLX". It is noted that some results were very close to the actuals, particularly in instances where the direct labor dollars were close to the calculated average monthly direct labor of $585.0. As displayed, the largest variances were at the minimum ($374.0) and maximum ($813.0) labor bases. In organizations where direct labor is fairly constant, this projection technique is fairly accurate. If the base does fluctuate to extremes, formula adjustments could be made, plus or minus, which would compensate for that type of situation.

Expense Detail Projection

There are a number of different methods that can be used in projecting expense account detail as described below:

- Based on past history records and statistics, proportionate percentages to the total overhead can be developed and the expense spread by major expense categories or detailed accounts through the percent application.

- A successful approach in some organizations is to develop an individual expense rate per direct labor hour or based on other pertinent correlation factors such as headcount as in the case of fringe benefits.

- The "least squares" or regression statistical technique described in the latter part of this chapter.

- Another method is to go through the same process for each account development as discussed above for the total overhead expense—scattergraph approach.

The historical expense statistics must be thoroughly analyzed to determine the most effective projection procedure in any given organization because of their possible unique operations. Whatever the method, it should be geared to a mechanical application.

Least Squares Method of Projection

This type of projection is similar to the "scattergraph" technique principle. It is concerned with the prediction of variable "X" based on assumption of its relationship to a variable "Y". The method of least squares establishes a most probable relationship based on historical performance. If conditions in the past caused a certain relationship and it is assumed that similar conditions will exist in the future, then this type of predicting is considered valid. Generally, "Y" is related to "X" by a constant amount, plus a proportion of the value of "X" expressed mathematically as "$Y = a + bX$".

When this relationship is expressed graphically, the formula would be represented by a line—*a* would indicate the distance from the zero-point on the chart to the point where the formula line crosses the Y-axis, and *b* would give the slope of the line. More precisely, *b* expresses the tangent of the angle which the formula makes with the horizontal. As an example, the following charts illustrate this prediction philosophy.

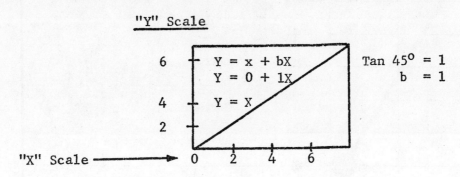

In the above chart, Y equals X and for every change in X there is an equal change in Y.

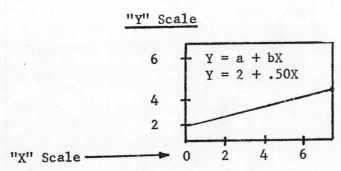

In the above chart, the formula indicates a Y—intercept or start point of "2" and a relationship of ½ X therefore $Y = 2 + .50X$.

Exhibit D displays the correlation established between overhead and direct labor dollars using the least squares approach in establishing a formula for projecting overhead expense.

As noted, eleven months of data were used. Calculations were performed mechanically and the results displayed on this exhibit. In addition to deriving the projection formula (overhead equals 46,000 + 1.2X), the chart also provides a rapid and visual means of making projections. For example, if it was required to determine an approximate overhead value for a labor dollar amount of $100.0, you would simply note the point of intersection on the vertical scale which indicates an approximate overhead value of $165.0.

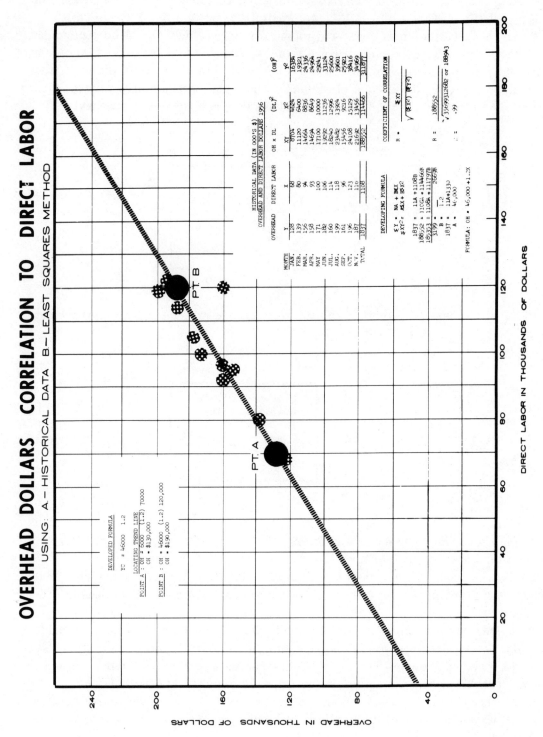

Exhibit D

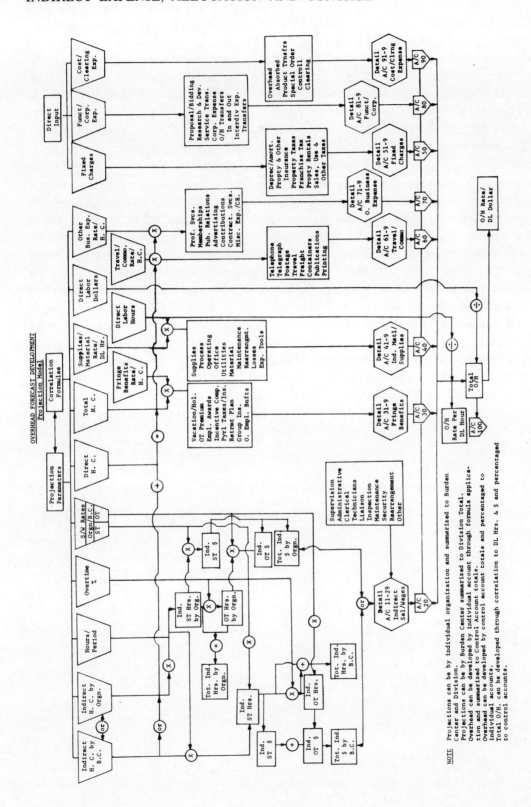

EXHIBIT E

NOTE: Projections can be by individual organization and summarized to Division.
      Center and Division.
      Projections can be by Burden Center summarized to Division Total.
      Overhead can be developed by individual account through formula applica-
      tion and summarized to Control Account totals.
      Overhead can be developed by control account totals and percentaged to
      individual accounts.
      Total O/H can be developed through correlation to DL Hrs. & $ and percentaged
      to control accounts.

The same procedure can also be used in developing formulae for expense categories or individual accounts as noted previously.

The two dark circles (points A & B) in Exhibit D represent statistically developed points from formula application in order to provide the basis for drawing the trend line. The checkered circles represent the overhead plots against the labor dollars.

All types of correlation projections are possible through the least squares approach to projecting indirect expenses. This technique must be thoroughly understood and applicable however in order that it can be effectively used as a projection tool.

A typical model of an indirect expense projection process is displayed in Exhibit E wherein certain correlation formulae are used to develop the various expenses. Indirect headcount can be a direct input projection or based on a percent of direct manpower and priced as shown on this exhibit. Fringe Benefits are correlated to total headcount as well as is Other Business Expenses and Travel/Communication. The reasoning being that these expenses are *generally* based on the increase of decrease of personnel. Supplies and Material expenses are correlated to a rate per direct labor hour based on the experience that as more hours are used, the greater will be these expenses. Certain costs are predeterminable and enter the system as direct input such as Fixed Charges, Corporate Allocations and Clearing Expenses. From this model a rate per direct labor hour or a percentage of direct labor dollars is developed for application purposes in terms of usage for proposal or product pricing, negotiations and booking expenses.

Indirect expense is one of the governing criteria in selling a product and, therefore, should receive its proper emphasis from the standpoint of control in expense incurrence, allocation, organization responsibility, budgeting and in monitoring actual expense status with respect to planned expenditures.

6

Travel Analysis,
Expenditure and Control

Business travel is a "sleeper" expense that usually fails to receive its appropriate emphasis when management evaluates the financial aspects of its operations. This is not to say that travel costs are ignored, but rather their magnitude or significance is obscured because they are included in broader categories of cost analysis and reporting.

In one organization of approximately 7,000 employes, there was an average of 350 employes on the road spending approximately $88,000 per week and time from work was 14,000 manhours per week. The irony was that until the travel analysis activity was mechanized, it was not known on a timely basis that there were 50 people traveling to a similar destination and ten of which were attending the same seminar.

COMPUTERIZING THE TRAVEL SYSTEM

Defining the Requirements

In order to design, develop and implement the computerized travel system, there are some very definite needs that have to be considered which are noted as follows:

1. Identification of travelers by organizational units for expenditure responsibility and monitoring.
2. The amount of travel advances and type (cash, company check, traveler's check, etc.). This is necessary for cash requirement planning and further, it represents in the aggregate the approximate travel cost or expense commitment.
3. Analysis of the need for and validity of the trip from management's view. How many employes are traveling for the same reason and have past results warranted this expenditure?
4. Evaluation of commonality of trips to the same destination. Could one traveler accomplish a number of tasks at the same destination rather than sending four travelers—consolidated trip tasks are feasible.
5. Provide summaries of advances, expenses and liquidations to functional execu-

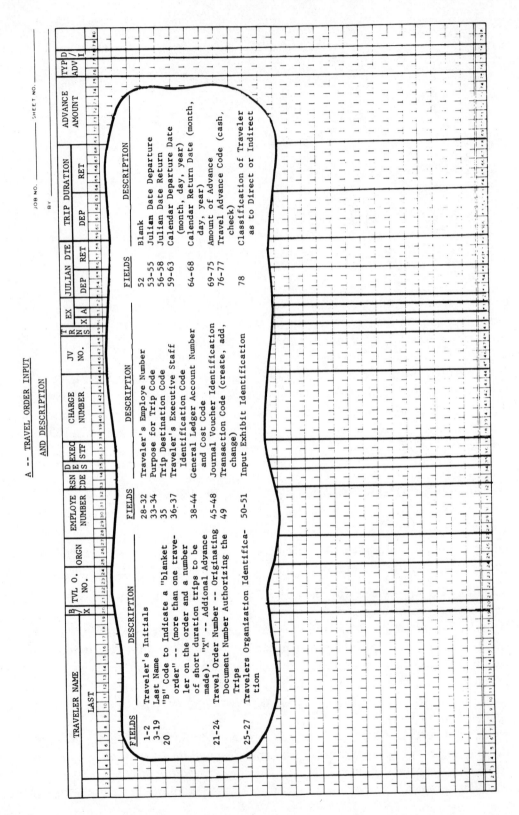

A -- TRAVEL ORDER INPUT
AND DESCRIPTION

FIELDS   DESCRIPTION

1-2   Traveler's Initials

3-19   Last Name

20   "B" Code to Indicate a "blanket order" -- (more than one traveler on the order and a number of short duration trips to be made). "X" -- Addional Advance

21-24   Travel Order Number -- Originating Document Number Authorizing the Trips

25-27   Travelers Organization Identification

FIELDS   DESCRIPTION

28-32   Traveler's Employe Number

33-34   Purpose for Trip Code

35   Trip Destination Code

36-37   Traveler's Executive Staff Identification Code

38-44   General Ledger Account Number and Cost Code

45-48   Journal Voucher Identification

49   Transaction Code (create, add, change)

50-51   Input Exhibit Identification

FIELDS   DESCRIPTION

52   Blank

53-55   Julian Date Departure

56-58   Julian Date Return

59-63   Calendar Departure Date (month, day, year)

64-68   Calendar Return Date (month, day, year)

69-75   Amount of Advance

76-77   Travel Advance Code (cash, check)

78   Classification of Traveler as to Direct or Indirect

EXHIBIT A

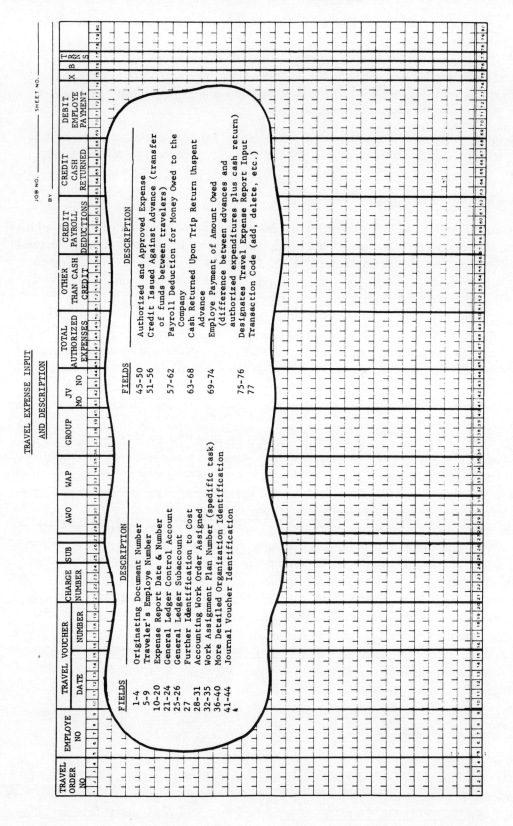

TRAVEL EXPENSE INPUT
AND DESCRIPTION

JOB NO. _____   SHEET NO. _____
BY _____

FIELDS   DESCRIPTION

1-4   Originating Document Number
5-9   Traveler's Employe Number
10-20   Expense Report Date & Number
21-24   General Ledger Control Account
25-26   General Ledger Subaccount
27   Further Identification to Cost
28-31   Accounting Work Order Assigned
32-35   Work Assignment Plan Number (specific task)
36-40   More Detailed Organization Identification
41-44   Journal Voucher Identification

FIELDS   DESCRIPTION

45-50   Authorized and Approved Expense
51-56   Credit Issued Against Advance (transfer of funds between travelers)
57-62   Payroll Deduction for Money Owed to the Company
63-68   Cash Returned Upon Trip Return Unspent Advance
69-74   Employe Payment of Amount Owed (difference between advances and authorized expenditures plus cash return)
75-76   Designates Travel Expense Report Input
77   Transaction Code (add, delete, etc.)

EXHIBIT B

tives so that each can evaluate his own organization in terms of travel costs and their necessity.

6. Eliminate manual recordkeeping and summary calculating effort.
7. Provide timely information of aged outstanding balances so that the proper action can be taken to obtain settlement of the account directly with the employe or through an automatic payroll deduction.

To satisfactorily meet the above needs, it is almost mandatory to mechanize the travel accounting function because of the clerical effort and cost involved to do it manually.

Data Collection from Source Documents

In any computerized system, one of the basic, but most important elements which govern successful operations is the input into the system. This means it must be valid and entered into the proper location fields which have been reflected in the coding process. The Travel Order Document input and its description is shown in Exhibit A. The data is entered from the above source document.

It is noted that each item has its appropriate field length. There may be instances when all of the information is unavailable when the traveler departs on his trip, but it can be entered later through an "add" transaction "B" in column 49 on a supplemental input form. Changes and deletions can also be effected to the initial record by the proper transaction codes. Coding of data is necessary in order to compact the input and resident tables in the files are used to identify the information in the appropriate description on its output.

The initial input sets up the record in file and must always include travel order and employe number since these are the basic key identifiers to the traveler's records. A transaction code must always be included on the input in order for the program to perform its function of what to do with the data. The other information is also important in order to fulfill various processing and reporting needs.

When the traveler returns, he prepares the Expense Report Document. Upon proper review, approval and coding by the accounting travel section, this data is entered directly from the document in the appropriate fields as detailed in Exhibit B.

The expense information is used to supplement the record created from the travel departure report. Both input formats are important in that Exhibit A provides trip detail and advances and Exhibit B gives the expense detail and liquidation of the advance amount.

In addition to the above input which is on a current basis, the initial history record input must be provided through the use of the same input forms. Table code descriptions are entered on a separate format.

Input Data Processing

When the input and output requirements have been resolved, the next need is to consider the processing requirements. Exhibit C displays the sequence of events in the computer processing activity.

As shown in this exhibit, the cards are processed to tape if not entered directly online and listings are provided to the originating organization as support and reference to the

MECHANICAL TRAVEL PROGRAM PROCESSING

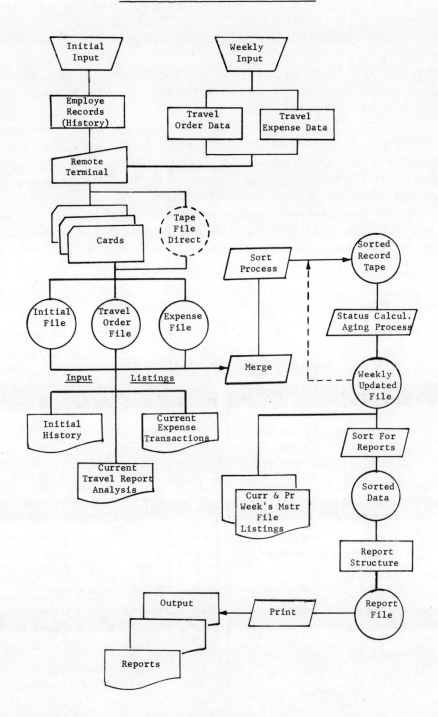

EXHIBIT C

transaction. The output listing is in the same format as the input entered except travelers are sorted by travel order and employe number sequence within executive staff code.

The initial history or master file represents the records from the manual employe travel register at the start of the mechanical system. This is a large input effort, but must be done in order to maintain the continuity and transition from the manual to mechanical reporting.

The new input and master file data is merged and the sorts, calculations and aging processes are performed so that the storage file properly represents updated information to satisfy current travel status reporting.

The various sorts include travelers by executive staff organizations, destination, trip reason, direct and indirect classification, organization, charge number and journal voucher number. The updating includes the algebraic addition, subtraction and reconcilement of current input advances and expenses to the traveler's account, staff group and company totals as well as journal voucher amounts.

The computer reports and summarizes direct, indirect and total travelers for both current and prior week. If the traveler's name appears more than one time in a particular period, he is included only once in the total reported traveler headcount for that period.

Data Identifications

In order to compress input, table codes must be established in the program. The

PROCESSING PARAMETERS

TRANSACTIONS

CODE	DESCRIPTION
B	TRAVELER DELETION
X	ADJUSTMENT OF ADVANCES

EXECUTIVE STAFF REPORTING

CODE	LEVEL
AA	PRESIDENT
BB	VP-OPERATIONS
CC	VP-ENGINEERING
DD	CONTROLLER
EE	DIR. IND. RELATIONS

DIRECT CHARGE IDENTIFICATION

ACCT	
164 165	DIRECT PERSONNEL & CHARGES

REASON FOR TRIP

CODE	DESCRIPTION
1	IND. ASSOC. CONF/SEMINARS
2	TECH. LIASON W/CUSTOMER
3	CONTRACT/NEGOTIATIONS W/VENDOR
4	DIRECT CHARGES
5	CUSTOMER NEGOTIATIONS

DESTINATION

CODE	LOCATION
A	WASHINGTON, DC., VA., MD.
B	NYC AREA
C	HUNTSVILLE, ALA.
D	FT. WORTH, TEXAS
E	EL PASO, TEXAS (FT. BLISS, ETC.)

ADVANCE IDENTIFICATION

CODE	DESCRIPTION
1	PETTY CASH
2	GENERAL DYNAMICS CHECK
3	TRAVELER'S CHECK

EXHIBIT D

extent and detail of the tables are dependent upon organization needs. Exhibit D is an example of codes established to designate narrative descriptions for destination, staff groups, trip reason, etc.

The codes in the exhibit are self-explanatory except for two special transaction codes listed. An entry coded "B" is made for an individual traveling on a "blanket order" which indicates that the trip is flexible and/or that a number of trips or travelers are authorized against the same travel order. An "X" code entry signifies that there is an adjustment to be made to the amount of the traveler's advance. The purpose of this code is to make sure that the supplemental advance has been entered and properly identified in the records.

Other common transaction codes are used to indicate an instruction to the computer for performing a specific task and are described as follows:

Code	Description
A	Create new record (history record or new input)
B	Add to record—data was lacking in the initial input
C	Change a record—error in previous input or the need for adjustment to the file record
D	Delete record
E	Retrieve record. This is used for online activity and permits the display of a record from the disk file

An example of actual input and its coding is shown in Exhibit E, although for purposes of presentation it is not in the same sequence as the input format.

TRAVEL ORDER INPUT DATA

TRAVELLER NAME	TRANS		EMPLOYE NO.	ORGN	STAFF IDENT.		DIR/IND	TVL O NO	CHG NO	
M. R. Smith	B	BLANKET CODE DELETION	72640	27	QUALITY ASSURANCE	BB VP ENGRG	D	1550	165	DIRECT CHARGE
H. M. Jones	X	ADVANCE AMOUNT CHANGE	56421	10	CONTROLLER DEPT.	CC CONTROLLER	I	139	600	OVER-HEAD

RSN CDE		DEST CDE		ADV AMT	TYPE ADV	ADD ADV COD		DURATION OF TRIP		
								FROM	TO	
2	TECH LIASON WITH CUSTOMER	B	NYC AREA	100	11 PETTY CASH	X	NO WIRE ADVANCE	08/15/67	08/18/67	NOT REPORTED IN SUBSEQUENT WEEK
3	CONTRACT NEG. W/ VENDOR	C	HUNTSVILLE, ALA.	50	33 TRAVELER'S CHECK	X		08/20/67	09/10/67	REPORTED IN PRIOR & CURRENT WEEK'S ACTIVITY

EXHIBIT E

It is noted that if the description data were "spelled out" in narrative on the input, it would take three or four cards or a number of direct input lines into the system in order to enter the data. This would be a time-consuming, repetitive task.

General Types of Output

The batch output is concerned with the following reporting in broad categorization:

- Listing of the current input data and combined listing of current and prior period active traveler records.

- Analytical data concerned with travel order input which provides varied summary information by staff organization and company totals relative to destination, reason, charge numbers and direct and indirect designation. Exhibit F indicates the type of reporting from the travel order input.

- Summaries are provided from the expense report input which are concerned with the differences between advances and credits (approved expenses and/or cash returns), aging of the unpaid balances and payroll deductions.

- Segregated reports are provided for the staff groups for travel control purposes so they can review and monitor their subordinates' travel activities, expenditures, status and overall group's performance. The reports are similar to those prepared for the overall company travel activity.

SPECIFIC REPORT DESCRIPTION

There are a number of reports generated mechanically from this system as shown in the Exhibit G flowchart and described below.

1. *Travel Order Analysis*—a listing of current week's active travelers in employe number sequence and travel order number. Shows all of the travel order detail with an overall summary for the organization at the end of the report. An example of output format (1) is as follows:

REPORT NO XXXXX   (1)   <u>TRAVEL ORDER ANALYSIS</u>   W/E 10/27/69

(Current Week)

TRAVELER NAME	TRAVEL ORDER NO	EMPLOYE DEPT NO	DEST	CHG NO	REASON FOR TRIP	DURATION DEP	DURATION RET	ADVANCED DOLLARS	D I	HOW PAID	ADDNL ADV
M. R. SMITH	1005	10 768	NYC	600	SEMINAR	10/20	10/30	200.00	I	CASH	NO

	SUMMARY FOR W/E 10/27/69	ADVANCE AMOUNT
	CASH	$200.00
	TRAVELER CHECK	.00
	COMPANY CHECK	.00
	TOTAL ADVANCES	$200.00

NO. TRAVELERS <u>0</u> DIRECT <u>1</u> INDIRECT <u>1</u> TOTAL

DETAILED OUTPUT REPORTING

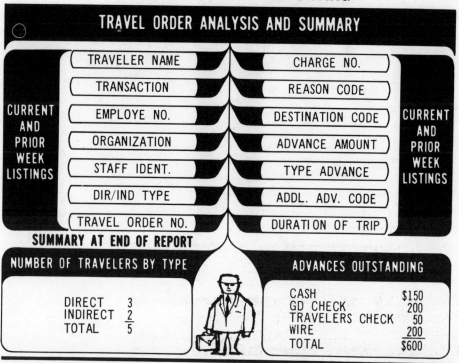

TRAVEL ORDER ANALYSIS AND SUMMARY

CURRENT AND PRIOR WEEK LISTINGS

TRAVELER NAME	CHARGE NO.
TRANSACTION	REASON CODE
EMPLOYE NO.	DESTINATION CODE
ORGANIZATION	ADVANCE AMOUNT
STAFF IDENT.	TYPE ADVANCE
DIR/IND TYPE	ADDL. ADV. CODE
TRAVEL ORDER NO.	DURATION OF TRIP

CURRENT AND PRIOR WEEK LISTINGS

SUMMARY AT END OF REPORT

NUMBER OF TRAVELERS BY TYPE

DIRECT	3
INDIRECT	2
TOTAL	5

ADVANCES OUTSTANDING

CASH	$150
GD CHECK	200
TRAVELERS CHECK	50
WIRE	200
TOTAL	$600

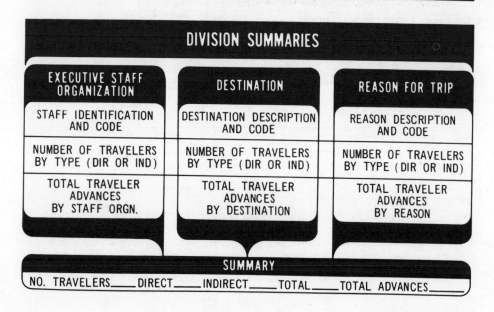

DIVISION SUMMARIES

EXECUTIVE STAFF ORGANIZATION	DESTINATION	REASON FOR TRIP
STAFF IDENTIFICATION AND CODE	DESTINATION DESCRIPTION AND CODE	REASON DESCRIPTION AND CODE
NUMBER OF TRAVELERS BY TYPE (DIR OR IND)	NUMBER OF TRAVELERS BY TYPE (DIR OR IND)	NUMBER OF TRAVELERS BY TYPE (DIR OR IND)
TOTAL TRAVELER ADVANCES BY STAFF ORGN.	TOTAL TRAVELER ADVANCES BY DESTINATION	TOTAL TRAVELER ADVANCES BY REASON

SUMMARY

NO. TRAVELERS____ DIRECT____ INDIRECT____ TOTAL____ TOTAL ADVANCES____

EXHIBIT F

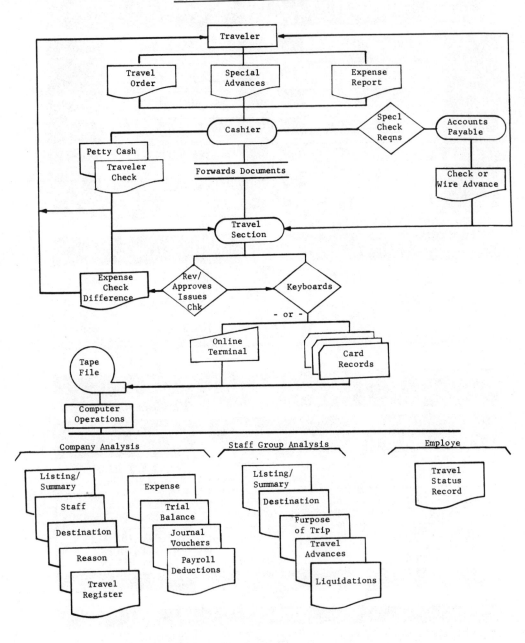

EXHIBIT G

2. *Travel Order Analysis (active current and prior period data)*—the listing is similar to the above except that it combines the active prior period travelers with the current week in order to reflect the overall status of all travelers "on the road." The report structure and summary is similar to that in (1) above.

3. *Staff Organization Analysis (active current and prior period active)*—the listing is similar to (1) and (2) above in that it presents the same detail for each individual staff group. This report is distributed to the travel section, staff executive and company management.

4. *Staff Organization by Destination*—at end of each staff group's report is the following summary:

(4) CONTROLLER FUNCTION SUMMARY

(By Destination)

DESTINATION	DIR	IND	TOTAL	ADVANCE
NYC	0	1	1	$200.00

5. *Staff Organization by Reason*—this is an additional summary at the end of the staff group's report and is presented as follows:

(5) CONTROLLER FUNCTION SUMMARY

(By Reason)

REASON	DIR	IND	TOTAL	ADVANCE
SEMINAR	0	1	1	$200.00

6. *Total Company Analysis by Organization*—this is a summary listing of traveler headcount totals and advances by staff organization.

(6) ORGANIZATION SUMMARY BY STAFF GROUP

STAFF GROUP	DIR	IND	TOTAL	ADVANCE
CONTROLLER	0	1	1	$200.00

7. *Total Company Analysis by Destination and Reason*—this summary is similar to the staff organization examples in reports (4) and (5) above. It achieves the same

purposes of traveler activity evaluation and control except on a company-wide basis.

8. *Traveler Expense Transaction Listing*—this is a listing of the detailed expense input for updating the traveler file resulting from his trip return. The format of this report is as follows:

(8) TRAVEL EXPENSE TRANSACTIONS

Employee No.	Tvl O. No.	Voucher No.	Voucher Date	Numbers Dept. Grp	Wap	Chg No.	Expense Auth	Cash Return	Other Credit	Payroll Deduct	Paid Empl	TRNS
768	1005	72640	10 / 71	10		600	175.00	15.00	10.00			A

9. *Employe Travel Register*—for immediate reference to an employe's travel status by travel order number, this report is invaluable for answering questions and determining overall company totals. It is formatted as follows:

(9) EMPLOYEE TRAVEL REGISTER

TRAVELER'S NAME	EMPLOYEE NO.	TRAVEL ORDER NO.	ACCT NO.	DEPT	TOTAL AUTH.	OTHER CREDITS	DEBITS (INC.ADV.)	OWE EMP	OWE CO
M. R. SMITH	768	1005	600	10	175.00	25.00	200.00	.00	.00

10. *Organization Travel Advance Liquidation*—this report is prepared for each employee twice a month to indicate his individual travel transactions. It keeps his travel account status current and makes possible the reduction of telephone calls to the travel section for information relative to his account. The report layout is as follows:

(10) EMPLOYE TRAVEL RECORD

TRAVEL ORDER NO.	VOUCHER NO.	VOUCHER DATE	ADVANCES/ DEBITS	TOTAL CREDITS	OWE EMP	OWED CO	DUE AMOUNTS AGED U/30 DA	DUE AMOUNTS AGED 31-60 DA	DUE AMOUNTS AGED 60-40 DA
1005	72640	10	200.00	200.00	.00	.00	.00	.00	.00

11. *Staff Travel Advance Liquidation*—this report is similar to (10) above except that the employes' names are listed within each staff group and this report is distributed to each staff organization for their review and action—particularly if the account is delinquent based on the "aging" status.

12. *Travel Trial Balance*—this report is an overall company status report and is similar to that described for (11) above—staff travel advance liquidation. It provides summary totals for top management review and action. It highlights the extent of delinquencies in each traveler's account as well as indicates the cost of his travel activity.

13. *Payroll Deductions*—when a deduction is made, it is reported on the following format which is forwarded to the Payroll Section for action (this process is performed mechanically based on criteria that is set forth by policy and program instruction):

(13) <u>PAYROLL DEDUCTION</u>

TRAVELER'S NAME	EMPLOYEE NO.	TRAVEL ORDER NO.	TRAVEL VOUCHER NO.	ACCOUNT NO.	AMOUNT

The extent of the above mechanical reporting is, of course, dependent upon organizational needs. Reporting by various organizational levels, charge numbers or other criteria is no problem. The proper sorting in the program and report structuring will achieve most any requirement. Proper planning in system design and "built-in" flexibility will yield the desired results. Sales territories can be substituted for destinations, sales managers for executive staffs, code variations for reasons, etc.—the opportunity is unlimited in the model described above.

COMPUTER ANALYSIS REPORTING

The various computer processes and reports described above provide considerable analysis and statistical data for analysis of all aspects of the travel activity and at all levels —employe, organization, staff group and total company. The summary statistics provide management with an overview of their travel activities for purposes of surveillance and control. Problem areas are readily identified specifically and decision action can be readily effected. Out-of-control travel activity can be assessed and associated with organizational responsibility which in turn has the means of determining and resolving problems to the employe level. Excess expenditures and travel activity as well as travel account delinquencies can be readily established through the mechanical travel system.

ONLINE PROCESSING/REPORTING

The primary objective in this activity is to determine the information that is required rapidly and on a current status basis. The Travel Section, having been exposed to many inquiries from travelers, accounting, operating groups and management, can most generally provide the appropriate guidelines in this determination.

An example of a coded message and the reply is noted below:

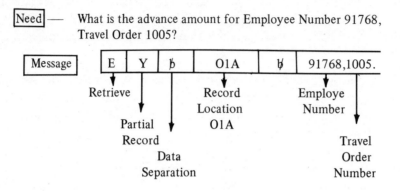

Need — What is the advance amount for Employee Number 91768, Travel Order 1005?

Reply — Advance amount for employe no. 91768, TO no. 1005 is $150.00.

In addition to retrieving data, you can create a record, change or add to it by using the appropriate transaction code and the other required identifiers and input information.

AUDIT TRAILS/CONTROLS

The data validity in any mechanical system is dependent on audit trails and controls. The extent of controls to be established is a matter of complexity, need and cost involved in sophisticating the program. In the above system, the following guidelines are minimal in order to achieve the maximum control with the least effort and expense:

- The employe travel order and expense document numbers are used to provide the audit trail to all required information relative to the employe. The staff group designators represent the audit trail determinant to organization activity.

- The travel order and expense voucher table should contain the lowest and highest controllable numbers in sequence and any other number would be cause for rejection.

- Only designated journal voucher numbers with associated general ledger account numbers can be entered into the system.

- Only proper code designations for staff, destination, reason for trip and other data will be accepted.

- Table file of authentic employe identification numbers.

- No input will be acceptable unless it has the appropriate keys of record location, transaction code, employe number, travel or voucher number.

A computerized travel control system is a practical means to timely evaluation of an organization's complete travel activity. It provides the tool for assessment of need for travel and measurement of tangible results. Although this system is most feasible for larger organizations with heavy travel activity, it does not preclude the need for certain aspects of reporting in smaller organization—either manual or mechanical. It provides for maximum recordkeeping and reporting with minimal clerical time and cost.

7

Computer Utilization Cost
Control and Allocation

In many organizations, computer usage costs have become a major expense that requires close scrutiny and analysis by management in order to be assured of its relative value in terms of cost versus benefits, productive utilization, proper accumulation and allocation of costs and that there are adequate procedures established to control computer operations.

COSTS INVOLVED

Exhibit A indicates the general type of costs associated with a computer operation which are the basis for its cost accumulation process. The extent, size and complexity of these costs are dependent upon the computer organization's operations.

Cost Identification

As computer costs are incurred, they should be identified to the appropriate work order in order to provide a means for their accumulation and, subsequently, their allocation to the users of computer services.

An example of an established computer work order to which costs are charged is shown below:

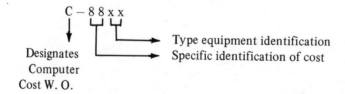

C – 8 8 x x

Designates
Computer
Cost W. O.

Type equipment identification
Specific identification of cost

COSTS INVOLVED IN COMPUTER OPERATIONS

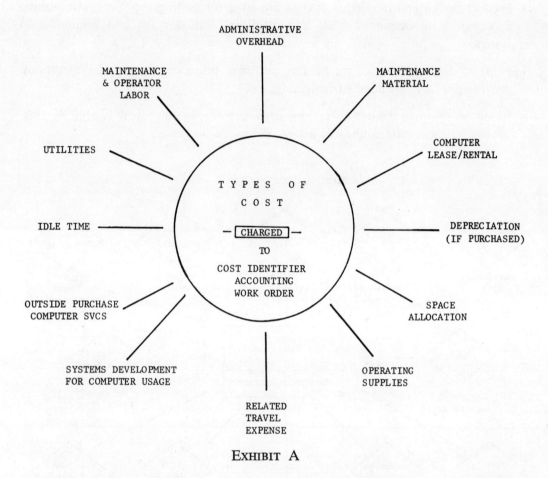

EXHIBIT A

The type of data represented by the work order designators allows for summarizing costs by specific type and equipment. Detailed costs can be ascertained by equipment type and cost description (labor, material, etc.).

MULTIPLE COMPUTER USERS

Exhibit B displays the various major user organizations and their type of activity which can be conducive to computer usage.

If properly used, the computer can serve as the "hub" for accommodating all types of input and its manipulation to service all organizations reporting needs. As an example, consider the following:

- Operating data provides performance statistics and cost data for the accounting system.

- Product design and development data are used for costing a project, establishing approximate productional needs and furnishing data for the cost accumulation system.

- Planning data can be used for bidding purposes, projecting anticipated operations, providing a basis for detailed budgeting, etc.

- Based on selective data from various organizations, management is able to plan, control, test alternate courses of action and make decisions.

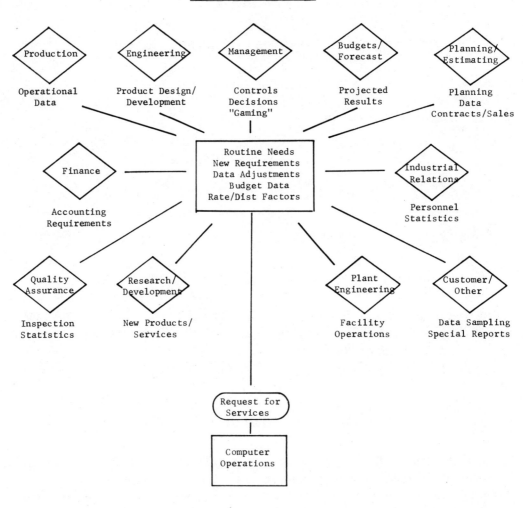

MULTIPLE COMPUTER USERS

EXHIBIT B

COST ACCUMULATION AND ALLOCATION PROCESS

User organizations are allocated computer costs on the basis of the routine production jobs performed by the computer center and a result of requests for new computer services. In the latter situation, the user organizations initiate a requirement request which is forwarded to computer operations as shown in Exhibit C.

This request contains pertinent information which identifies the submitting organization, job description, charge number (direct or indirect requirement), the processing required and its priority in terms of user needs. This request is screened by computer operations (noncomputer operating personnel) to determine the adequacy of information submitted, whether there is a duplication of reporting, whether the job can be scheduled, if it is properly approved, what resources are necessary and if the budget will accommodate the cost of the task. Other criteria can be added to this review process dependent upon the authority and responsibility vested in this group and management direction.

Service Request Decision

If the request does not meet the review criteria, it is returned to the user organization for more explanation, substantiation or whatever the concerned problem involved was for its disapproval.

If the request is approved, it is scheduled, the required steps taken for its accomplishment and the time recorded for the job performance. The recording of lapsed time for completion (including setup and other pertinent effort involved) is then entered on tape records.

Cost Allocation

The time involved on either a productional effort or new request is priced based on a predetermined calculated rate per hour and the cost of the individual tasks are reported. Although the rate is computer-generated based on the previous month's actuals (described below), the cost accounting function has the responsibility to monitor the rate for accuracy, adequacy and make pertinent adjustments as required. The cost allocations are therefore based on computer time usage (direct and indirect) multiplied by the rate—costs are reported in terms of organization, project and other detail required relative to the allocation distribution.

COMPUTER RATE CALCULATION AND APPLICATION

As noted in Exhibit D, certain inputs and processing are required in order to develop the application rates.

COST ACCUMULATION AND ALLOCATION PROCESS

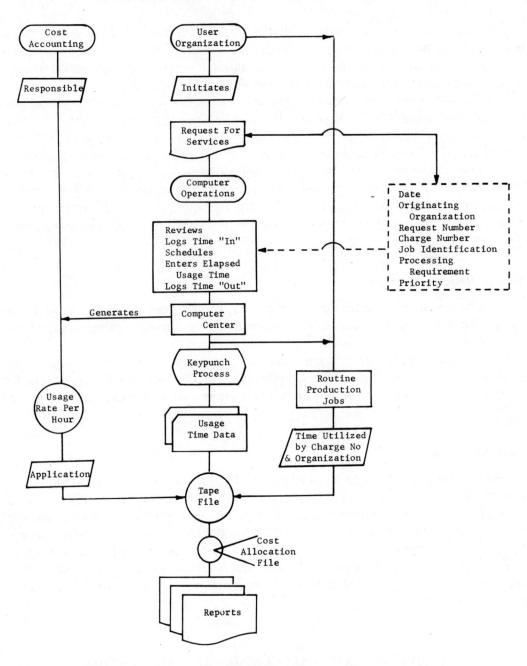

EXHIBIT C

COMPUTER RATE CALCULATION AND APPLICATION

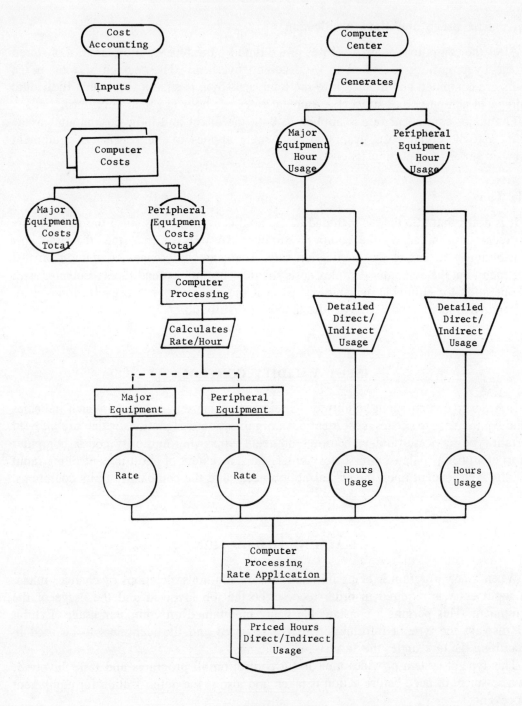

EXHIBIT D

The cost accounting function provides the accumulated computer costs input which is segregated for the prime processing computer(s) and peripheral or supporting equipment. All direct and indirect costs are included in the total cost data.

Equipment Usage and Rate Application

After the computer center processes usage time by the type of equipment, it is stored on file by project or identified to organization overhead. The segregated total usage hours are computed and divided into the total costs by a mechanical process. Individual segregated computer and support equipment rates per hour are then developed.

The major equipment rate is applied to both the direct and indirect computer usage hours and the dollar costs generated. The same applies to the peripheral equipment usage in order to apportion its costs.

Idle Time

It is noted that idle time is included in the total computer costs since the rental hours represent costs billed by the computer supplier. In view of this, the idle time cost distribution is a part of the application rate. There are differences of opinion on this treatment, but the computer complex costs should reflect all expenditures associated with its operation for equitable distribution. Even if the computers are organization-owned, a similar treatment should govern idle time cost distribution.

INPUT VALIDITY CONTROL

In order to control input validity or its rejection, a master file is used which indicates valid equipment type codes, cost identifiers, organization designations which are allowed certain type services, valid work order numbers, approving authority codes, computer effort identifier associated with a work order, etc. The extent of audit in controlling input validity is dependent upon the organization's needs and the complexity of its operations.

MACHINE UTILIZATION

When a new program is being initiated and/or additions, deletions or changes made, an input entry is required in order to describe the job involved and the usage of the equipment. This permits a constant file being maintained on computer usage. Exhibit D1 displays the type of information that is required and the identifiers to be used in describing the task under the "asterisked" columns.

This type of system provides a clear cut control on all programs and tasks involved, an assessment of need before action is taken and also is the authorization for equipment processing.

MACHINE UTILIZATION
NEW PROGRAM / JOB NUMBER

PROGRAM NO.	JOB NO.	JOB DESCRIPTION	K/P COLS	*	**	***			****
1–6	7–10	11–50	51–52	53	54	55	56–77	78	79–80
								1	A

* COMPUTER CODE
** TYPE OF RUN
*** FREQUENCY CODE
**** CARD TYPE

LEGEND:

** TYPE OF RUN

A – APPLICATION PROGRAM
C – CARD TO TAPE
D – DOT LIST
F – FARGO
I – INGP
K – KAISER LIST
P – PRINT
Q – REPRO
R – RPG
X – FIXIT

*** FREQUENCY CODE

A – DAILY
B – SEMI-WEEKLY
C – WEEKLY
D – BI-WEEKLY
E – MONTHLY
F – BI-MONTHLY
G – QUARTERLY
H – TRI-ANNUAL
I – SEMI-ANNUAL
J – ANNUAL
K – AS REQUIRED

**** CARD TYPE

A – ADD PROGRAM
B – ADD PROGRAM AND JOB
C – CHANGE PROGRAM
D – DELETE PROGRAM

EXHIBIT D1

AUDIT TRAILS

All output from the system can be traced back to the input document and sources of data by request number and the data contained therein. Detailed transaction listings on a weekly basis are compared to the input and if there are variances, they are investigated with reference to the source documents. Benefiting or user organization reference to the file is another means of tracing data back to its point of origin and verifying any unusual transactions entering the system.

REPORTING

There are a number of reports prepared from the computer utilization system both for internal computer operations control and reference as well as for the user organizations. Representative examples of these reports are as follows:

Transaction Listing (Computer Operations)

Week No	Request No	Job Code	Orig Orgn	Work Order	Type Equipment						Total Cost
					A		B		C		
					Hrs	Cost	Hrs	Cost	Hrs	Cost	

Transaction Listing (Organization)

Week No	Work Order	Request No	Job ID Code	Requestor Name	Production		Development		Total	
					Hrs	Cost	Hrs	Cost	Hrs	Cost

Budget Comparison (Organization or Project Detail)

Project	Work Order	This Period						Project To-date					
		Actual		Budget		Variance		Actual		Budget		Variance	
		Hrs	Cost	Hrs	Cost	Hrs	Cost	Hrs	Cost	Hrs	Cost	Hrs	Cost

The reports in addition to the above will vary for computer operations and the user organizations. Computer operations need to know such performance data as: total computer time utilization, idle time, downtime and for what reason, outside purchased time and why, behind schedule and what reports, job run times, reruns necessary and why and what jobs, budget comparison to actuals, unmatched suspense, analysis of computer load, etc.

The user organizations are more concerned with: rejection of input, was schedule met, action taken on service request and cost, etc.

ESTABLISHING COMPUTER USAGE BUDGET

One of the most effective means of evaluating and controlling computer usage costs and, in turn, computer operation costs is through the establishment of a budget system. This means that all user organizations must plan their computer usage in advance and obtain the necessary approvals before the computer center will undertake to do the tasks requested. The planned and approved computer requirements also serve another purpose—it allows the computer organization to make its plans, schedules, priorities, etc. The planning of computer usage provides the cognizant management with an opportunity to review and scrutinize the costs to be incurred and, like any other cost projection, the requirements must be substantiated. Further, based on the approved plan submissions, the computer center prepares their budget which, in turn, is carefully reviewed since it, too, is a part of the overall cost to the major organization's planned expenditures of operation.

Usage Budget Processing

Exhibit E indicates the processing involved in preparing the budget plan for computer usage.

The user organizations prepare and submit their approval proposals on pre-established forms which indicate their planned usage, organization and project identification, type equipment and other pertinent data by monthly period. The planned usage is for both the routine and anticipated requirements. These forms containing the requirement details are forwarded to computer operations who perform the review as indicated in Exhibit E.

A composite is made by computer operations of all the tasks, time required by type equipment and the associated cost. This information and their recommendations are then forwarded to management for their review. It is possible the screening process will reveal that more computer usage time is planned than is available or the costs are out of proportion with past history experience.

Monitoring and Controlling Computer Costs

Each month, a report is prepared mechanically for the total operation costs which is segregated by user organizations indicating the actual cost incurrence comparison to budget with the resulting variance. Another report shows the variance at the project level. All variances must be reconciled and explained and, if beyond certain tolerances, management decisions are necessary to correct the situation. Application rate comparisons are also followed closely as they may affect contract cost over/underruns, negotiations, meeting competition, profit effect, etc. The budget data is entered on magnetic tape for mechanical comparisons to the actuals generated monthly.

ESTABLISHING COMPUTER USAGE BUDGET

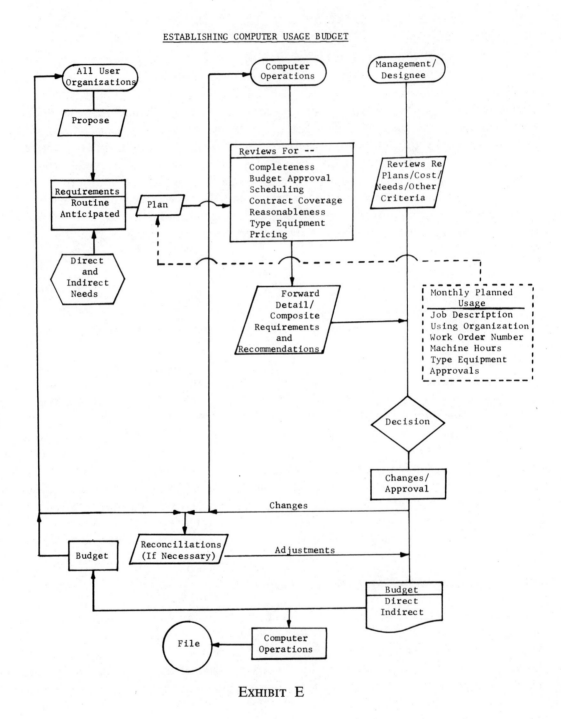

EXHIBIT E

SUMMARY OF INPUT/OUTPUT AND MASTER FILE DATA

Input	Output	Master File
Request Number	Suspense Code Report	Completion Date Scheduled
User Organization	Cost Reports	Machine Hours/Dollars
Number	Project	Week and Month and
Charge Numbers	Work Order	Year-to-date
Project	Task	Budget Variance (Hours
Work Order	Machine Type	and Dollars)
Task	Organization	Month and Year-to-date
Machine Type	Work in Process	Division Code
Job Code	Budgest Comparison	Processing Work Number
Requestor's Name	Status Reports	G/L Account Number
Equipment Code		Equipment Standard Rate
Budget		Suspense Control Code

Input	Output
General Ledger Account	Adjustment Number
Journal Voucher Number	Journal Voucher Number
	Charge Number Description

The above represents the primary data that is input into the computer utilization system from the services' request forms and the budget plan. The reporting results from this input and the involved computer processing.

The mechanization of recordkeeping and reporting computer utilization statistics will provide for: more timely, varied and detailed reporting, more accurate computer cost accumulation and its proper application, computer-generated application rates, more and varied statistics for measuring computer center performances and budget versus actual comparisons and variances in detail and summary.

8

Implementing a Mechanized Plant, Property and Equipment

One of the basic elements of cost that affects many facets of a business enterprise is the responsibility of the accounting function involved with the acquisition, recordkeeping and obsolescence monitoring of its plant, property and equipment. In many organizations, this is the largest single investment in doing business. This functional area requires close scrutiny and attention by all levels of the organization.

To achieve the proper control of the thousands of assets required in a business enterprise, appropriate identification must be assigned for efficient recording and processing of the information needed to satisfy financial reporting, taxation, budget comparisons, location, functional responsibility and depreciation calculations.

CONSIDERATIONS INVOLVED IN MECHANIZATION

The following steps are considered as essential requisites and recommended in assessing the current procedures for the initial "take-off" point and development of the computerized process:

- A flowchart displaying the manual procedure.

- An overall mechanical process flowchart which displays the approach to mechanization and indicates the input processing and output.

- Resolving output information that will be needed for recording and reporting so that the basic detailed file records can be determined in terms of composition, field length and file organization.

- Development of various code tables in order to achieve proper classification of data for initiating program action, sorting, calculating, summarizing, reporting and retrieving.

- Assigning record file and other code identifiers that will achieve compressed data entry.

- Procedure for computerization of depreciation.

- Establishing appropriate audit trial links and controls.

Capital Asset Data Flow

Exhibit A indicates the general mechanical process concerned with the fixed asset program.

As noted on this chart, input data enters into the system through a terminal device and is edited and audited before the processing cycle starts. The master file is created, sorted and summarized for other file input records in order to create various reports as indicated at the bottom of this exhibit. The alpha characters (A-D) represent file identifiers.

The master file data flow is displayed in Exhibit B and indicates the specific information that is contained in this file.

available such as depreciation rate and also the type of transaction data that is periodi-

This exhibit indicates the initial record, subsequent additions as the data becomes cally entered into the system. Records are updated as well as the various files.

Acquisition Document Input

The input requirements as shown in Exhibit C are described below with their appropriate field locations (entry can be card or terminal data).

Input card Format 1 represents the expenditure request data and is the initial input derived in the acquisition cycle. The document number will be the prime identifier for this record. The fields are described as follows:

Expenditure Request

Field	Identifier	Description
1	Input Card	Differentiates card input to record
2–6	Expend. Request No.	Request document number
7–10	Expend. Request Date	Request document date
11–14	Originating Organization	Organization originating request
15–19	Request for Purchase No.	Document number
20–23	Request for Purchase date	Document date
24–28	Purchase Order No.	Document number
29–32	Purchase Order Date	Document date
33–38	Estimated Price	Represents P. O. amount or estimate (considered as a purchase commitment)

39-42	Quantity	Number of units
43–55	Item Description	Asset nomenclature
56–60	Asset Model	Identifying number
61–65	Asset Serial	Identifying number
66–68	Vendor Code	Established identifying code
69–79	Vendor Name	Self-explanatory
80	Transaction Code	Transaction code identifying type of action to be performed within program

Input card 2 represents additional basic information when it becomes available from the purchase document and is added to the record through this card. The prime identifier is the purchase order number which is the record linkage to the Card 1 file. Its fields are described as follows:

Procurement Document

Field	Identifier	Description
1	Input Card	Differentiates card input to record
2–6	Purchase Order No.	Document number identification
7–10	Purchase Order Date	Document date
11–14	Work Order No.	Assigned by Cost Accounting of the asset item to be used for special task within contract
66	Activity	Activity for which asset is to be used: 1 — Contract requirement 2 — Internal use to accomplish ordinary organization needs 3 — Interdivision effort 4 — Foreign requirements 5 — Other
67–73	Location	Physical location by building of the asset and the organization who has possession/ responsibility
74–75	Type	A two-digit alpha-numeric code designation for the type of asset as, for example, typewriters, desks, oscilloscopes, scales, etc.. This code allows for more detailed and specific item reporting.
76	Transaction	Transaction code signifying the type of action to be performed within program such as: A — Create record B — Add data to existing record C — Change record D — Delete

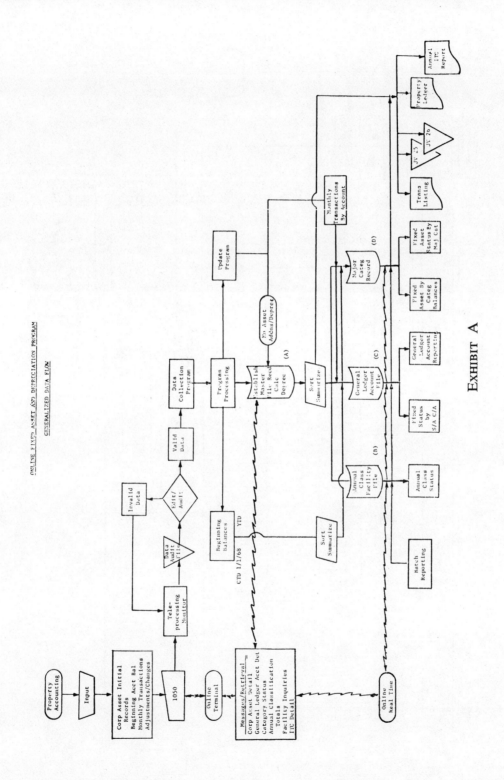

ONLINE FIXED ASSET AND DEPRECIATION PROGRAM

GENERALIZED DATA FLOW

EXHIBIT A

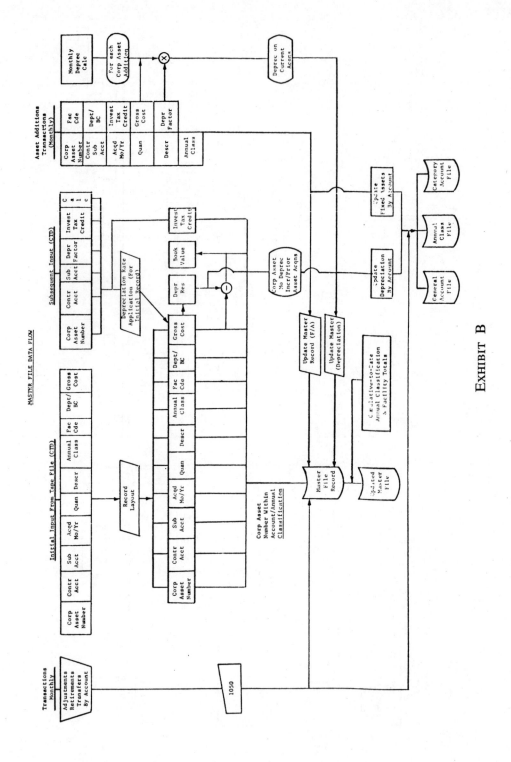

EXHIBIT B

OVERALL MECHANICAL PROCESS

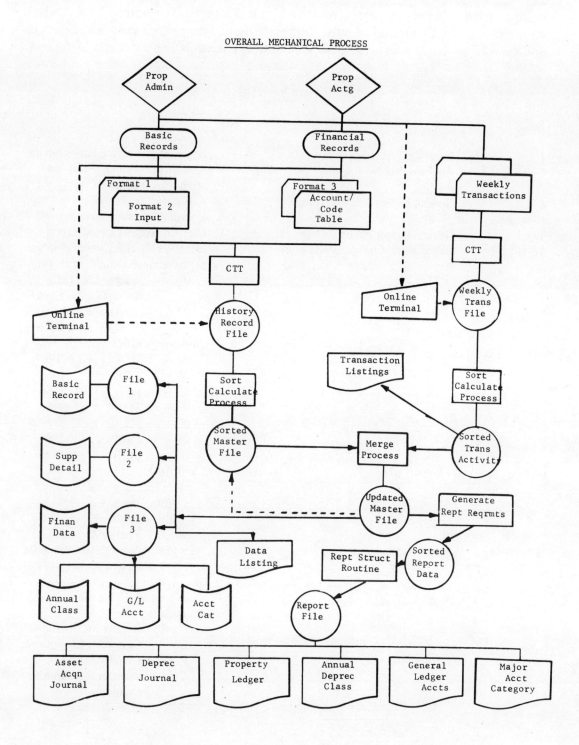

EXHIBIT C

Input Card 3 represents data provided by the Property Accounting Group which information is strictly finance oriented. It provides actual acquisition costs and depreciation rates to be used for expense and book value. The fields are described as follows:

Financial Input Data

Field	Identifier	Description
1	Input Card	Differentiates card input to record
2–7	Asset Control No.	Identification number assigned when asset is acquired
8–10	General Ledger Account—Prime	Account control number for recording and summations
11–12	General Ledger Account—Sub	Detailed account identification
13–14	Depreciation Classification Code	Identifies classification of item for depreciating. Examples of this are:

01 –	Straight Line (SL) Acquired before 1967	
02 –	Sum of the Year Digits (SYD) Acquired before 1967	
03 –	SL Acquired in 1967	
04 –	SYD " ". 1968	
05 –	SL " " 1968	
06 –	SYD " ". 1968	
07 –	SL " " 1969	
08 –	SYD" " 1969	
09 –	Other " 1970	

Field	Identifier	Description
15–16	Facility Code	Identifies asset to major physical location (could be one or many):

AA –	Facility X
BB –	Facility Y
CC –	Facility Z

Field	Identifier	Description
17–20	Acquired Mo/Yr	Acquisition date of asset by month and year. Required for tax analysis and reporting
21	Acquired Code	Code for identifying the source of acquisition:

C –	Inplant construction
G –	Customer/ Government
P –	Direct Purchase
T –	Transfer from another Division
O –	Miscellaneous

Field	Identifier	Description
22–26	Department/Burden Center	Identification to a department or burden center who maintain possession
27	Calculation	Calculation code identification that indicates to the program that depreciation rate will be applied to either gross cost or book value: X – Gross Cost Application Y – Book Value
28	ITC	The code identifies assets subject to investment tax credit which only applies to the first year of asset acquisition. The codes are as follows: 0 – Non-qualified 1 – 4 to 6 years of life 2 – 6 to 8 years life 3 – 8 years and over
29–31	Asset Item Quantity	Number of units or items involved in acquisition
32–44	Asset Item Description	Nomenclature of asset item
45–48	Depreciation Rate	A four-digit depreciation percent is inputted for application to asset cost/book value. This is entered by line asset item when acquired or can represent a cumulative percent, particularly, on old assets being inputted into the system from historical records.
49–58	Gross Cost	Represents the cost of asset acquired including freight, taxes or other miscellaneous expense involved.
59–68	Depreciation Reserve	Represents in current month the total amount of depreciation to-date on a fixed asset. This is mechanically calculated and/or can be programmed to accept a direct input, particularly, on initial input.

Field	Identifier	Description
69–78	Book Value	Represents difference between the Gross Cost and Depreciation Reserve.
79	Disposal	When an asset is disposed, a code will be entered which will indicate the type of disposal: 1 — Sold 2 — Transferred to another Organization 3 — Obsolescent/Scrapped 4 — Cannot be found/loss writeoff 5 — Other
80	Transaction	Transaction code identifier as described in Format Two above

Batch Processing

Exhibit D indicates in general the processing necessary not only for creating the initial historical records, but also for entering the current period transaction data.

When data is entered into the system, it is audited in terms of the validity of the asset assignment number and general ledger account identification. Further, all of the other required descriptive data must be entered (not necessarily at the same time) as shown in Exhibit E. The magnitude of the audit is contingent upon the system designer's program controls established.

The outcome of the computer processing provides sorted files which are then used to generate various disk data files for purposes of online retrieval.

The transaction tape file after sorting is merged with the historical records in order to provide an update of the records for current period reporting.

The depreciation is calculated and the book value computed for each asset which in turn is summarized to general ledger account and asset category totals.

The annual depreciation classification, File 4, is a sort of the data contained in File 3, described above. All of the asset items are classified according to the annual depreciation classification within an account and facility. Facility code (asset location) is the major sort with the general ledger account being secondary and the depreciation classification is the minor sort. Asset costs and depreciation expense or reserve are segregated by current period, year and cumulative-to-date.

MECHANICAL BATCH PROCESSING

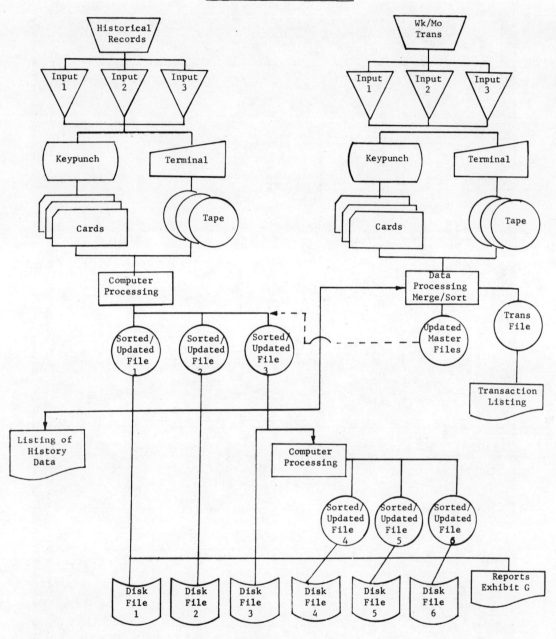

EXHIBIT D

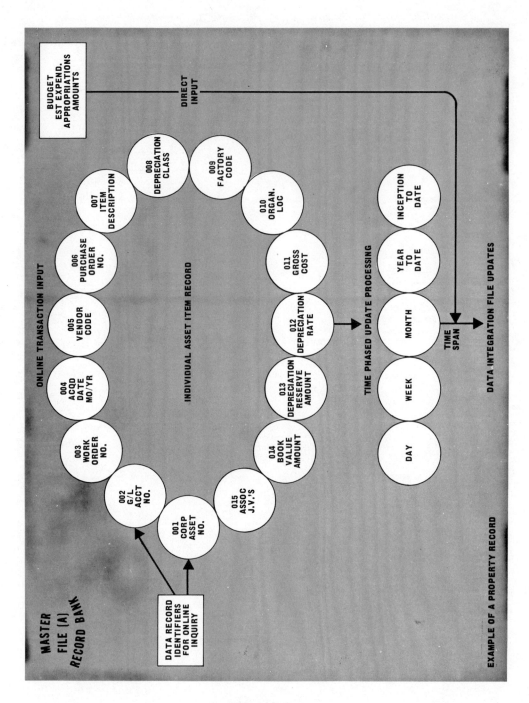

EXHIBIT E

The general ledger asset account, File 5, is also derived from the basic File 3. The sort is by control and subaccount number. This file contains the gross cost or beginning balance value. The gross cost value is entered if the asset item is being entered into the record for the first time and the beginning balance represents the beginning balance carryover from the prior period. As additions are made to a general ledger account in terms of new acquisitions, they are placed in the "addition" location field. When transfers, sale or obsolescence occurs, this data is entered in the "deletion/reduction" field and represents a decrease to the asset account total.

With respect to the depreciation record, File 6, the reserve or beginning balance is similar to that discussed above for the fixed asset account relative to gross cost and beginning balance. As depreciation is expensed by period, it is entered into the "addition" field and the reductions/deletions represent decreases to the depreciation accounts.

Obsolescence

This subject is defined as the loss of the usefulness of a capital asset due to the technological advancement displacement, retirement age of the asset which is established upon acquisition, change in asset need or usage decision, physical wear and tear from usage, revised operational requirements, etc. There may or may not be a salvage value dependent upon the situation or cause of obsolescence.

In this chapter, the "depreciation" nomenclature is synomous and utilized for describing the accounting treatment of the obsolescence process concerned with a capital asset. The discussion on this subject is premised on the fact that when a capital item is acquired, an estimated life of usefulness is established or assigned and the appropriate method of periodic discounting the value of the asset is decided upon. Most organizations have established practices that govern the procedures of depreciation and they are in accordance with tax regulation criteria and substantiation. Some of the types of depreciating assets mechanically, calculations and reports involved are outlined below.

Depreciation Calculation

Depreciation is computed to reflect decreases to asset values because of physical wear and tear, deterioration as well as obsolescence due to technological changes or new innovations. The application of depreciation factors under the manual process is generally made to the gross cost by major category of accounts; for example, furniture and fixtures, machinery and equipment, mobile equipment, etc. The reason for this is that in large organizations particularly, with thousands of asset items, it is prohibitive from the standpoint of clerical effort involved and timeliness of data availability.

In the mechanical process, depreciation application to individual items is a simple task with summations to various categorization and book values generated. Computing depreciation by asset item provides the necessary book values immediately at the time of an asset's disposal or when fully depreciated. All records are updated simultaneously. The mechanical system also provides the capability to compute depreciation by general ledger control account, asset category or in grand overall total.

The depreciation factors are based on organization policy and three methods are commonly used—Straight Line (equal spread by period over a predetermined time span); Sum of the Year's Digits and Double Declining—the latter two methods afford the maximum depreciation in the early estimated life of the asset. In the mechanical process, it makes no difference what depreciation procedure is used because the program is geared to accept any input factor and apply it to the specific acquisition cost designation.

In some instances, the depreciation factor is applied to the book value rather than gross cost. This situation occurs primarily when the item is transferred from one organization to another and has been partially depreciated and also in the double declining process.

Computer Generated Depreciation Factors

The processing procedure for developing depreciation factors mechanically is noted as follows:

1. When an asset is acquired and the decision is made as to the type of depreciating method to be used, a code designating the computation is entered into the system—for example, "X" would indicate straight line, "Y" for the sum of the year's digits and "Z" for double declining.
2. Simultaneous with the calculating procedure code input, the estimated years' life would be entered and also the "scrap" value, if any, beyond the estimated life of the asset.
3. In the case of straight line, the program would divide 100% by the life of the asset and the derived percent would be applied to the asset gross cost less scrap value if applicable. If the asset was acquired in mid-year, then the actual months of possession would be divided by 12 and a percentage developed. This percentage would be applied to the total year's depreciation developed above in order to obtain the appropriate depreciation in the first year of acquisition. Thereafter, the depreciation expense would be on a full annual basis but spread by period increments.

   If the asset is disposed of before the estimated life was reached, the computer would calculate the proportionate share of depreciation in the year of disposition and combine with the prior period cumulative to date depreciation in order to obtain total depreciation to date for asset value computation.
4. In the case of the sum of year's digits, the number of years' depreciation would be added together and the last year's number would be divided first by the above summed total to derive the application percentage. The depreciation factor would be applied to the gross cost to obtain the first year's depreciation value. As in the case of straight line above, the same procedure would govern to obtain the appropriate depreciation in the year of acquisition or disposal.

   An example of the procedure is as follows for an asset acquired in January, costing $120, with a 3 year life:

Year(s)	Process			Depreciation
3	$3 \div 6 = 50\%$	x 120 =		$60
2	$2 \div 6 = 33\ 1/3$	x 120 =		40
1	$1 \div 6 = 16\ 2/3$	x 120 =		20
6				$120

The above assumes there was no scrap value involved.

5. In the double declining (DD) process, it is assumed that in order to avoid infinity in depreciating an asset, depreciation would be calculated for the first two years on the DD basis and the remainder of the years would be based on utilizing the sum of the years' method. This is a common procedure and straight line could be substituted for the sum of the years. An example of this procedure follows with the assumptions that the asset cost was $150, acquired in January, estimated life of 4 years:

Cost	Process	Depreciation	Method
$150	$- 4 = 37.50 \times 2$	$ 75.00	DD
75	$150 - 75 = 75$		DD
	$- 4 = 18.75 \times 2$	37.00	DD
	$75 - 37 = 38$		DD
38	$2 - 3 = 66\ 2/3\% \times 38 =$	25.33	SYD
38	$1 - 3 = 33\ 1/3\% \times 38 =$	12.67	SYD
	Total	$150.00	

The factors developed by the computer would be outputted for reference and/or use possibly as a direct input in the future if the occasion so warranted.

Segregating Data for Tax Needs

The computerized property system provides the capability for segregating property information for tax payments and investment credit purposes. The procedure involved is as follows:

1. For each asset acquisition, there is an established sales factor which is applied to the gross cost in order to accumulate the sales tax paid each period for purposes of expense reporting.
2. The computer also outputs, at the appropriate required time, a listing of the gross acquisition costs of the various asset items and the depreciation that has been taken to date on those items. This listing is forwarded to the country authorities who in turn, based on their tax factor application derive the amount of property taxes to be paid. The taxes are generally based on calculated and revised book values.
3. Previously, there was established by the IRS a provision for investment tax credit

allowances. The capability in this program permitted segregation of data into four categories which are as follows:

Identifier	Categories
0	Asset item not qualified for tax credit
1	4–6 years life
2	6–8 years life
3	Over 8 years life

The master file was sorted monthly and asset items segregated as shown above. The designations were established at the time of input entry. The output report indicated current period and year-to-date costs as well as the eligible tax. The percent application used was 7% allowance for items with their life over eight years. Two-thirds of 7% for items in the 6–8 year category and ⅓ of 7% for items in the 4–6 year group. The credit was taken in the year of asset acquisition.

Audit Trail and Control

The primary audit of input data is accomplished through a visual and keypunch verification check when it is initially punched on cards or keyboarded on the terminal device. The program, however, should contain the capability to verify, internally, the input of:

> Control and subaccount numbers
> Annual classification (Depreciation Procedure)
> Tax codes
> Facility and Transaction Codes

If the data cannot be matched to that contained in the tables, it is rejected by the system. In case of asset control number, it is matched against a file to determine if it is currently in existence or if it falls within a span of numbers assigned to asset acquisitions.

The record fields are identified as to whether the data should be alpha or numeric.

Record codes are another control which checks the number of records before and after processing in order to make sure that no records were lost in the input activity.

To protect the validity of the data contained in the reporting records 4, 5, 6 no changes can be made to these files without being first reflected in the detailed File 3. This is accomplished through the use of transaction code usage in Field 80 of Input Two.

Batch Reporting

There are many, varied reports which are produced from this system as displayed in Exhibits F and G. Having organized the proper file records, any number of report variations are possible. The following discussion is concerned with the individual reports that are most common to the majority of organizations.

REPORTING

ASSET DETAIL FILE (F-1)

PURCHASE/SHOP ORDER			WORK ORDER			ASSET				LOCATION		CUS	ACTV	TYPE	CONT
NO	DATE		NO	DATE		QUAN	DESCRIPTION	MODEL	SERIAL	BLDG	ORG	CDE	CDE	CDE	CDE
	OPEN	CLOSE		OPEN	CLOSE										

VENDOR		INVOICE			RECEIVING	
CDE	NAME	NO	DATE	AMOUNT	NO	DATE

PROPERTY LEDGER (F-2)

ASSET CONTROL NO	G/L ACCT		DEP CLS CDE	FAC CDE	ACQD			DEPT/ C A L C	ASSET			DED RATE	GROSS COST	DEP RES	BOOK VAL
	PR	SUB	CDE	CDE	MO	YR	CDE	BC	C I T C	QUAN	DESCRIPTION	RATE	COST	RES	VAL

ANNUAL CLASSIFICATION STATUS (F-3)

G/L CONTROL A/C	DESCRIPTION	AN CLS CDE	ACQUISITION COST			DEPRECIATION			BOOK VALUE		
			CURR	YTD	CTD	CURR	YTD	CTD	CURR	YTD	CTD

EXHIBIT F

ACQUISITION JOURNAL VOUCHER (G-4)

G/L ACCT		DESCRIPTION	AMOUNT	
PR	SUB		DR	CR

DEPRECIATION JOURNAL VOUCHER (G-5)

G/L ACCT		DESCRIPTION	AMOUNT	
PR	SUB		DR	CR

INVESTMENT TAX CREDIT (G-6)

TAX CREDIT		ASSET CONTROL NO	G/L ACCT NO	ASSET		ACQUISITION COST
CDE	DESCRIPTION			QUAN	DESCRIPTION	

GENERAL LEDGER ACCOUNT STATUS (G-7)

G/L ACCT		DESCRIPTION	BEG PERIOD BAL	DR	CR	ENDING BALANCE
PR	SUB					

MAJOR CATEGORY ASSET STATUS* (G-8)

G/L ACCT CONTROL	DESCRIPTION	BEG PERIOD BAL	ADDITIONS	REDUCTIONS	ENDING BALANCE

*Grouped and summarized by asset accounts, depreciation and book value.

EXHIBIT G

Transaction Listings—This listing reflects the input into the program. It is out-putted in a similar format of its Inputs One and Two.

Asset Detail File (F-1)—This report is used by the organization responsible for property accountability (Plant Services, Coordinating Agency, Property Administration, etc.).

Property Ledger (F-2)—reports each detailed asset item within general ledger sub and control accounts and annual classification. This record serves as an update of all asset items, their cost, depreciation-to-date and book value.

Annual Classification Status (F-3)—this report reflects the status of the asset depreciation classifications within general ledger account and facility. It is produced monthly and provides varying period data by account and facility. Depreciation is provided for straight line, sum of the year's digits or other recognized depreciation methods.

Acquisition Journal Voucher (G-4)—this report reflects the debit and credit entries to the fixed asset accounts during the monthly period for the general ledger system. It includes adjustments as well as the acquisition costs for reflection in the accounting records.

Depreciation Journal Voucher (G-5)—this report reflects the debit and credit entries for the depreciation accounts during the period. The depreciation values reflect the obsolescence amounts for previously acquired assets as well as those in the current period.

Investment Tax Credit (G-6)—This report reflects the gross acquisition costs which are subject to a tax credit according to a predetermined and assigned code described in the input.

General Ledger Account Status (G-7)—this report reflects the status of the fixed asset general ledger accounts. The balance of each account is shown at the beginning of the period, and the transactions affecting it in terms of debit and credit with the resultant ending balance value.

Major Category Asset Status (G-8)—this report reflects the status of a grouping of fixed asset general ledger accounts. It is a monthly status report that is used for top management reporting in terms of hierarchy summaries. The data is summarized by asset, depreciation and book value groupings.

The above represents the minimal scope that can be achieved in the reporting cycle with respect to batch processing. The scope of the reporting is dependent, of course, upon organization needs.

ONLINE PROCESSING/REPORTING

The primary requisite for online operations is to have well organized files on disks which are available for either online processing or retrieval. Exhibit H reflects the online processing.

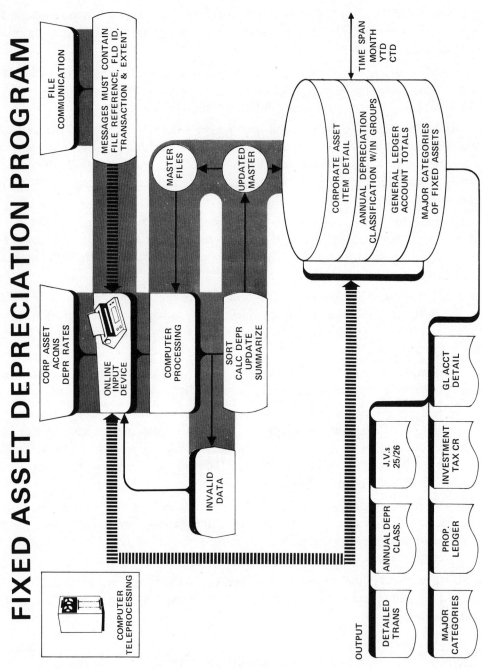

FIXED ASSET DEPRECIATION PROGRAM

Exhibit H

Commercial Products/Services

As shown in Exhibit A, the enterprise either automatically receives follow-on orders for its standard products or negotiates possible new terms based on economic or other governing conditions. The prospective customer may also solicit on his own a request for a product quotation based on an advertisement or through referral by other satisfied customers. The sale may further be consummated through direct solicitation by an organization's salesman.

In any case, there is a review of the offer relative to the criteria shown in the exhibit and other possible pertinent considerations. The purchase order follows next with generally an initial verbal agreement. The sales procedure is rather simple and uncomplicated once the agreement has been made as to volume, price and delivery schedule.

Government Agencies

There are many more considerations involved with government business which require specialists to interpret the needs and this is further complicated particularly in the development of exotic new products such as missiles, spacecraft, advanced vehicle capabilities, etc. The review is also more detailed requiring considerable negotiations and documentation. Competition is very keen for major multi-billion dollar contracts.

Contracts are issued as cost plus fixed fee, fixed price with and without incentive, time and material, etc. In many instances, the guidelines are rather explicit as to what is expected in terms of performance from the end product. The problem is that, in many cases, the organization has to initiate product development from the "drawing board" to its ultimate physical shape or form including performance tests.

Further complications arise from negotiating unreimbursable expenditures, labor and overhead rates, funding, progress payments and other requirements of a government contract. Then, too, there may be an inadequate definition of specifically what it is or what it will look like upon completion. Progress is followed closely with its attendant detailed reporting. Contract changes, amendments and redirection are a common occurrence.

CUSTOMER SALES FILE

In the mechanically oriented organization, particularly, the detail of the sales order is either punched on cards or entered via a remote terminal device directly on tape as shown in Exhibit B.

A transaction listing is prepared for review and reference and the tape record is used further to update the previous customer history master file and simultaneously update the backlog system. Each customer file is maintained separately with all of its associated detail. Reference can be made to individual sales with quantities, price, terms, deliveries and current status of the customer order.

CUSTOMER FILE UPDATE

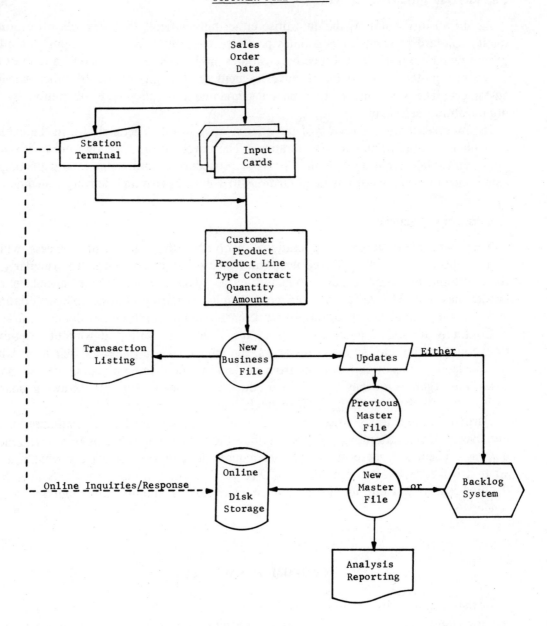

EXHIBIT B

SALES ANALYSIS REPORTING

Predetermined formats comparing past performance and budgets with current period data provide management with a tool to rapidly evaluate the overall sales position and progress. The detailed reporting permits analysis of sales by customer, contract, product,

product line, sales order, territory and individual salesman. The type of report formats for sales analysis, review and evaluation are noted as follows:

Product/Item Line Sales Analysis

(Summary Totals by Product Item/Line)

Product Line/Item	Contract/ Sales Order	Customer	Sales Amount (000)						
			Curr Period	Budget	Var	YTD Act.	Budg	Var	Last Year

This type of report segregates contract and sales orders by product line in order to determine status, profitability and problem areas for management review and action. A product line represents a summary category assigned or associated to a number of related type contracts on which effort is directed toward a specific and common end-result product or service; for example, a type of missile, weapon system, vehicle, ship, service, etc. In commercial firms, a product line would be classified as a type of automobile, shoes, furniture, typewriters, etc.

Customer Sales and Summary Analysis

Customer	Contract/ Sales Order	Sales Amount (000)						
		Curr Period	Budget	Var	YTD Act.	Budg	Var	Last Year

Salesman/District Sales Analysis

(Summary Totals by Salesman & District)

Salesman and/or District	Customer	Product Item/Line	Sales Amount (000)						
			Curr Period	Budget	Var	YTD Act.	Budg	Var	Last Year

Type Contract/Sales Order Analysis

(Summary Totals by Contract or Sales Order)

Contract/ Sales Order	Customer	Product Line/Item	Sales Amount (000)						
			Curr Period	Budget	Var	YTD Act.	Budg	Var	Last Year

Mechanically, the above information is readily available for batch output and/or "on call" through the online capability.

SALES BACKLOG DEVELOPMENT

The inventory of undelivered commitments or sales backlog is expressed in terms of products or services to a customer. It can represent "firm" business on hand which is supported by documentation (sales order, contract, letter of intent, etc.) or pending business which may have been negotiated but the physical sales order has not been issued. Based on anticipated negotiations and needs of customers, backlog would also include "probable" type new business for planning future operations. A combination of these three classifications then represents the basis for planning the amount of effort, organization direction, production, resources required, etc., which would be necessary to meet and fulfill customer requirements and commitments.

Computing Backlog Balances

Undelivered products or services' values are computed by adding new business volume (classified as new orders booked, sign-ups, negotiated sales, etc.) to a beginning balance and reducing this amount by the sales or deliveries actually made or planned as in the case of projections. The ending backlog balance value is also influenced by any adjustments resulting from changes or re-direction to the contract conditions or sales agreements in terms of quantities to be delivered, costs and fees, funding or contract limitations.

Exhibit C displays the computations involved in the development of the ending backlog and/or outstanding commitments.

EXHIBIT C

COMPUTING BACKLOG BALANCE

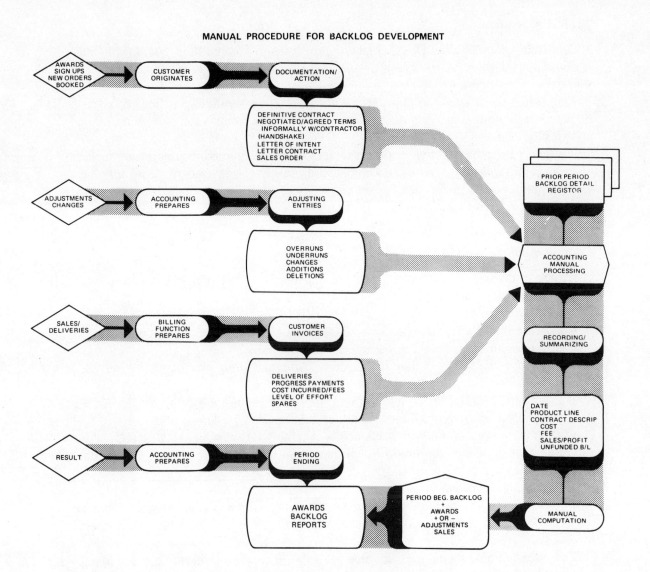

MANUAL PROCEDURE FOR BACKLOG DEVELOPMENT

EXHIBIT D

In order to control and identify backlog data properly for analysis and planning, code numbers are assigned for a specific work order (detailed level of reporting), contract, product line, functional organization, customer and type of contract. These classifications assist the organization in their detailed assessment of backlog status.

Typical Operation

As displayed in Exhibit D, the manual processing for computing backlog in most organizations consists of recording awards, sales orders, agreements, adjustments and sale delivery invoices.

The customer initiates the appropriate documentation signifying an award, sign-up or purchase commitment. This documentation represents definitive contracts negotiated and specifies the terms of the agreement.

There are a number of obvious disadvantages to manual recordkeeping which include magnitude of reporting required, error potential due to the myriad of detail involved, satisfying multi-organization needs, excessive clerical effort and inadequate management control and decision-making data.

Computerized Backlog System

Exhibit E displays the processes involved and the reporting that is possible to overcome the manual system deficiencies.

Input Requirements

- Current month's transactions in terms of new orders booked, adjustments, sales/ deliveries and miscellaneous contracts' reference table.
- Reference table files containing customer identification, product items/services, product line description, contract number and type.
- Prior period master file containing year and inception-to-date detail for costs, fees, total award, sales, profit, funded and unfunded backlog balances and total.
- Prior period master file of miscellaneous or minor contracts' backlog detail.
- File of current active contracts by product line for audit requirements of input data entry.

Processing Involved

Current month transactions are keyboarded from source documentation using an input device which produces either punched cards or transmits data directly to the tape or disk files.

The current transactions are combined with the prior period master file in order to update the files for current period reporting and also to serve as the basic master file in the subsequent period's processing. All contracts with zero or negative balances are segregated for special reporting and analysis.

Current month's data for miscellaneous contracts is compared to the miscellaneous contract master file for update and reporting.

Structured reports are created and stored on tape for printout processing.

Although many more detailed steps are involved in the overall processing, Exhibit E above summarizes the various considerations in the program and reporting.

COMPUTERIZED DEVELOPMENT/CONTROL OF BACKLOG DATA

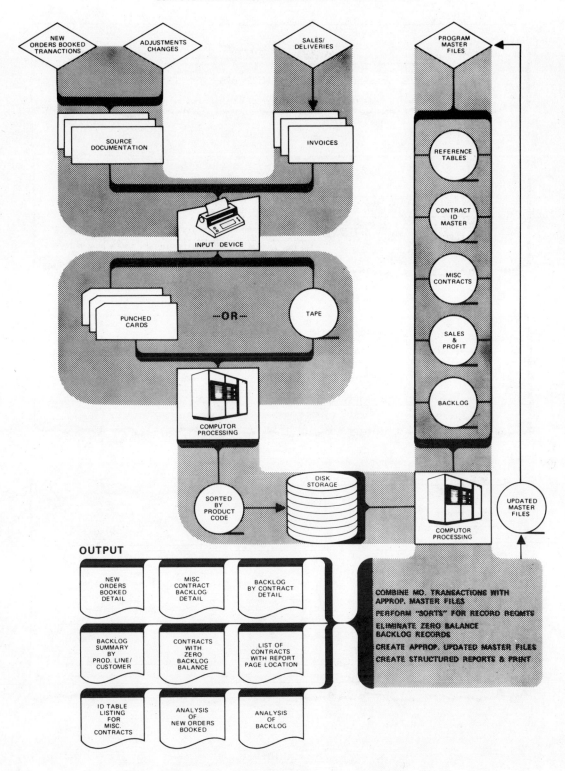

EXHIBIT E

REPORT NO.   NEW ORDERS BOOKED DETAIL   **MONTH ENDING XX/XX/XX**

PROD. LINE	PROD. CODE	CONT TYPE	G/L ACCT	CUSTOMER	REMARKS	CONTRACT NO.	CONTRACT DESCRIPTION	CURRENT MONTH	YEAR TO DATE
AM	326	FP	511-11		FOLLOW ON			50,000.00	100,000.00

SUMMARY SUB TOTALS FOR CUSTOMERS WITHIN PRODUCT LINE TOTAL WITHIN DIVISION TOTAL

BACKLOG BY CONTRACT DETAIL

REPORT NO.'   CONTRACT NO.   CONTRACT DESCRIPTION —   **MONTH ENDING XX/XX/XX**

DATE	PROD. LINE	G/L ACCT	PROD. CODE	CONT TYPE	REMARKS	COST	FEE	AWARD	SALES DATE	SALES	BACKLOG BALANCE	PROFIT
JAN	AT	511-58	143	CPFF	SERVICES	90,000.00	5,400.00	95,400.00	JAN	13,500.00	81,900.00	900.00
FEB	AT	511-58	143	CPFF	SERVICES				FEB	12,000.00	12,000.00	900.00
FEB 1969 BALANCES						90,000.00	5,400.00	95,400.00		25,500.00	25,500.00	1,800.00

MONTH AND INCEPTION TO DATE RUNNING TOTALS BY CONTRACT WITH TOTAL DIVISION SUMMARY AT END

BACKLOG SUMMARY BY CUSTOMER AND PRODUCT LINE
(MONTH & INCEPTION TO DATE SEPARATE LISTINGS)

REPORT NO.   PRODUCT LINE AM — —   **MONTH ENDING XX/XX/XX**

	COST	FEE	AWARD	SALES	BACKLOG	PROFIT
CUSTOMER TOTALS	100,000.00		100,000.00	60,000.00	40,000.00	1,800.00
	50,000.00		50,000.00	10,000.00	40,000.00	300.00
PRODUCT LINE AM TOTAL	150,000.00		150,000.00	70,000.00	80,000.00	2,100.00

MONTH AND INCEPTION TO DATE TOTALS BY CUSTOMER WITHIN PRODUCT LINE WITH DIVISION TOTAL

ANALYSIS OF BACKLOG
IN 000'S

STANDARD REPORT   **PERIOD ENDED XX/XX/XX**

PRODUCT LINE	JANUARY 1 BACKLOG	NEW ORDERS	SALES	TERMINATION & OTHER ADJUSTMENTS	ENDING BACKLOG ACTUAL	ENDING BACKLOG BUDGET
GOVERNMENT						
PRIME						
	500	300	200	< 10 >	590	620
	200	100	150		150	100
SUBCONTRACT						
APPLIED PHYSICS	100	50	60		90	80
MISC	120	50	70		100	90
TOTAL	920	500	480	< 10 >	930	890
COMMERCIAL						
	50	75	40		85	80
	40	20	15		45	50
TOTAL	90	95	55		130	130
GRAND TOTAL	1010	595	535		1060	1020

EXHIBIT F

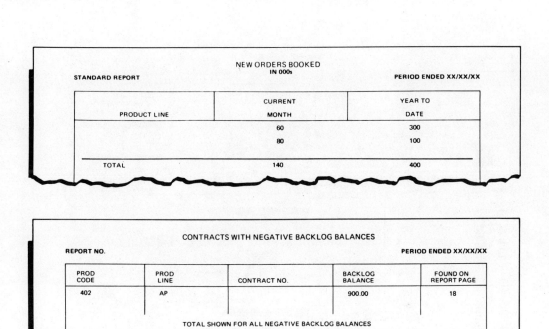

NEW ORDERS BOOKED
IN 000s

STANDARD REPORT   PERIOD ENDED XX/XX/XX

PRODUCT LINE	CURRENT MONTH	YEAR TO DATE
	60	300
	80	100
TOTAL	140	400

CONTRACTS WITH NEGATIVE BACKLOG BALANCES

REPORT NO.   PERIOD ENDED XX/XX/XX

PROD CODE	PROD LINE	CONTRACT NO.	BACKLOG BALANCE	FOUND ON REPORT PAGE
402	AP		900.00	18

TOTAL SHOWN FOR ALL NEGATIVE BACKLOG BALANCES

CONTRACTS WITH ZERO BACKLOG RELEASES
(CONTRACTS DELETED FROM BACKLOG REPORT)

REPORT NO.   PERIOD ENDED XX/XX/XX

PROD CODE	PROD LINE	CONTRACT NO.
554	AP	

SURVEY SHOWS NO. OF RECORDS DELETED DURING PERIOD.

MISCELLANEOUS CONTRACT BACKLOG DETAIL
INCEPTION TO DATE

REPORT NO.   PERIOD ENDED XX/XX/XX

CUSTOMER	IDENT. NO.	PROD. CODE	CONTRACT NO.	COST	FEE	AWARD	SALES	BACKLOG	PROJECT

SUMMARY IS BY SUBTOTAL FOR EACH CUSTOMER AND GRAND TOTAL

EXHIBIT G

BACKLOG DATA PROCESSING & COMMUNICATION
ONLINE APPLICATION

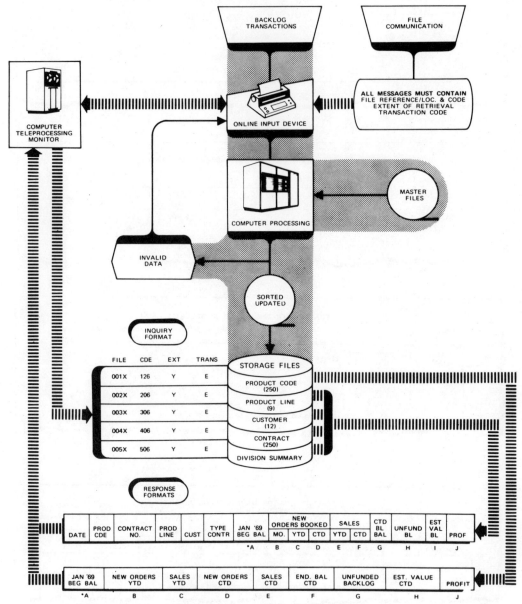

EXHIBIT H

Reports from the System

There are approximately nine formal reports or listings which are outputed and illustrated in Exhibits F and G.

ONLINE COMMUNICATION

Exhibit H displays the online application process.

The master files are necessary in order to accommodate batch reporting. The disk files are used for testing alternate courses of action and "gaming" without disturbing the validity of the actual report files.

Record storage location codes are established for ease of access and are included in each message for data location identification.

Codes are assigned to each contract, product line, customer and type of contract in order to compress input and achieve proper and unique identification to specific data stored.

A reference table in the file will include codes designating the "extent" of data manipulation or retrieval and transaction instructions. An "X" code, for example, indicates that all information is being affected whereas the "Y" identifier represents a partial-record effect.

The transaction codes used in this system are described as follows: "A" for creating a record; "B" for adding to the record; "C" for changes; "D" for record deletion and "E" for displaying a segment or complete record.

All messages to the computer must contain: file reference/location, data code, extent of retrieval and a transaction code. If a message is incomplete, it will be rejected and the remote station advised. In a partial record retrieval process, reference must be made to the specific data involved. For example in Exhibit H, "J" is the identifier for "Profit."

Two typical data requirements, messages and computer response are illustrated below:

1. <u>Requirement.</u>   Add "Profit" of $60.00 to contract code 126.

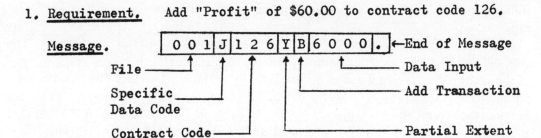

   <u>Response from Computer.</u>   "Contract code 126 profit now reads $60.00".

2. <u>Requirement.</u>   Delete "contract code" 120 from the file.

   <u>Message.</u>   `0 0 1 | b | 1 2 0 | X | D | .`

   <u>Response from Computer.</u>   "Contract code 120 record deleted".

Properly coded, the computer can perform any requirement—change, retrieve, update and report.

The advantages of an online capability are multifold in that backlog information can be updated continuously thus providing timely data. Detailed and summary information is readily accessible to all authorized users. Customer current backlog status is readily and rapidly determinable. It affords the capability to simulate the results from various data input and manipulation.

NEW BUSINESS DECISIONS AND ACTION

The primary aid to management decisions and taking appropriate action is based on significant information which isolates and highlights problem areas. Sales analysis reports, for example, provide clues as to specific problem areas that require attention such as delayed deliveries, need for new business and unprofitable product lines.

Trend Analysis Charts

In addition to the reports, there should also be provided trend charts which graphically measure performance against the plan. They can be at any level or variation of the sales activity—customer, product/service, contract, district, salesman, etc.

Exhibit I illustrates the type of chart that can be produced mechanically.

For example, all of the backlog balance data resident in the file can be chart displayed "on call" at the station device on a continuing updated basis including the projected or planned backlog balance. This display indicates the trend of the undelivered backlog position relative to the starting point as well as the budgeted volume. Information is available by specific product line or program and in total for the organization. This chart, when used in conjunction with the other two displays in this exhibit indicate immediately where a specific problem exists—sales and/or new business bookings.

The Sales portion of the exhibit is similarly constructed to that of the backlog. The rise and fall of sales deliveries naturally influences the backlog balances. The analysis of this chart indicates that the sales are consistently uniform by period. The trend in total parallels the planned projections. By individual program, however, there are variances between the actuals and the projected budget. In Program D, for example, it is noted that the actual sales will be less than projected and, therefore, a more detailed analysis is required to determine the cause. The situation may be the result of delayed deliveries, funding limitation, insufficient manpower level, changes in contract terms, etc. Decision and action may be necessary.

The New Orders' display illustrates the receipt of new business. An analysis of this chart indicates that no new business was received in the months of January and February. Further, that the months of March and June had the largest new orders volume. The trend during the year, excluding January and February, would indicate that the aggregate total budgeted would be realized. As in the case of the sales analysis,

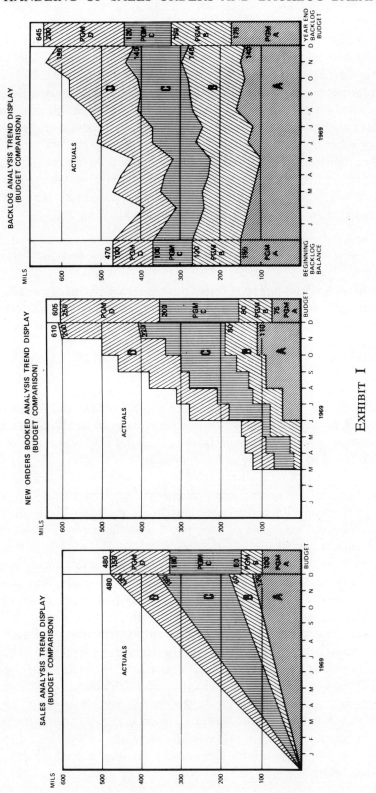

EXHIBIT I

the problem exists with the individual program. Program D's trend would indicate that it would be below budget. An evaluation is therefore in order as to "why." It could very well be redirection of the program, loss of a customer(s), marketing problems or an optimistic budget which would signify management attention for corrective action.

Reference to further detail supporting the chart displayed information should identify any problem to a contract, customer or functional area of responsibility. The problem may be associated with delays in awards or sales orders, funding, manpower activity, recordkeeping or other difficulties.

Periodic or "on demand" graphic displays can simplify the work of the analyst, planner and management in their review and evaluation of backlog status. Trend line reporting is a valuable technique for assessing future operations, the validity of an organization's projections and specific problem areas requiring action.

COMPUTER-GENERATED SALES PROJECTIONS

For purposes of budget and financial forecasting, backlog balances must be developed in order to reflect the complete financial plan since it is one of the main considerations in establishing the level of effort, cash flow, resources, new product development, market penetration, facility expansion, etc.

Sales Projections

The sales/deliveries can be mechanically developed for review and resolution through the establishment of a reliable correlation with a set of independent data that will provide parameters for computing sales trends and volume. Exhibit J is an example of how this is accomplished based on the "least squares" approach.

Direct manpower effort or total direct labor costs are generally considered a reliable and valid correlation to sales volume (this determination, however, will probably vary by individual organization). In commercial enterprises particularly, it could very well be past performance trends in terms of anticipated customer needs in addition to other sales intelligence and judgment.

From the plotted point correlation, a statistical formula is developed mechanically. As noted on this exhibit, a series of actual plot points were made. The computer calculates the formula which, when applied to a projection of effort (manpower, direct labor hours or dollars), will provide the anticipated sales volume values. In addition to the formula results, however, it is also necessary to interject judgment and experience factors to reflect peaks and valley points resulting from the number of work days in a month or other known variable and projected economic or environmental conditions.

Points 1 and 2 shown on the above exhibit represent calculated statistical values for locating your connecting line which can also be utilized for making visual projections. For example, if your manpower effort was established at a "100", then the point that it intercepts the line would indicate a sales volume level of "110". The same projection reasoning could apply that, by establishing a sales volume, a level of effort could be obtained from the chart.

MECHANICAL PROJECTION OF SALES VOLUME
(Least Squares Computed Formula)

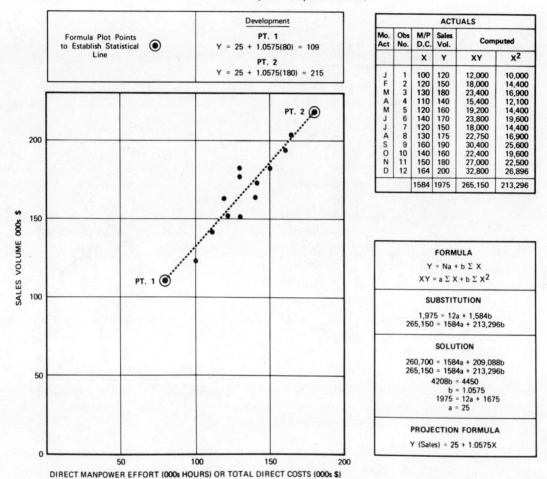

Formula Plot Points to Establish Statistical Line	Development
	PT. 1
	$Y = 25 + 1.0575(80) = 109$
	PT. 2
	$Y = 25 + 1.0575(180) = 215$

				ACTUALS	
Mo. Act	Obs No.	M/P D.C.	Sales Vol.	Computed	
		X	Y	XY	X²
J	1	100	120	12,000	10,000
F	2	120	150	18,000	14,400
M	3	130	180	23,400	16,900
A	4	110	140	15,400	12,100
M	5	120	160	19,200	14,400
J	6	140	170	23,800	19,600
J	7	120	150	18,000	14,400
A	8	130	175	22,750	16,900
S	9	160	190	30,400	25,600
O	10	140	160	22,400	19,600
N	11	150	180	27,000	22,500
D	12	164	200	32,800	26,896
		1584	1975	265,150	213,296

FORMULA

$$Y = Na + b \Sigma X$$
$$XY = a \Sigma X + b \Sigma X^2$$

SUBSTITUTION

$1,975 = 12a + 1,584b$
$265,150 = 1584a + 213,296b$

SOLUTION

$260,700 = 1584a + 209,088b$
$265,150 = 1584a + 213,296b$
$4208b = 4450$
$b = 1.0575$
$1975 = 12a + 1675$
$a = 25$

PROJECTION FORMULA

$Y \text{ (Sales)} = 25 + 1.0575X$

EXHIBIT J

CONTROLLING MANPOWER LEVELS

Manpower levels can be controlled generally based on the volume of business on hand or anticipated. After the sales forecast has been prepared and the level of effort established to accomplish the planned deliveries, a manpower requirement level is determinable. The inventory level also has a bearing on the effort required to meet the schedules and at the same time maintain a planned inventory balance consistent with management policy. The level of direct manpower effort based on sales can be projected and controlled through the use of the correlation technique displayed in Exhibit J.

Although the above discussion relates primarily to direct manpower, the indirect to direct ratio will generally govern the number of indirect support personnel necessary to

"Anticipating the Cure!"

EXHIBIT K

be compatible with the direct level. The final determinant to the level of manpower and its control is a management prerogative. Budget versus actual manpower reporting is the basis for management to continually review its status and initiate the proper action to effect its control.

Sales and its attendant backlog represents the "life blood" of any successful organization. Without its consideration in the planning process, no valid or concrete objectives can be determined or projected. A caricature of what can happen to "lagging" business is displayed in Exhibit K wherein the "shot in the arm" of new business provides one of the major solutions to an organization's problems.

10

Administering the Product Pricing and Billing Process

One of the most basic and fundamental functions performed in any organization that produces a product or furnishes a service for sale is product pricing. In order to determine a sales price, an organization must know or be able to estimate fairly accurately the cost of a product and this, added to its profit margin requirements becomes the sales price.

New products are particularly difficult to price because of many unknown factors that could occur during the development process such as under-estimating the number and type of operations involved, the amount of material required, cost of manpower, the associated expenses, learning curve etc.

In the standard product organizations, pricing is generally accurate if costs have been closely monitored and recorded.

COST AND SALES RECORDS

In a computerized system, there are a number of record files that are used to accumulate the total costs of a product or service. Depending upon the complexity of the reporting process, costs are generated by an accounting work order, task, product item, sales invoice number, contract, lot, burden center, organization, etc. Each of these cost category segregations provides the means for pricing a product, billing the customer, monitoring performance, establishing controls, budgeting and actual comparisons, financial statement reporting and management decision-making. Even though a sales price has been established and negotiated, costs are accumulated not only for future estimating and support of product price, but also to determine the true profit of the sales delivery.

Weekly Cost Reporting

Although the most important costs are accumulated basically on a daily basis (labor and payables), they are summarized on a weekly cycle as shown in Exhibit A.

WEEKLY COST REPORTING FOR BILLING PURPOSES

Direct Labor and Overhead Costs

WIP ACCT NO	CONTRACT/PRODUCT IDENTIFICATION	ACCOUNTING WORK ORDER	BURDEN CENTER	COST CODE	WORK DEPT	HOURS		LABOR DOLLARS			OVERHEAD	CORP ALLOC	TOTAL
						DIRECT	OT	DIRECT	OT	TOT			

Prepared weekly showing that week's activity, month and year-to-date. Summaries are by contract.

Accounts Payable Reporting

Week Ending

ACCTG NO	ACCOUNT		CONTRACT CODE	CONTRACT/PRODUCT IDENTIFICATION	ACCOUNTING WORK ORDER	TYPE COST CODE	VENDOR NO	VOUCHER		DUE DATE		AMOUNT
	NO	SUB						MO	NO	MO	DAY	

Prepared weekly showing totals by type cost (material, tooling, freight, subcontract, etc.) and summarized to contract totals.

Interdivision/Company Activity

INTERDIV/CO		ACCT NO	ACCOUNTING WORK ORDER	ISSUING ORGANIZATION		TYPE EFFORT CODE	CONTRACT/PRODUCT IDENTIFICATION	CONTRACT CODE	AMOUNT
MO	DATE			NAME	DATE				

Prepared weekly showing totals by "doing" organizations and contract summary.

EXHIBIT A

OVERALL COST ACCUMULATION

RECORD FORMAT

Contract/Product
Identification

Identification/
Voucher Number

Period

Description   J F M A M J J A S O N D

Labor/Overtime

Week 1
Week 2
Week 3
Week 4

Total Labor

Overhead

Factory

Week 1
Week 2
Week 3
Week 4

Total

Engineering

Week 1
Week 2
Week 3
Week 4

Total

Corp. Allocation

Total Overhead

Description   J F M A M J J A S O N D

Material Costs

Week 1
Week 2
Week 3
Week 4

Total Material   *

Direct Freight   *
Direct Travel   *
Subcontract   *
Special Tooling   *
Other Direct Costs
Inventory   *
Interdiv/Co   *
Subtotal
Fixed Fee   *

Total   *

* Data reflected in Government Standard Form 1034

EXHIBIT B

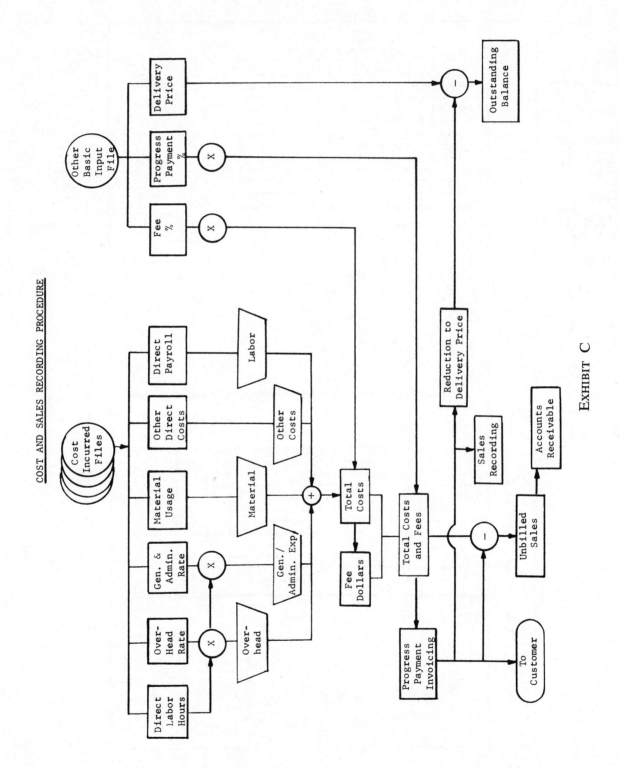

EXHIBIT C

Direct labor and its associated overhead is accumulated by work in process accounts which designate whether it is a cost plus contract versus a fixed price commitment or commercial sale. Contract or product identifiers are necessary in order to designate the type of effort and customer involved. An accounting work order is assigned which is generally associated with a specific type of task description. It is necessary to identify the organization burden center for performance measurment. The cost code designates the type of effort performed in terms of employe classification or task—engineering, manufacturing, etc. The work department indicates where the effort was or is being expended which is used as one criteria for budget and performance measurement. The balance of the report indicates direct hours and overtime expenditure as well as the associated dollars. Direct overhead and corporate allocation rates per direct labor hour or dollar are projected and applied based on past actuals and inputted into the system.

Accounts payable reporting represents direct and indirect expenditures for material, subcontract, tooling, test equipment, etc. which is identified by a cost code.

Interdivision and/or intercompany activity costs are generated by the performing organizations and, although actual cash transactions are generally not involved, they, nevertheless, represent legitimate costs in the billing process.

The above weekly cost data is summarized into monthly totals for financial reporting and contract status recording and evaluation.

Exhibit B displays a month-to-month cost accumulation record format of not only the contract/product costs by element, but also the fees and delivery price.

Exhibit C was developed as an overview of the overall cost accumulation and billing system on a fixed price contract with progress payments.

From the report files, the elements of costs are extracted and summarized in order to determine the total cost. To this total is applied a fee rate in order to determine the fee dollars or vice versa; sales price divided by 100% plus fee percentage equals total costs which deducted from sales equals fee dollars. The agreed on progress payment percent is applied to the total costs in order to determine the amount of the progress payment that can be billed to the customer.

The progress payment billed is deducted from the total costs and fees incurred to derive the outstanding unbilled sales.

Exhibit D reflects a commercial cost and sales recording activity which compares the planned costs of a priced delivery as versus the actual costs generated.

Based on historical experience, a sales delivery price is negotiated with a customer which includes a planned profit percent. The profit percent plus 100% divided into the product delivery price results in obtaining the total cost included in the sales price. In the actual cost accumulation system, the total costs are obtained from basic performance records, summarized and then compared to the projected costs in the sales price.

Exhibit D1 illustrates the commercial sales commitment cycle in which quantity and product costs are accumulated in inventory before shipment or, if shipped immediately, are recorded in inventory control registers. When items are shipped, a profit margin is applied to the costs to obtain the sales delivery price which is billed to the customer. The individual customer outstanding commitment file is adjusted by item/lot quantities and

COMMERCIAL COST AND SALES RECORDING

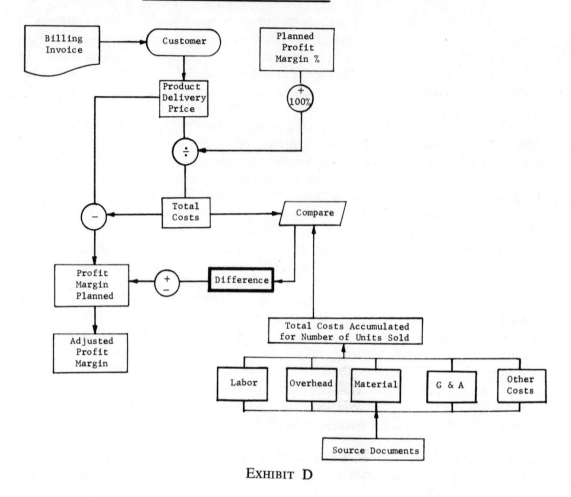

EXHIBIT D

sales price amounts for file updating. Various reports are produced which indicate the individual customer commitment status, product line and total organization updated position.

STATUS OF INDIVIDUAL SALES COMMITMENTS

In order to track effectively the status of sales commitments, a number of records have to be maintained to provide the data necessary for analysis, product pricing and customer invoicing. Exhibit E reflects examples of types of records that are maintained for sales commitment analysis and invoicing.

The first format is primarily government oriented, the second commercial and the third represents services performed. The data is obtained from the cost records as well as the billing process. It is by individual contract sales order or service and further detail can be provided by specific tasks (work order or project designations) where appropriate.

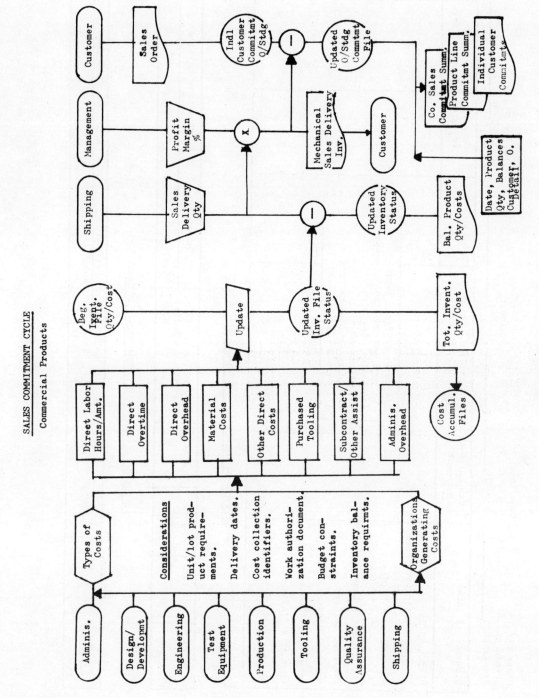

SALES COMMITMENT CYCLE
Commercial Products

EXHIBIT D1

COST AND SALES COMMITMENT STATUS

Government Business

Contract/
Product
Description

Commitment
Ident.
Code

Customer
Ident.
Code

Report
Period
Covered

Elements of Data	Total Current Commitment (a)	Total Costs to Date (b)	Previous Submission (c)	Remainder (d)	Current Submission (e)	Remaining Contract Bal. (f)
Direct Labor						
Hours - Straight Time						
- Overtime						
Dollars - Straight Time						
- Overtime						
Total Labor Dollars						
Overhead Dollars						
Material Costs						
Other Direct Costs						
General and Administrative						
Fee Dollars Total Costs						
Sales Value						

(a) Contract Price Terms
(b) Cost Accumulation System
(c) History Record
(d) Equals (b - c)
(e) Customer Invoice Data
(f) Equals (a) - (b + e)

STATUS OF COMMERCIAL BUSINESS COMMITMENTS

Sales Order Ident. No.	Territory	Customer Code	Quantity	Product Descript.	Sales Dollar Value	Delivered		Remaining Balance	
						Quantity	$ Value	Quantity	$ Value

STATUS OF SERVICE COMMITMENT PERFORMANCE

Service Ident. No.	Customer Code	Type of Service	No. Hours (if applic.)	Dollar Value	Performance		Remaining Commitment	
					Hours	$ Value	Hours	$ Value

EXHIBIT E

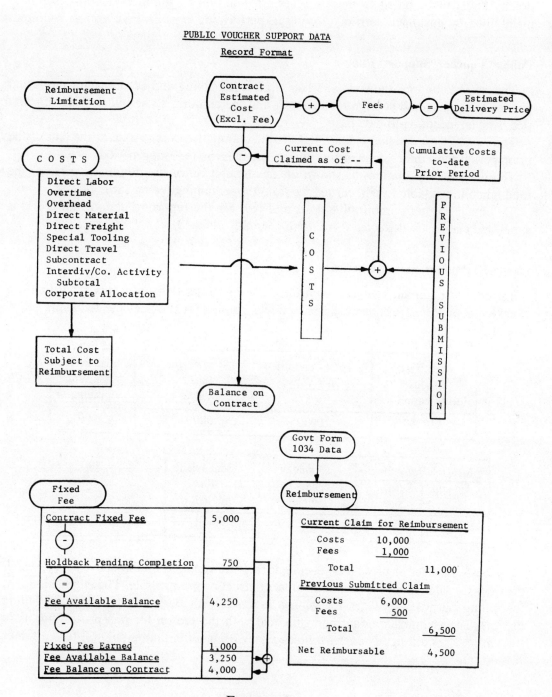

PUBLIC VOUCHER SUPPORT DATA

Record Format

EXHIBIT F

The data is maintained on an inception-to-date basis and provides the amount of dollars that can be billed to the customer. In addition to summary records, status is maintained by customer, territory, contract, performing organization, etc. as required.

Public Voucher Support Data

This record contains the costs and fees eligible for billing and accompanies the actual invoice to support and substantiate the cost and fee amounts to be billed. The information is on an inception-to-date basis.

The current cost claimed column reflects the cumulative cost to-date at the end of the prior period plus the costs incurred during the current reporting period.

The fixed fee calculations as shown on this exhibit reflect the holdback portion, the total amount available to bill, earned fees and the remaining fee on the contract.

To obtain the net reimbursable costs and fees for the reporting period, the previous submitted claims are deducted from those currently claimed.

Contract/Product Status Checklist

In order to maintain adequate control of contract sales delivery status at all times, a checklist is produced mechanically on a weekly basis that provides the following information:

Contract/ Product Identification	Total Committed Sales Value	Shipped and/or Billed Value	Eligible for Current Billing
A12367	10000	5000	1000

Ineligible for Billing		Value of Balance to Complete	Scheduled Date For Completion
Amount	Reason Code		
1000	A	3000	1/21/71

As costs and fees or profit are generated, they are reported on the above report which provides the sales status for each individual contract or product sale. The eligible amount for billing purposes provides the billing function with data for initiating the billing process. The ineligible amount is highlighted with the reason for non-processing, as in this case "A" would signify contract holdbacks; "B" funding limitation; "C" for customer request, etc.

PROGRESS OR PARTIAL AND TIME PAYMENTS

Progress Payments

Fixed price contracts often contain a provision for partial payment of costs prior to completion of a sales delivery. This is particularly true on long lead delivery items. In

SUMMARY OF COST CLAIMED

Contract No.	Date of Claim	Work Orders		Cost Claimed for the Period				
				Beginning Date of Contract	TO	Current Submission Date		
Description			ITD Total Claimed Costs	Curr. Costs Claimed	Total Costs Claimed	Prev. Reqstd Costs	Costs Curr. Claimed
Labor							
Overhead							
Material							
Other Direct Costs							
Material Inventory							
Total Direct Costs			10,000	2,000	12,000	8,000	4,000
General and Administrative							
Corporate Office Allocation							
Total Other Expenses			2,000	300	2,300	1,800	500
Total Costs Incurred			12,000	2,300	14,300	9,800	4,500
Deduct Holdback - 20%			2,400	460	2,860	1,960	900
Subtotal			9,600	1,840	1,440	7,840	3,600
Subcontractor Payments			2,500	500	3,000	2,200	800
Costs Applicable to Progress Payments			12,100	2,340	14,440	10,040	4,400

Summary Data

Description	Values
Total Contract Deliveries	5,000
Liquidation % - (90)	4,500
Net Billing Balance	500

Description	Contract Negotiated
Contract Value Negotiated	50,000
% Progress Payment Limitation (90)	45,000
Amount Elegible on Deliveries	5,000

EXHIBIT G

essence, this means that as costs are incurred, only the negotiated progress payment percentage can be billed to the customer. The cost data applicable for progress payments is developed mechanically in the format shown in Exhibit G.

The information used in this exhibit is derived in the following manner for current costs claimed:

- Direct costs are obtained from the basic weekly reports or monthly from the cost ledger with the exception of material inventory which is extracted from the inventory schedule.

- Payments to subcontractors are obtained from the accounts payable billing report.

- The costs are totalled and a 20% holdback rate, for example, is applied to obtain the holdback amount.

- The total cost claimed column (prior period's totals) are combined with current costs to obtain total costs claimed.

- The previously requested cost amounts are obtained from the prior period's billing submission and subtracted from the current total costs claimed to derive the costs currently claimed.

- In the summary data at the bottom of this exhibit, total contract deliveries represent the amount of actual billings for deliveries on the contract.

- The 90% negotiated liquidation is applied to the contract deliveries in order to obtain the liquidation amount of progress payments.

- Contract value represents the total dollar value in the contract terms.

- The limitation percent is applied to the contract value to obtain the total progress payment limitation amount and the difference represents the eligible amount for billing on final delivery.

Progress payment liquidation can be developed through a mathematical equation application as follows:

$$\frac{\text{Progress Payment \%}}{100\% + \text{Fee \%}} = \text{Liquidation \% applied to holdback}$$

Time Payments

Many sales are negotiated with varying payment terms dependent upon the sales invoice and/or type of contract. Time payments can be based on delivery segments, costs incurred, contract progress or other special terms. Partial payments can be computed at 85% of costs and liquidated on the basis of 85% of the sales price which then takes into consideration the fee "pickup." In commercial business, terms could be negotiated on the following illustrating bases:

- 10% on signing contract; 5% per month for 10 months and the balance of 40% upon sales delivery.

- 6% signup; 30% over the next six-month period and the balance on delivery.

- Equal % recovery by period to the scheduled delivery date with penalty for not meeting the agreed upon delivery date.

In most commercial firms dealing with standard products, the terms are generally 100% payment 30 days after delivery.

RECONCILING BILLING DATA WITH ACTUAL COSTS AND PROFITS

In order to be assured that the actual costs and profit records are in balance with the billed and unbilled data in the billing function files, a comparison is made each month-end by contract or sales order. Any differences are investigated and adjustments made to the appropriate files so that both record files are in balance.

The reconciliation process as displayed in Exhibit H is described as follows:

- Cost data is developed on a weekly basis and is tape-to-tape transferred into the billing file as well as the cost ledger system.

- The files are updated weekly for the month, year and inception-to-date totals.

- Profit margin is applied to the costs in the billing records to obtain profit billing amount which is totalled with cost for a sales delivery billing price.

- Costs that are billed to the customer are segregated from those that are unbilled. The data files reflect cost and profit segregation for analysis, comparisons and future estimating criteria.

- Fee rates from an internal computer table are applied at month-end to the cost ledger data in order to obtain a cost and fee file based on the cost accumulation records.

- The billing and cost accumulation files are compared at month-end and if the records differ, an exception report is produced which is analyzed and adjustments made—generally to the billing records as reconciliation to the actual cost records.

This type of mechanical reconciliation saves countless hours of manual effort and provides a timely means for detecting errors immediately through audit trails capabilities and making the necessary adjustments.

MECHANICALLY GENERATED BILLING DOCUMENTS

Having generated a billing file, the next step is to prepare the billing documents mechanically. The ordinary routine invoices that are based on standard product de-

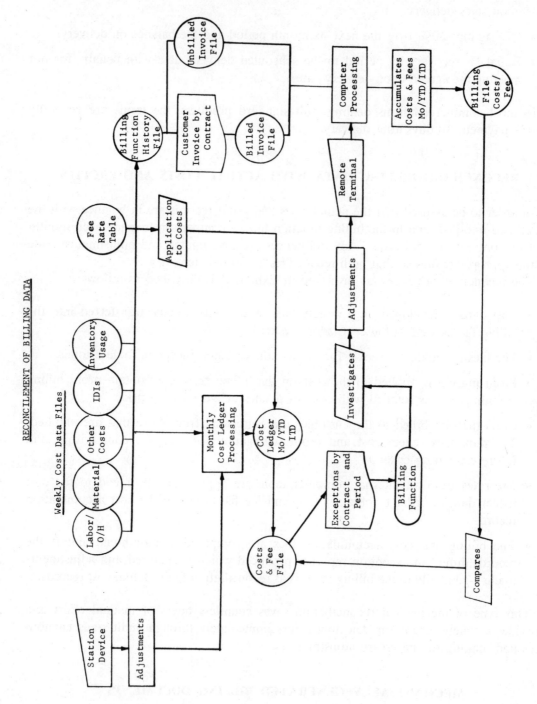

RECONCILEMENT OF BILLING DATA

EXHIBIT H

liveries pose no problem. The customer address file provides the necessary data for addressing the invoices to the proper customer locations. Quantities and standard unit prices (including profit margin) provide the details for the invoicing process. The formatting of the invoice output can either be on preprinted forms or program-generated invoice formats.

Military or government agency type billing is more involved. For example, on CPFF billing, detailed support data must accompany the invoice as illustrated in Exhibit E. The summary of invoice data is formatted below (Government Standard Form 1034):

Number and Date or Order	Date of Delivery of Service	Product or Services (Description, Contract Item Number, etc.)	Quan/ Hours	Unit Price		Amount
				Item Cost (Product)	Rate Per Hr. (Services)	

Other information on this form includes date of voucher, contract number and date, requisition number and date, invoice receipt date, etc.

Partial deliveries and payments on fixed price contracts are probably the most difficult to achieve mechanically because of the progress payment aspect on DD250s, time and material and engineering services' contracts. However, the mechanical billing files do contain the required detail and summary information. Through the use of a coding location identifier, the data can be extracted in the manner required for the Summary of Costs Claimed, Forms 9–50 and 1195 (note Exhibit G for invoice support content).

COMPUTER-GENERATED PROJECTION OF CASH RECEIPTS

Cash receipts from customers are predicated on actual deliveries, level of effort performed or other contract or agreement criteria.

Commercial Products

Standard commercial products with a predetermined and negotiated sales price and delivery schedule can be projected in the following manner:

- Knowing the scheduled dates of delivery and the priced quantity, this data would be entered into the computer file. The records would include not only firm business deliveries, but also a projection of the potential new business anticipated to be delivered.

- The computer would schedule the delivery sales values by time period and contract or product. A summary by period would be made for all contracts and/or product lines.

- Based on experience, a lag factor would be developed which would indicate the time span between "ship out," invoicing and cash receipt. Unless there are unusual conditions, the delivery price should be a cash receipt in approximately 30–40 days from date of delivery.

- The mechanical process would lag the delivery invoice amounts for the projected period and the result represents the projected cash receipts by period based on projected sales deliveries. This data is further analyzed and adjusted to reflect judgment, anticipated unusual situations and possible management direction on the final data.

The billing files are a very valid and useful source for determining lag factors between shipment and the physical cash receipt.

Cost Plus Fixed Fee (CPFF) Contract Collections

Based on a level of effort projection by contract and element of cost, this type of collection activity is not difficult to achieve mechanically. Generally speaking, man-power effort can be fairly accurately defined by period based on contract terms and translated into direct labor costs. With a negotiated overhead application rate, indirect expenditures can be developed. A ten-day lag after cost incurrence and invoicing should provide the cost collection forecast for these two elements of cost.

Material and other direct costs are generally minor unless they involve considerable subcontracting effort, special tooling, etc. A thirty lag period after cost incurrence and invoicing should provide the cash receipt projection for these costs.

A preliminary cash receipt schedule can be mechanically developed and through analysis and application of judgment, a reliable estimate made of anticipated cash receipts. Changes and adjustments can be readily inputted into the system. Exhibit H1 depicts the CPFF flow of data for contract collection.

Fixed Price Contract Activity

Exhibit I displays the fixed price contract data flow which results in various files, reports and the cash receipt and collection files. For fixed price contracts, an item delivery schedule is prepared and time-phased for the life of the specific contract. This schedule is then the determinant for cash receipt projections. In long lead delivery items, the anticipated level of effort is projected and a progress payment factor applied to determine the amounts that can be billed. Time lagging the item delivery schedule with its associated dollar values and the predicted level of effort invoicing by ten days results in the projected cash receipts.

In the case of new business projections, the proposal to the customer indicates delivery scheduling which then becomes the basis for cash receipt projections. Past experience factors derived from delivery schedules and invoicing provides the basis for establishing criteria in making the projection assumptions.

The above exhibit indicates the various files used in the actual billing process. The projection of invoicing and cash receipts are less involved in the forecast process because there are no "actuals" to be considered—delivery schedule, level of effort, progress payments and the lag of collection receipts are the major criteria.

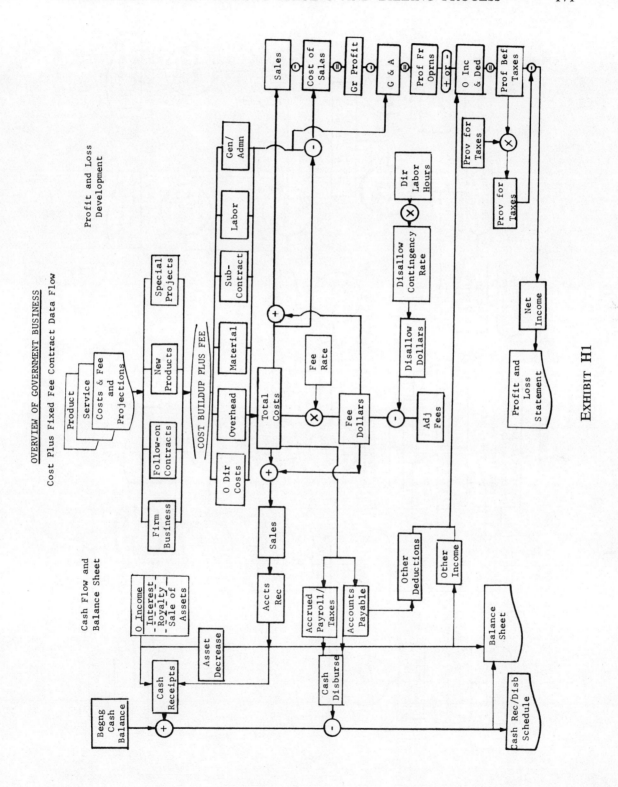

EXHIBIT H1

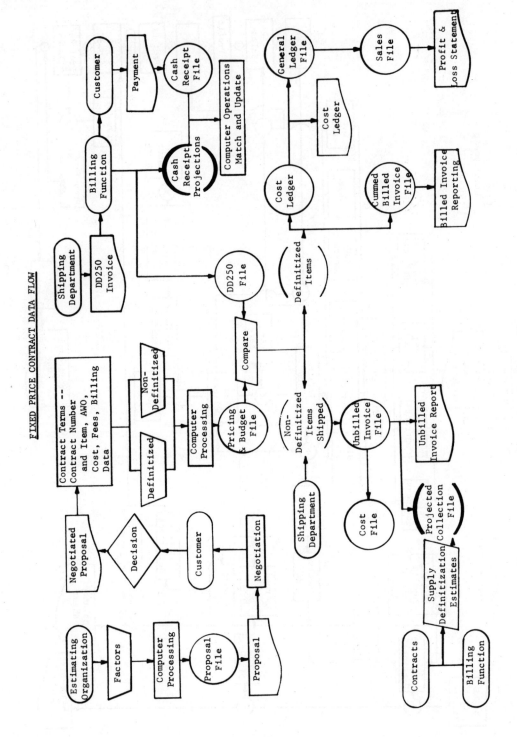

FIXED PRICE CONTRACT DATA FLOW

EXHIBIT I

COMPUTER-GENERATED STATISTICS FOR PRODUCT PRICING

In order to provide the planners, estimators and other concerned individuals with the appropriate data for a product pricing, it is necessary that certain pertinent and actual statistics be developed for analysis, interpretation and use in the preparation of future price or sales proposals.

Exhibit J represents a generalized flow of information and the type of data that would be required in order to generate the specific analytical statistics which would aid in the pricing activity.

After the contract or sales order has been negotiated, the operating plan or procedure is forwarded to the responsible and appropriate prime control organizations such as research and development (new product), engineering and production control in terms of their involved effort.

The responsible organization establishes the detailed requirements and forwards the appropriate work authorizing documents to the performing organization where accounting work assignment and work orders are designated and incorporated into a mechanical master file.

Collection of Cost Statistics

The costs are generated in terms of their specific type such as labor, material, travel, reproduction, subcontract, etc., and categorized or recorded against predetermined identifiers as shown in Exhibit J. This identification provides audit trails to the type of cost generated as well as the organization(s) involved.

The costs incurred are further summarized to the type of effort involved which could be the production cost of a specific product in its entirety and detailed to major components, sub-assemblies and parts or items of the product. This is necessary for detailed costing and support of the sales price negotiated particularly on government agency business. Different types of effort generally involve specific cost collection identifiers, for example:

- Major Product/Component—accounting work order and shop order
- Tooling　　　　　　　　　—tool order serial number
- Test Equipment　　　　　—test equipment item number and unit
- Spare Parts　　　　　　　—spare part accounting or production work order
- Special Costs　　　　　　—work assignment number or authorization

The cost data generated for the particular effort involved is then accumulated in the cost collection system from which various reports are derived. It is noted that costs are segregated and collected in a form compatible for comparison to the original negotiated estimates. This comparison provides statistics for future estimates and indicates deviations from the originally planned or projected costs to accomplish the various tasks required.

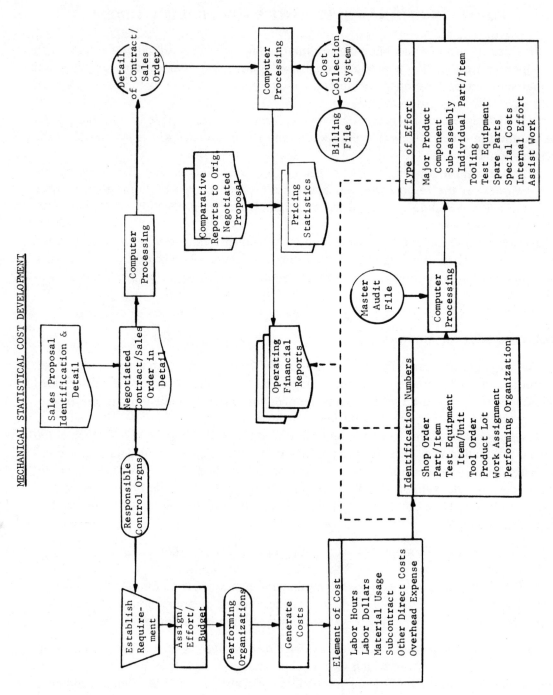

MECHANICAL STATISTICAL COST DEVELOPMENT

EXHIBIT J

Product Lot Hour System

Before production requirements are released for effort to commence, quantities are established and segregated into the number of lots and their comparative sizes. This action is necessary due to the conformance requirements involved in part and price commonality that may exist.

Direct labor hour expenditure and associated quantities with parts, components and end item products are accumulated during the production process cycle. The hours collected are also increased by pertinent experience factors to reflect production scrap and rework loss due to part configuration change and/or improper production practices and operator errors.

The hours are collected by shop order number within part number and summarized to accounting work order, type task or contract item, component and end product total. Through various sorts of the data, reports to serve different purposes are generated— statistical analysis, actual versus projected requirements comparisons, basis for future pricing, etc.

Various reports are produced from the computerized product pricing and billing process which delineates the specifics of accomplishing a task; for example: labor activity, quantity and price of material, subcontracting commitments and expenditures, travel necessary for liaison purposes, special tooling and/or test equipment and scrap and rework effort and costs.

With computer-generated statistics, the information provides the pricing organizations with more comprehensive data for future estimates, product cost analysis and performance measurement.

The computerized process provides the link between the negotiated sale, accumulation of costs, invoicing the customer, analyzing variances and providing the statistics for future price/sales proposals.

The functions of product pricing and billing provide the means to accumulate accurate costs, to price the product and/or service, invoice the customer, receive payment on a timely basis and provide statistics for future projections.

11

Structuring the
Mechanical General Ledger System

Every organization, irrespective of its size and complexity (proprietorship, partnership or corporation), which operates in the business world environment must maintain some type of general ledger accounting system. Data must be collected, recorded and identified to establish ledger accounts in order that they can be properly classified and entered into the appropriate records for further financial report summations.

BASIC SYSTEM REQUIREMENTS

Establishing the Chart of Accounts

The basic need for a general ledger system is to properly establish the account structure. Considerable care and planning must be devoted in order that the account organization will satisfy the needs of an organization and provide flexibility to meet changing requirements.

The establishment of account assignments and their identification is generally the responsibility of the controller's office who issues the directives concerned with additions, deletions and/or changes in the chart of accounts. The extent and complexity of the chart of accounts is dependent upon an organization's needs.

The account structure however, should be kept simple, logical, readily understandable and compatible to the needs of the organization's environment relative to its recordkeeping and reporting.

Transaction Entries

All entries into the general ledger must be via journal vouchers which represent the transactions that have occurred during a given period and identified to the chart of accounts.

176

The journal voucher format, as shown below, is typically the same in context in most organizations and includes the journal voucher number and month, the control and subaccount (as applicable) and the debit and credit amounts. There may be one or several accounts entered on one journal dependent upon complexity of the transaction.

Journal Voucher Format

Journal Voucher			Ident	General Ledger			
				Account		Amount	
Month	No.	S		Prime	Sub	Debit	Credit

The numeric month represents the time period in which the transaction occurred. The journal voucher numbers are established to designate the type of transaction (cash, receivables, sales, etc.) and the "S" is for an alpha identification if the transaction is a supplement to the main journal. The column headed by "Ident" designates that the journal is an original entry or the reversal of a prior entry. The account and debit/credit amounts are self-explanatory.

As shown in Exhibit A, all accounting organizations have responsibility for the preparation and submission of journals as they affect their operations. The time schedule for preparation is dependent upon the availability of the basic or raw data and management dictates.

In some organizations, it is noted that the journal format may be expanded to include other segregations of data in order to meet the needs of the detailed expense and cost subsidiary ledger requirements at the same time. This is particularly desirable for the mechanization process. The additions to the format shown above would be as follows:

Expense Ledger				Work Order or Orgn	Cost Ledger			
Account		Amount			Account		Amount	
Prime	Sub	Debit	Credit		Prime	Sub	Debit	Credit

The work order identification number would be used for cost ledger transactions and the "organization" is used for the expense ledger entries.

Exhibit A also reflects some of the other systems that are affected by journal voucher input such as cost ledger, backlog (sales aspect), contract or product sales/profits/costs, product line (shoes, automobiles, missiles), inventory, etc.

Reporting

All of the journals generally flow to the general ledger section which is responsible for the audit of the data and its recording in the register. The audit primarily consists

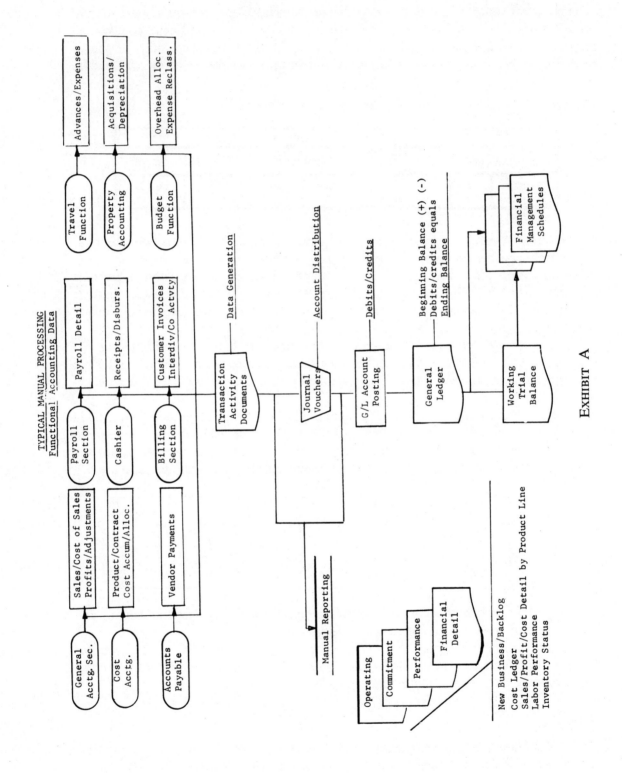

TYPICAL MANUAL PROCESSING
Functional Accounting Data

General Acctg. Sec. → Sales/Cost of Sales Profits/Adjustments → Payroll Section → Payroll Detail → Travel Function → Advances/Expenses

Cost Acctg. → Product/Contract Cost Accum/Alloc. → Cashier → Receipts/Disburs. → Property Accounting → Acquisitions/Depreciation

Accounts Payable → Vendor Payments → Billing Section → Customer Invoices Interdiv/Co Actvty → Budget Function → Overhead Alloc. Expense Reclass.

Data Generation → Transaction Activity Documents

Account Distribution → Journal Vouchers

Debits/Credits → G/L Account Posting

General Ledger

Beginning Balance (+) (−)
Debits/credits equals
Ending Balance

Working Trial Balance → Financial Management Schedules

Manual Reporting

Operating
Commitment
Performance
Financial Detail

New Business/Backlog
Cost Ledger
Sales/Profit/Cost Detail by Product Line
Labor Performance
Inventory Status

EXHIBIT A

of making sure that the accounts are proper (coincide with chart of accounts and appropriately reflect the transaction). Also, the debit and credit amounts must be verified that they are equal in total.

The general ledger includes the description and number of the account, calendar month of the data, journal voucher number, beginning balance by control and sub-accounts, the transaction (journal voucher) activity (either debit or credit amount), and the ending balance.

Each control account and its subaccounts are generally assigned a separate page in the register for ease of reference and analysis. A typical format of a ledger page is noted as follows, but it can vary dependent upon accounting's needs:

Control Account Number_____							
Description_____							
Date		Account		Description (with reference to subaccounts)	JV No	Debit	Credit	Balance
Mo	Da	Prime	Sub					

The journal voucher number reference is provided to establish an audit trail back to the journal detail for verification of the data.

The ending general ledger balances and post-closing adjustments are summarized to the working trial balance schedule and the data is balanced. This information is then used in the preparation of the two prime financial schedules—the balance sheet and the profit and loss statements.

THE COMPUTERIZED APPROACH

The capability to minimize clerical operations, gain more reporting flexibility, speed up preparation of schedules, establish simulation of alternative decisions and set a basis for comparing the information to budgets and forecasts can be most effectively achieved through a mechanized process. Exhibit B typifies the transition from a manual to a computerized system of transaction.

As indicated in this exhibit, computerized data banks including journal vouchers are a logical solution to a computerized general ledger which is the basic source of data for the financial statement development.

Journal Voucher Preparation

Exhibit C portrays the flow of data under the mechanical system. As in the manual process, the responsible organizations originate the input data. Ideally, the data is extracted from the source documents, themselves, in prescribed and data-sequenced formats directly onto keypunched cards or magnetic tape via the remote device. When

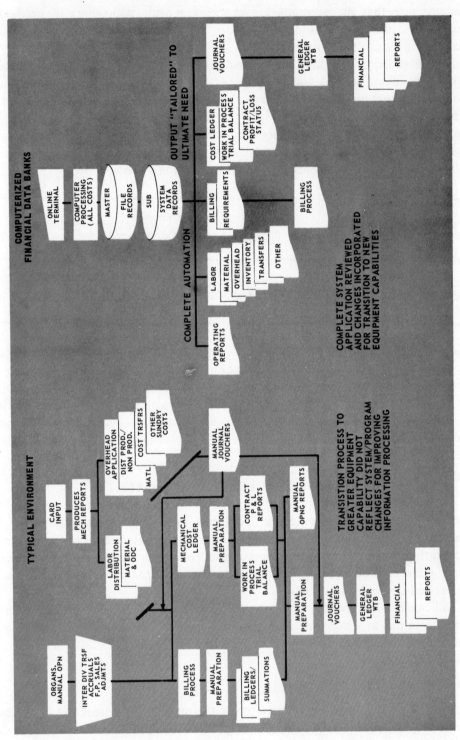

EXHIBIT B

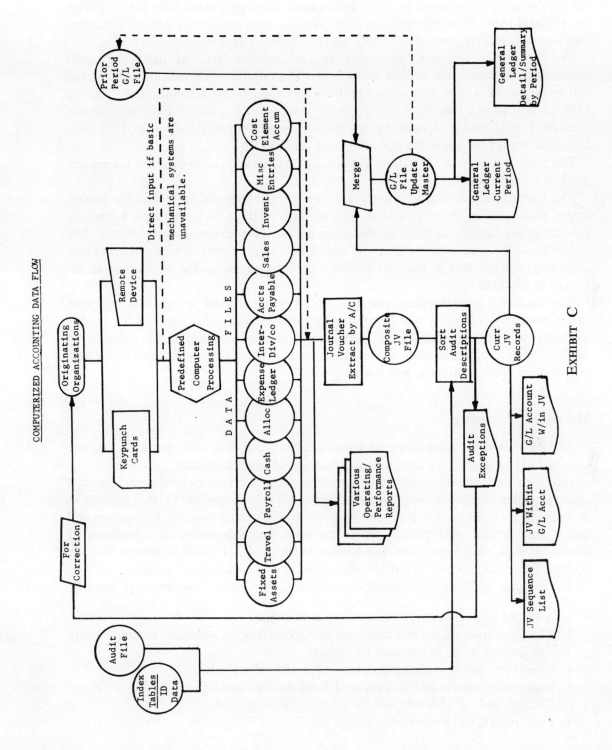

COMPUTERIZED ACCOUNTING DATA FLOW

Direct input if basic mechanical systems are unavailable.

Originating Organizations

Remote Device

Keypunch Cards

For Correction

Predefined Computer Processing

DATA FILES

Fixed Assets
Travel
Payroll Cash
Alloc
Expense Inter-Ledger Div/co
Accts Payable
Sales
Invent
Misc Entries
Cost Element Accum

Prior Period G/L File

Merge

G/L File Update Master

General Ledger Detail/Summary by Period

General Ledger Current Period

Journal Voucher Extract by A/C

Composite JV File

Sort Audit Descriptions

Curr JV Records

Various Operating/Performance Reports

Audit Exceptions

G/L Account W/in JV

JV Within G/L Acct

JV Sequence List

Audit File

Index Tables ID Data

EXHIBIT C

the data is already contained in other mechanized basic programs, then these systems are adjusted in order to provide that their satellite program output will be formatted into journal vouchers conducive for the general ledger system utilization.

The data will be extracted by journal voucher number, account, debit and credit amounts for the composite journal voucher file. The information is mechanically sorted and audited as to validity with respect to the proper journal and account numbers in the table as well as determining if the accounts are correctly associated to their related journals. Invalid data is reported as "exceptions" to established standards and returned to originating organizations for correction and reentry.

The valid journal voucher current file is sorted and structured to produce the reports as shown in Exhibit C.

The current journal voucher transactions are merged with the prior month's general ledger master file in order to update that file and produce both the current period's general ledger register as well as the summary file of previous periods' detail. The advantage of the latter report is that you can audit trail the transactions for any account beginning with the first of the year balances up through the period of time being reviewed or analyzed.

The successful general ledger system is contingent upon valid journal voucher input in the proper fields in order that program processing be effective in meeting the storage and reporting requirements of the system. All journal voucher input either from mechanical files or adjustment entries must contain account identification associated with a debit and credit entry and amount.

Mechanical Processing

Exhibit D is quite comparable to Exhibit C with the exception that it is oriented toward what happens in the mechanical processing of this information.

Basically, the computer processing should consist of a two-cycle system. The first cycle produces the preliminary reports which will be forwarded to the accounting department for their review and audit relative to the journal voucher listings, general ledger and working trial balance. After the audit and submission of corrections or additional data, the second cycle will be run which produces the final journal voucher listings, general ledger, working trial balance and pertinent financial schedules.

The program manipulations include the following steps in the mechanical processing:

1. All input data will be transcribed to magnetic tape.
2. The input transactions will be sorted on tape to journal vouchers within account.
3. The general ledger master will be updated.
4. Line codes will be assigned and report records will be created.
5. Preliminary reports will be produced from the first cycle.
6. Changes and/or additions will be entered and processed.
7. Final reports will be produced from Cycle 2.

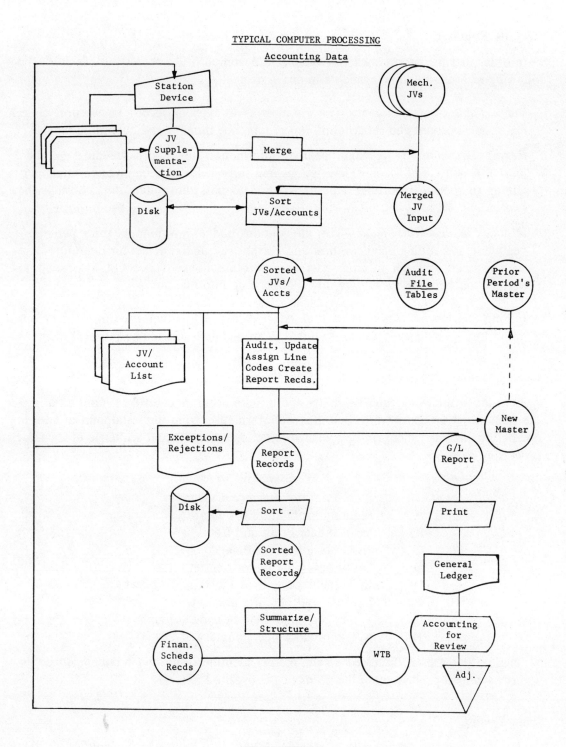

TYPICAL COMPUTER PROCESSING
Accounting Data

EXHIBIT D

Records Required

In order that the proper data is available to accomplish the processing required, the following records should be available in this system:

Index Table—contains control information as to type of record transaction code, class code, account and subaccount, report type line number and column number.

Report Designations—contains control information to report schedule number, journal voucher and account descriptions and three fields of accumulative totals pertaining to specific reporting. This file is used to pass the update data through the system.

History File and Other Data—This file contains budget information, prior period(s) beginning and ending balances, past and current cumulative totals for operating data such as sales and net income, past period transactions by account associated to journal voucher entries and working trial balance information.

Exhibit E displays the flow of general ledger data which is then used in the development of the trial balance, balance sheet and as an update to the online retrieval file.

Record Coding Processing

In order to achieve greater flexibility and a more accurate control of input data, it is desirable to set up codes which will identify information from the standpoint of ease in coding instructions which can designate specific identification and sequence of data for processing purposes.

Examples of this would be as follows:

Code	Working Trial Balance Categories
A	Monthly Profit and Loss data
B	Year-to-date Profit and Loss
C	Asset portion of the Balance Sheet
D	Liabilities in the Balance Sheet
E	Investment portion of the Balance Sheet
F	Expense and clearing accounts
G	Direct costs and their clearing account
H	Major product line summary

These codes are, as discussed above, merely identifiers and any number can be assigned, again, dependent upon the needs of the organization.

Line Coding

The computer processing system includes a line code table which identifies all data to a line and column location as they would appear in the working trial balance and

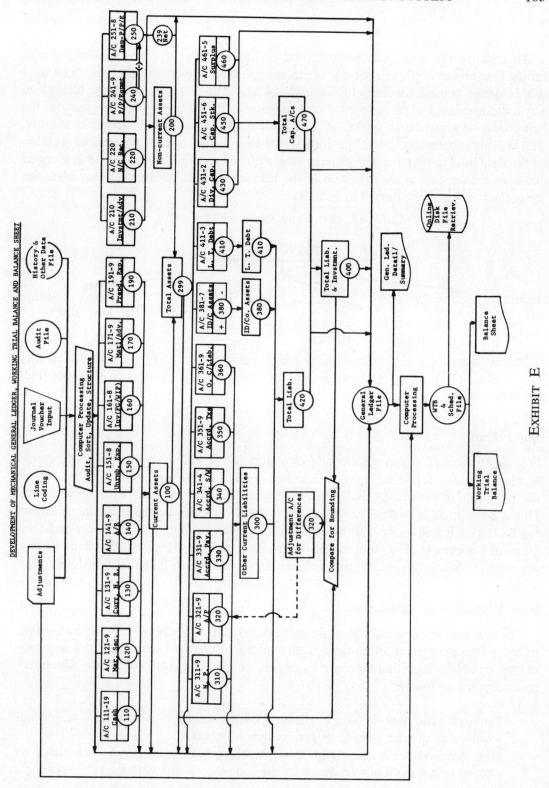

DEVELOPMENT OF MECHANICAL GENERAL LEDGER, WORKING TRIAL BALANCE AND BALANCE SHEET

EXHIBIT E

financial reports. In essence, it is the link between the general ledger account number and the line item concerned.

An effective line code can be composed of any number of characters in order to satisfy the varying needs of different organizations. The line coding that has been used in this system consists basically of seven characters. The first four represent identity to a specific schedule and its number. For example, for the balance sheet designation, the first character would be an alpha "B" and three digits of the specific schedule number. The next two characters in the line code would be assigned to the line number location of the data as it is stored in the general ledger file. The cash item would be line coded "01" since it appears as the first item in the balance sheet. The last character identifies the column in which the data is to be located.

Illustration of the Line Code Assignment

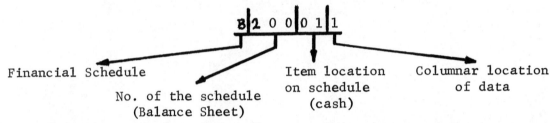

In the balance sheet, you could have four columns of data: (1) actual this month, (2) beginning of the year, (3) budget and (4) variance. Line coding is very important for online processing and retrieval.

Audit Trails

Since all accounting records are subject to auditing by either outside firms or internal accounting personnel, there must be a means built into the mechanical process which will allow you to continually audit the data from the beginning input to the end results. This is done through internal program instructions. An entry on the financial schedules can be readily traced to the trial balance, to the ledger, to the journal voucher and then the source document. The audit can also be performed from the other direction—source document to journal to ledger, trial balance and line code to financial schedules.

Data Controls and Verification

Controls are very necessary in a mechanical program in order to validate data before its entry into the system, otherwise, invalid information could jeopardize the accuracy of the complete reporting system. Examples of the controls which are absolutely necessary are as follows:

1. *Input*

   Table of valid journal voucher and account numbers. Association of journal vouchers to specific general ledger account numbers.

   Predetermined debit and credit totals before input is submitted as a check to whether or not the totals produced by the computer match with the submission.

2. *Ledger Totals' Verification*

One of the control features for establishing the validity of the general ledger balances is to have the computer add all of the debits and credits to the prior month's ending balance in order to obtain the current month's ending balance. If the result ties in with the balances generated from the detail, then there is assurance that the general ledger accounts and amounts have been properly entered and computed.

3. *Accounting Personnel Audit*

Visual and audit check by personnel when they receive the preliminary reports.

Reporting from the General Ledger System

1. *Journal Voucher Listing in Sequence*

JV	Date		Amount		
No	Mo	Yr	Debit	Credit	Variance

The totals are reflected for each journal which may include a number of **account** transactions. The sort is by journal voucher.

2. *Journal Voucher Within General Ledger Account*

Account		JV	Date		Amount		
Prime	Sub	No	Mo	Yr	Debit	Credit	Variance

The sort is by general ledger account and the journal vouchers are identified to the accounts. Totals are shown by account number.

3. *General Ledger Account Within Journal Voucher*

JV	Date		Account		Amount		
No	Mo	Yr	Prime	Sub	Debit	Credit	Variance

The sort is by journal voucher and the accounts shown are totaled for each individual journal.

4. *General Ledger by Individual Account*

Account		JV	Beg.	Amount		
Number	Description	No	Bal.	Debit	Credit	Balance

The beginning balance is shown at the beginning of each period, the debit and credit transactions and the ending balance.

5. *General Ledger Summary*

This report is similar to (4) above except it includes all of the months' transactions and balances for the year. It provides a complete year's history for analysis and reference.

6. *Working Trial Balance*

Account			Amounts		Ending
Prime Sub	Description	Detail	Balance Adjustments		Balance

Prior to the preparation of all data for the various financial schedules, a working trial balance must be prepared. The line code assignment to the general ledger accounts is the basis for structuring a trial balance report. The trial balance account summaries can be directly related to specific items in the financial statements.

ONLINE ACTIVITY

Since the state of the art indicates that the direction is for online activity, it is necessary that the program be constructed in order that your records are readily accessible for making changes, deletions or retrieving specific data.

This is not a difficult task providing the files are so constructed that they can be readily accessed through a location identification coding system. If, for example, there was a need to access the cash account in the general ledger for a complete line of data, the "GL100000" code would be used. The code represents the following:

  GL—General Ledger

 10000—Control account identification for cash item

   0—Complete line. If only the beginning balance was being retrieved, then "1" (first column) would be used in lieu of "0".

Any combination of characters could be used providing they were initially structured in the system.

The same type of system would apply to working trial balance information except the beginning designation, instead of being a "GL" designation would be a "WT" locator account. The balance of the message characters would be the same as that discussed above for the general ledger.

A computerized general ledger system preceded by mechanical journal voucher preparation is of the utmost importance as a basic step to financial statement preparation. Journals that are not conducive to mechanization such as adjusting entries can be keyboarded directly into the system. All changes to the general ledger must be entered through journals in order to reflect the basic audit trial to the source document or computerized file in which the journal was developed.

In summary, the mechanical system provides the means for accelerating month-end closing, making timely changes to files, records and reports, results in decreased manual effort and provides a means for simulating the effect of alternative decisions.

12

Financial Data Integration and Control

CHANGE IS INEVITABLE

The challenge today and for the future is concerned with the proper organization of financial data in order that it can be systematically and effectively accumulated, manipulated, stored and readily available to satisfy multi-organization reporting needs.

Summarized below are the major and influencing factors in our current information environment which indicates that a change is necessary in data handling in order to achieve the mandatory needs in progressive organizations.

TODAY'S CHALLENGE

GROWTH IN DETAIL VOLUME
EQUIPMENT AVAILABILITY
CHANGING REQUIREMENTS
"STATE OF THE ART" PROGRESS
TIMELINESS IN DECISION MAKING

FLEXIBILITY IN CHANGING PLANS (BUDGETS, FORECASTS)
GREATER CONCENTRATION ON ANALYSIS VS MANUALLY GENERATED REPORTS
GROWING COMPLEXITY IN CUSTOMER REPORTING

COMPETITION FROM COMPETITORS (KEEPING UP WITH THE JONES')

IMPROVE PLANNING AND CONTROLS ON
      CONTRACT STATUS/PERFORMANCE
      CASH REQUIREMENTS
      MANPOWER LEVEL
      FIXED ASSET BUDGET
      DIRECT/INDIRECT RATIOS
      CONTRACTUAL REQUIREMENTS

A74419

Neglect of varied information needs results in customer and vendor dissatisfaction, loss of discounts, late customer billings, excessive working capital requirements, inefficient operation control, tardy or inadequate decision-making which all culminate in business losses and inefficiencies.

DATA PROCESSING EVOLUTION

Advanced information technology and its associated capabilities has made possible the achievement of sophisticated financial management information systems. Exhibit A displays the evolution and progress that has been occurring in the data processing field.

The changing climate has affected all aspects of information processing relative to equipment, programming and management reporting needs.

DATA PROCESSING EVOLUTION

SPACE AGE

PAST & PRESENT

TAPE STORAGE ORIENTED
UNSOPHISTICATED SOFTWARE
EXPENSIVE
COMPUTER USAGE CONFLICTS
FEAR OF PERSONNEL DISPLACEMENT

EQUIPMENT

THIRD GENERATION OF EQUIPMENT
DISC/MASS STORAGE
TIME SHARING
IMPROVED COST PERFORMANCE
ON LINE/REAL TIME
VIDEO/AUDIO RESPONSE
MICROFILMING
DIRECT ACCESS/RETRIEVAL

PROGRAM "PATCHING"
COMPETITION FOR TECHNICIANS
MULTI LANGUAGE CODING

PROGRAMMING

COMPUTER PROGRAMMING
SINGLE LANGUAGE
PERFORMED BY CONCERNED
    ORGANIZATION

GREW OUT OF NECESSITY
IMPROPER PLANNING
PIECEMEAL

MANAGEMENT INFORMATION

SYSTEMATIC ANALYSIS
SCIENTIFIC TECHNIQUES
DATA INTEGRATION
CLERICAL EFFORT MINIMAL
"STATE OF ART" SOPHISTICATION

A74421

EXHIBIT A

The most neglected area in information processing to date has been the relatively little emphasis and effort devoted to the importance of the planning required in organizing and determining management information requirements. Information is a most vital link or element of consideration in planning, managing, controlling and making decisions. It can be dynamic or dull and unmanageable. It can provide the guidance for improving your operation or misguide the user into inadequate or no decision-making.

A systematic approach, using scientific techniques with proper application and data integration, is the primary tool which will materially improve information development and processing. This procedure will allow you to simulate particular business conditions, test alternate plans and courses of action based on varied premises and eliminate much of the "guesswork" in the planning aspects of a business operation.

Changing Organization Relationships

Computer operations have also had a considerable influence and impact on organization relationship due to the advancement in information processing and potential data availability. To improve data handling and varied usefulness, it has forced the need to cross all organizational lines and functional activities. Exhibit B displays the overlapping relationship between organizations and their dependence on the computer and its capabilities.

CHANGING ORGANIZATION RELATIONSHIP

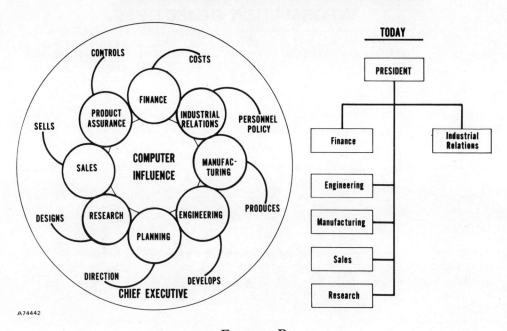

EXHIBIT B

Each organization has its own contribution to information "totality." As an operating activity occurs in each functional area, costs, scheduling and performance statistical information is produced and inputted into the system. This data then becomes the basis for integrating and summarizing to achieve planning, controlling, scheduling, costing and monitoring the progress of the effort.

All organizations will be originators as well as users of the data thus making them interrelated and dependent on each other for information with the computer being the "hub of the wheel" or processing controller and agent.

The computer's influence on organization relationship is a realistic inevitability. It offers capabilities beyond the reach of manual manipulation and interpretation of massive data. Specific information can be extracted selectively or on an exception basis. The computer files will be the central source of data reference whereby all concerned organizations will have the same "set of facts" for any contemplated, concerted action.

DEFINING INFORMATION OBJECTIVES

In order to define and achieve data integration to meet reporting objectives, consideration must be given to the type of data required, support programs and other necessary capabilities for accomplishing the requirements.

As shown in the Exhibit C, various capabilities have to be developed and utilized in satisfying information needs which are defined as follows:

INFORMATION OBJECTIVES

DATA BANK CONCEPT	MECHANIZE RECORDKEEPING	EFFECTIVE AND TIMELY REPORTING TECHNIQUES	FINANCIAL INTEGRATED REPORTING MODEL	TELEPROCESSING APPLICATIONS

TO RESOLVE

NEED FOR ACTION SIMULATION
TACTICAL & STRATEGIC DATA NEED
INCREASED REPORT REQUIREMENTS
VOLUMINOUS DETAILED REPORTING
MAGNITUDE CLERICAL EFFORT
FLEXIBILITY IN CHANGING PLANS
PRESSURE FOR ACCELERATED DECISIONS
EMPHASIS ON ASSET MGMT EFFECTIVENESS
ACCELERATED CLOSING
TIMELY / SELECTIVE DATA ACCESS
DATA INTEGRATION
DATA AUDIT AND CONTROL

EXHIBIT C

- Detailed source records must be mechanized in order to provide mass data accumulation, sorting and summarizing without information duplication to satisfy a number of needs.

- The data bank concept must be established for usage since it represents an advanced concept in file organization and storage.

- The teleprocessing applications are vital for immediate access and online retrieval of information. They provide the means for online decision simulation and testing varying courses of action.

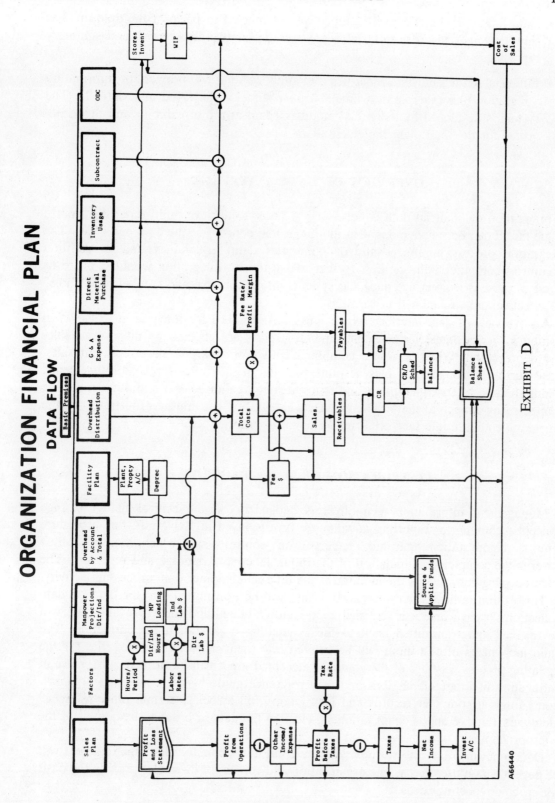

ORGANIZATION FINANCIAL PLAN

DATA FLOW

EXHIBIT D

A66440

- Data flow must be effectively defined and channeled to perform multiple updates simultaneously in order to develop file records for overall selective and summary reporting.

- Financial models must be constructed in a manner that will provide for information integration. An example of a financial plan model is displayed in Exhibit D. The system is developed by individual modules (data at top of exhibit) and then integrated for the total plan implementation.

OVERVIEW OF DATA INTERFACE

Integration of financial data is necessary in order to achieve multi-reporting from a single file. It can be synonymous with the intent and concept of the data bank files. The integration process minimizes and/or eliminates data redundancy and in addition maximizes computer utilization. A further expansion on integration would indicate its prime purpose is to interface data and systems into a cohesive and compatible "whole" for effective and streamlined processing.

An overview of data interface which illustrates the need for integration is shown in Exhibit E. As is noted, for example, operation costs are affected by manpower, sales and depreciation. When costs are combined with profit margin, they represent sales. Costs further affect the payables account and this in turn affects cash disbursements. The ultimate cash schedule, profit and loss statement, balance sheet and other reporting is affected by change to the basic costs. Data integration is a must as illustrated by the prevailing common interface of current accounting information.

INTEGRATION OF DATA RECORDS

Management information technology is dependent on the central file(s) storage concept technique for reporting advantages. As displayed in Exhibit F, this procedure requires remote station input into a teleprocessing control system which, in essence, then governs the complete manipulation of the input, its control, storage and reporting. The teleprocessing controller is the monitor of the internal computer data processing activity.

This exhibit indicates that incremental data will be transmitted into the detailed data collection system where it is screened as to validity, edited and sorted. Invalid data will be rejected and transmitted back to the originating organization for correction. The valid increments of cost input will be entered into their properly classified files for the updating process. Listings of the computer-accepted input will be printed out for use in verification of input submissions and as a reference guide by the concerned organizations. Internal computer records and instructions will associate certain other reference identifiers (charge and account numbers, etc.) to the data in order to update all of the appropriate files.

Data input may fall into various types of detail and summary files which content will be dependent on user needs. The organization and content of these files provide the basis for specific reporting needs.

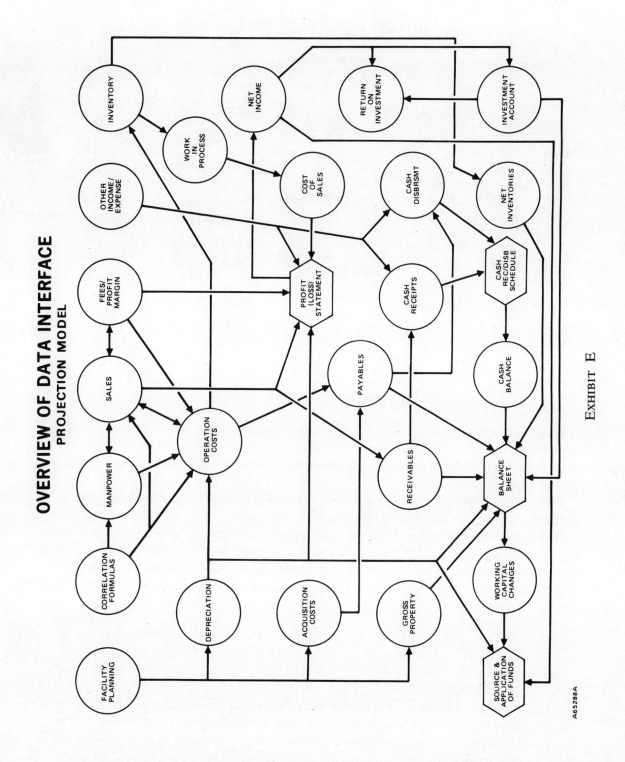

OVERVIEW OF DATA INTERFACE
PROJECTION MODEL

EXHIBIT E

A65288A

INTEGRATED RECORD PROCESSING

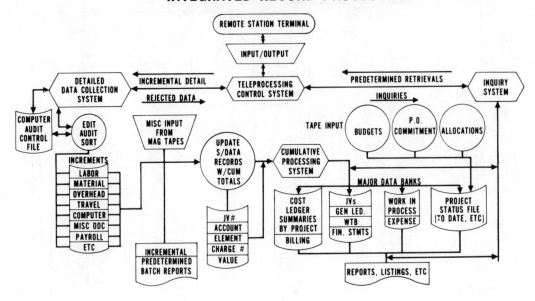

EXHIBIT F

DEVELOPMENT OF DATA BANK(S)

There are many different versions of a data bank depending upon the need of the organizations concerned. Data banks represent integrated storage file locations. They should be simple and contain only that information which is required to satisfy specific and multi-organization needs.

Exhibit G displays, in abbreviated form, how this concept provides the capability required and examples of data bank content.

In essence, the costs collected are inputted directly through a remote station terminal to the subsystem data banks. The cost ledger is classified as a file subsystem in that it contains considerable detail within its own system that is not required in the master files. Summaries of the data in these subsystem banks are further accumulated into a master summary base.

Establishing the Master Files

The master file represents strategic type of information which is used for management control, planning and decisions.

The contents of the master files are dependent upon an organization's decision as to the emphasis and utilization requirements it places on certain types of information. It is supported by data from the subsystem files. When management surveys its informational requirements, inevitably, they are concerned with the following "need to know" data:

- What is the status of effort remaining on a contract or undelivered sales?

- What was and currently is the net income from operations?

- Are the receivable balances excessive and what is the "age" of individual customer accounts—is there a problem?

- Is the inventory sufficient, too high or low?

- What is the situation with the cash position?

- Does the backlog require attention?

The above represents the type of summary data on which management decision and direction is based.

The theory of one vast data base storing all information is not practical because of its complication in file organization. Further, the instructions for online retrieval are too involved for the ordinary layman's personal involvement with file retrieval needs or "gaming." Another consideration is that the "search" time through a massive data base is costly in computer time as well as delays in retrieval.

DATA BANK CONCEPT

Exhibit G

AUDIT AND CONTROLS

Accurate reporting is not possible without the appropriate evaluation of the data coming into the system. All data should be thoroughly screened through program controls that will govern input validity. Audit files check the identification of all data in order to determine its acceptance into the file records.

As noted in Exhibit H, all transactions, changes, etc. must flow through a record controller program which verifies that data identifications are valid in terms of contract or sales order numbers, work order, general ledger account, etc.

CONTROLLING INPUT VALIDITY

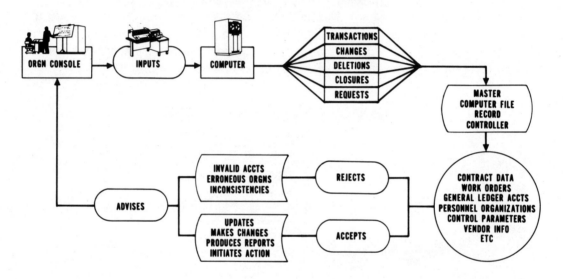

EXHIBIT H

If the input data is invalid or inconsistent with the program controls, it is rejected and an error message is relayed back to its originating station. If the input passes the screening process, then the program proceeds with the processing cycle of update and change.

It is essential that all accounting input data be entered directly from source documents by the organizations concerned because of their familiarity with the information and they can generally "sense" when the input is invalid by visual audit.

Transmission of documents and keypunch sheets to another organization for entry only leads to problems and error exposure. The subject of input validity and control cannot be overemphasized.

OPTIMUM UTILIZATION OF COMPUTER FILE RECORDS

"Pot of Gold" Utilization

Meaningful information is synonymous to a "pot of gold" in that it provides the "payoff" capability for planning, controlling and action decisions. Exhibit I indicates that source information at the lowest level flows through various computer processes in order to establish files that can be used in satisfying multitudinous reporting requirements pertinent to the needs of an organization, management and customer. This exhibit further illustrates the need for data integration.

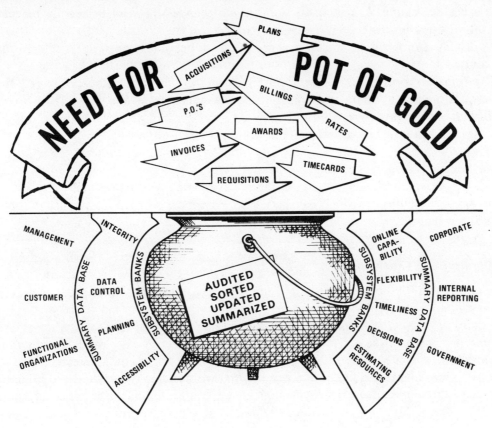

EXHIBIT I

This information is compiled at a number of subsystem levels in order to achieve the ultimate data summary requirements. Intelligent highlighting of timely and pertinent information for ease of analysis and interpretation can save countless hours of manual search, thousands of dollars in problem-avoidance through appropriate action and provide an organization with a competitive tool for successfully operating a business enterprise.

Management Planning

In establishing management plans, appropriate computer programs can perform practically all of the clerical functions currently necessary in order to achieve a projected plan of operation. In today's environment, the time span between the established plan premises and its manual mathematical development for analysis and evaluation is quite lengthy. This situation does not afford management an opportunity to review the complete substance of the plan adequately nor make changes that can be readily reflected and the adjusted results known on a timely basis.

As displayed in Exhibit J, initial premises, factors, decisions, etc. will be entered into the computer.

The computer controller, having received its input, will initiate the action required to produce preliminary data and guidelines for management evaluation relative to the finalization of the proposed plan and required subsequent deviation from the original premises can be rapidly incorporated to indicate the effect of the change. Computer storage files of historical data and program control and processing instructions are necessary for developing projection statistics.

In a typical situation today, masses of detail have to be reviewed manually and factors or parameters established which can be used for application to the anticipated conditions in the future.

Corporate Data Communication

In developing division and subsidiary information systems and data base, consideration must be given to corporate management needs as well as the individual division or subsidiary in terms of flexibility for meeting varying reporting needs. This is possible through utilization of the division record files which concept is displayed in Exhibit K.

Any corporate information plan must include a means for communicating directly with its divisions and subsidiaries in a manner that will provide timely, updated information in a short interval of elapsed time. Online communication is the most advanced capability and technique to overcome telephone calls, personal visits and considerable paper work flow from suborganizations in order to obtain the data needed for corporate consolidation purposes and analysis.

An online inquiry device at the corporate level would be tied in by telephone line to the various organizations' devices and data files. Information required would be "messaged" directly to a division or simultaneously to all of them. The query would conceivably be addressed directly to the organization's data base or the controller's remote station terminal.

If the inquiry is made directly to the division data base, an electrical impulse would also activate the pertinent division/subsidiary terminal device with indication that an

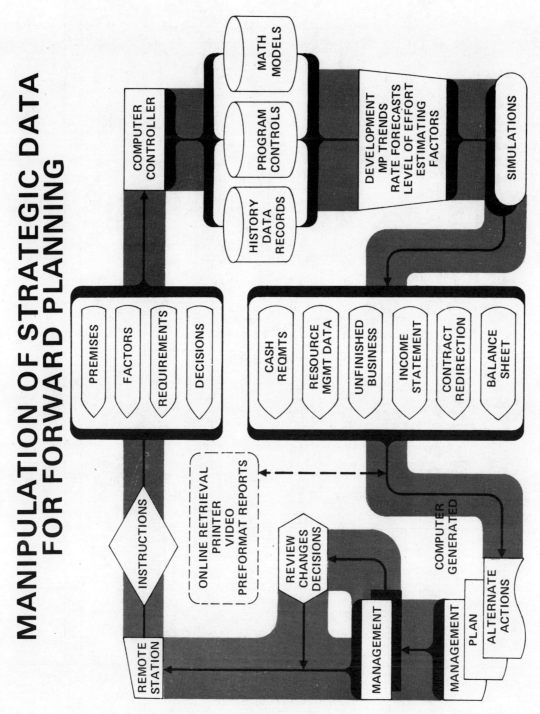

MANIPULATION OF STRATEGIC DATA FOR FORWARD PLANNING

COMPUTER CONTROLLER

MATH MODELS

PROGRAM CONTROLS

HISTORY DATA RECORDS

DEVELOPMENT
MP TRENDS
RATE FORECASTS
LEVEL OF EFFORT
ESTIMATING FACTORS

SIMULATIONS

PREMISES
FACTORS
REQUIREMENTS
DECISIONS

CASH REQMTS
RESOURCE MGMT DATA
UNFINISHED BUSINESS
INCOME STATEMENT
CONTRACT REDIRECTION
BALANCE SHEET

INSTRUCTIONS

ONLINE RETRIEVAL
PRINTER
VIDEO
PREFORMAT REPORTS

REVIEW CHANGES DECISIONS

COMPUTER GENERATED

REMOTE STATION

MANAGEMENT

MANAGEMENT
PLAN
ALTERNATE ACTIONS

EXHIBIT J

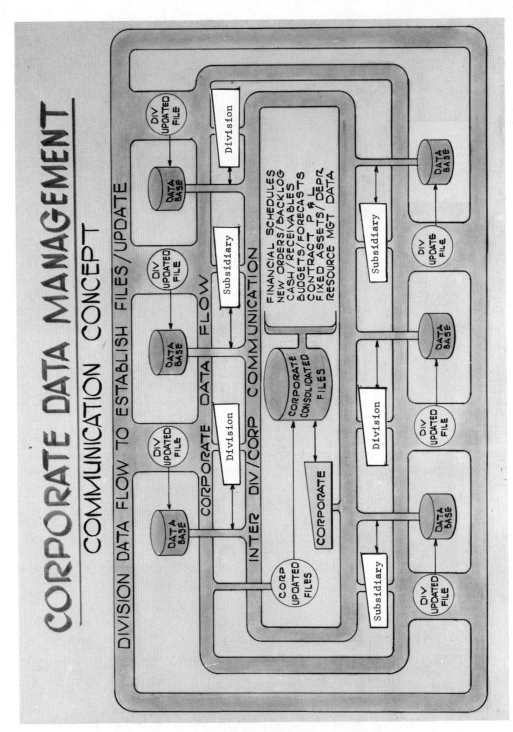

EXHIBIT K

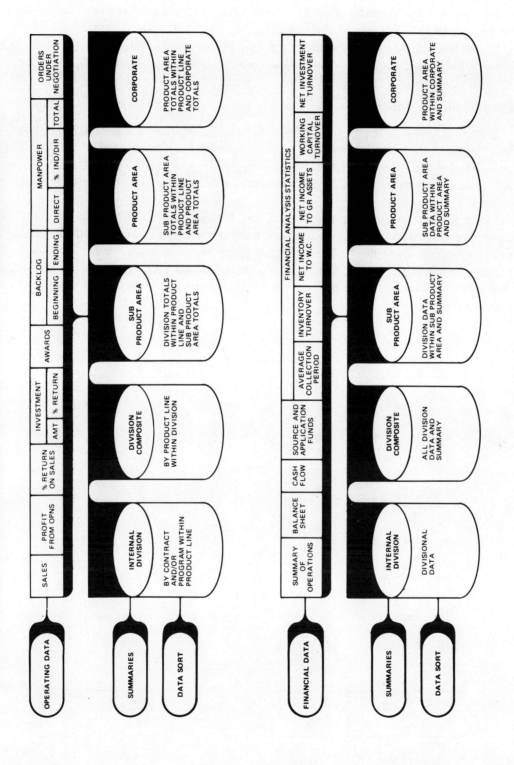

DATA REPORTING LINKED TO HIERARCHY SUMMARIES CONCEPT

EXHIBIT L

interrogation is being made of its files. Simultaneously, the information being retrieved by the corporate office would be printed out on the local station device.

In establishing the above communication, consideration should be given to what information should be summarized to hierarchy reporting and storage.

Data Reporting Linkage

Exhibit L displays the type of information to be reported for hierarchal summaries from the same data files used in a division or subsidiary. This method of file availability and updating for reporting is dynamic in that timely, relevant and accurate information is "on call" at any moment to top corporate management for their decision-making process.

Financial data integration and control are fundamental requirements of a sophisticated management reporting system. They provide the basic source of data for managing and controlling operations. The integration process, however, must be thoroughly planned to be effective and consider the "total" information aspect. To achieve data integration, computers must be the tool, systems must be the way and meaningful information must be the result.

13

Building Flexibility into the Financial Statement Report System

OVERVIEW OF FINANCIAL STATEMENT REPORTING

The primary objective of all financial accounting recordkeeping is to provide a capability for summarizing the detailed data into meaningful financial statements in order that an assessment can be made of performance, costs and profit for the operating statement and also to determine and evaluate the status of the balance sheet accounts. The successful enterprise is dependent upon this information for planning, controlling and decision-making. Exhibit A provides an overview for the considerations and needs of a financial management reporting system.

Acceleration of financial statement preparation provides management with a timely tool for determining the need to change direction, expand or contract operations, initiate borrowing if the cash position is too low, accelerate, if possible, the billing process if that is the problem with high accounts receivable balances, assess the inventory turnover, determine the adequacy of the return on sales and investment, etc.

COMPUTERIZATION APPROACH

The transition from manual to mechanical processing has already taken place in many organizations. Most organizations have mechanical labor distribution, accounts payable, payroll and other detailed data processing. To achieve the next step requires "bridging the gap" between detail and summary reporting. Exhibit B displays the origination of data, its flow through identifiers to the ultimate financial statement reporting.

Exhibit C displays the manual oriented procedures as versus the mechanical process objectives. The manipulation of data and its significance in compressing the time span of schedule preparation is highlighted in this exhibit.

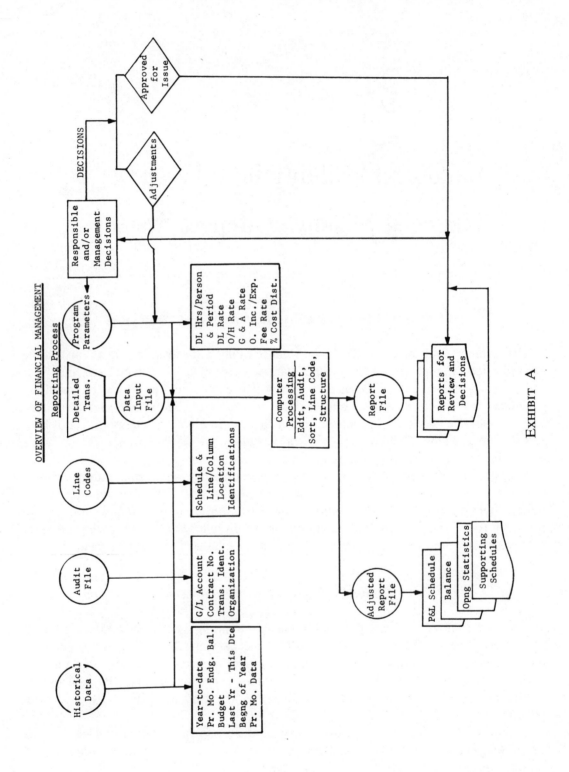

OVERVIEW OF FINANCIAL MANAGEMENT

Reporting Process

EXHIBIT A

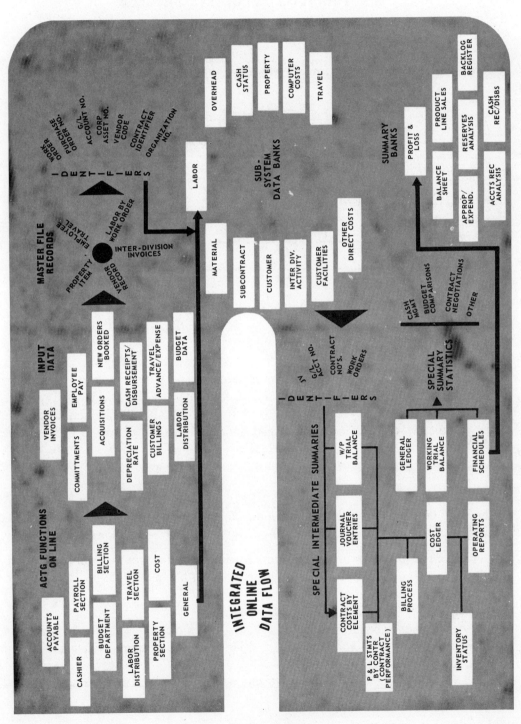

EXHIBIT B

FINANCIAL REPORTING PROCESS

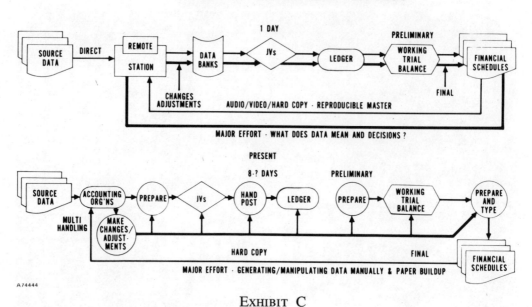

EXHIBIT C

As noted in Exhibit C, the manual effort involves multi-handling of data from its source to the preparation of the financial schedules. The major primary effort is, of course, the development and manipulation of the data. In the mechanical process, financial schedules could be achieved on the first workday after close. The accelerated effort mechanically would allow for detailed data analysis and action to be taken for problem solutions.

Processing

There are approximately five basic computer processes necessary in order to produce the end product—financial statements. They are summarized as follows:

1. The input of journal voucher information with general ledger account associations.
2. Development of the current period's general ledger file in detail as well as its update predicated upon prior period balances.
3. An update of the working trial balance records.
4. Processing non-account financial associated data which is necessary for the financial schedule analysis such as budget, prior period's information and data that is not reflected in the general ledger.
5. The actual production of all financial statements in the prescribed formats required.

Input Data

As will be noted in the description of the schedules, all of the data will be developed within the mechanical system. In the initial creation of the history, budget and miscel-

FINANCIAL STATEMENT MECHANIZATION

OPERATING DATA INPUT

JOB NO. __________ SHEET NO. __________

BY __________

T C	R C	ACCOUNT		SCHEDULE LINE CODE	AMOUNTS IN THOUSANDS						MISCELLANEOUS DATA OR DESCRIPTIONS
					CURRENT PERIOD	YEAR TO DATE	LAST YEAR		BUDGET		
		PR	S				PERIOD	TO DATE	PERIOD	TO DATE	
1	2	3 4 5	6 7	8 9 10 11 12 13 14	15 16 17 18 19 20 21	22 23 24 25 26 27 28	29 30 31 32 33 34 35	36 37 38 39 40 41 42	43 44 45 46 47 48 49	50 51 52 53 54 55 56	57 58 59 60 61 62 63 64 65 66 67 68 69 70 71 72 73 74 75 76 77 78 79 80

ASSET, LIABILITIES, INVESTMENT ACCOUNT BALANCES

JOB NO. __________ SHEET NO. __________

BY __________

T C	R C	ACCOUNT	SCHEDULE LINE CODE	AMOUNTS IN THOUSANDS					MISCELLANEOUS DATA OR DESCRIPTIONS
				CURRENT PERIOD	BUDGET	LAST PERIOD	BEGINNING OF YEAR	THIS DATE LAST YEAR	
1	2	3 4 5 6 7	8 9 10 11 12 13 14	15 16 17 18 19 20 21	22 23 24 25 26 27 28	29 30 31 32 33 34 35	36 37 38 39 40 41 42	43 44 45 46 47 48 49	50 51 52 53 54 55 56 57 58 59 60 61 62 63 64 65 66 67 68 69 70 71 72 73 74 75 76 77 78 79 80

DESCRIPTION OF INPUT

Column 1 - "TC" -- Transaction Code:	A - create record; B - add to record; C - change record; D - delete record
Column 2 - "RC" -- Record Code:	A - current period P & L; B - YTD P & L; C - assets; D - liabilities; E - investment account; F - expense clearing accounts; G - direct cost and clearing accounts; H - major product line summary; I - cash transaction; J - analysis of depreciation reserves; K - changes in sales and income by product line; L - status of property accounts; M - asset management statistics
Columns 3 - 7 - "Accounts":	General Ledger control and subaccounts
Columns 8 - 14 - "Schedule Line Code":	Identification to a specific record location by assigned report number, actual line location of data on schedule and the column location on schedule (this is further discussed in the General Ledger Chapter No. 2)
Other Columns:	Self-explanatory

EXHIBIT D

STATEMENT OF OPERATIONS DEVELOPMENT

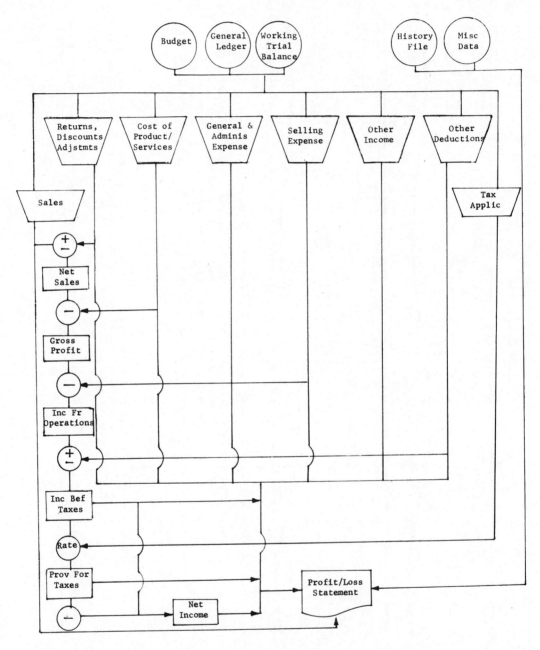

EXHIBIT E

laneous files, however, there will be considerable direct input or this input could be entered on a time available basis. The input formats that can be used for the various schedule files are displayed in Exhibit D.

The above two formats will accommodate all of the inputs required for the mechanized reports to be described in this chapter.

Profit and Loss

This schedule is basic to any operating organization and Exhibit E indicates the flow of data into this schedule.

This exhibit displays the computer operation of manipulating the data from its source to the actual mechanical production of the schedule. Each organization may have different terminology or items in its statement, but basically, this computing procedure governs in developing the profit and loss schedule.

The files indicated at the top of the exhibit can actually be one composite file which is updated monthly. The budget file is important for comparison to actuals, and for deriving variances. The history file provides statistics for future projection needs. The format of the profit and loss output is as follows:

Last Year This Date	Item Description	Current Period	Budget	Variance	Cumulative to Date

This income (loss) would be mechanically developed from the detail by contract, product, sales order and service in order that, in the analysis of the data, you can isolate problem areas specifically. Further, codes can be incorporated into the mechanization process which will summarize your activities in terms of a specific product, product line (related type activity), customer, type of effort (cost plus, commercial, fixed price, government, foreign, etc.).

Balance Sheet

This is a very important schedule in that it represents an organization's status at a point in time.

Exhibit F displays the processing of the information in the computer in order to generate this schedule.

Primarily, the data for the current period is derived from the information contained in the working trial balance file. It is possible that some reference may be necessary to the general ledger if more detailed account reporting is required in the balance sheet.

The budget file contains the planned anticipations from operations, comparison to the actuals mechanically and the computation of the variances.

The history file will contain the line item balances for the prior period, the beginning of the year and for the same reporting period last year. All of these comparisons aid in the analysis of an organization's progress or problems.

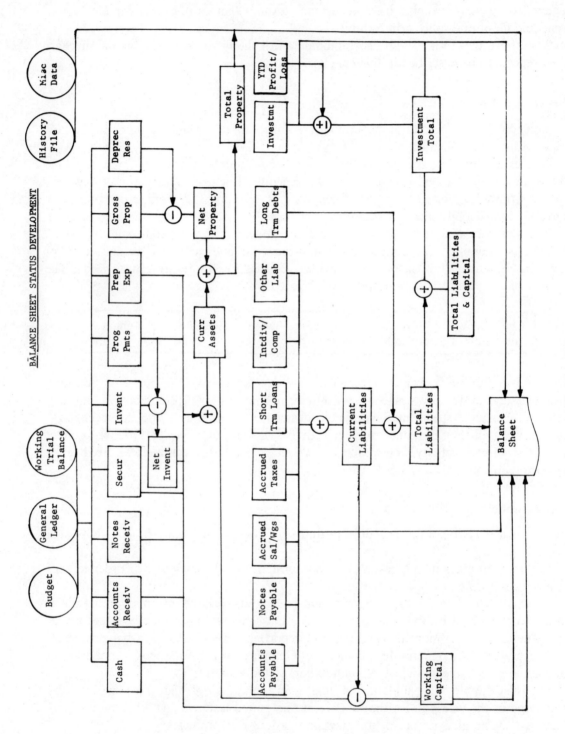

BALANCE SHEET STATUS DEVELOPMENT

EXHIBIT F

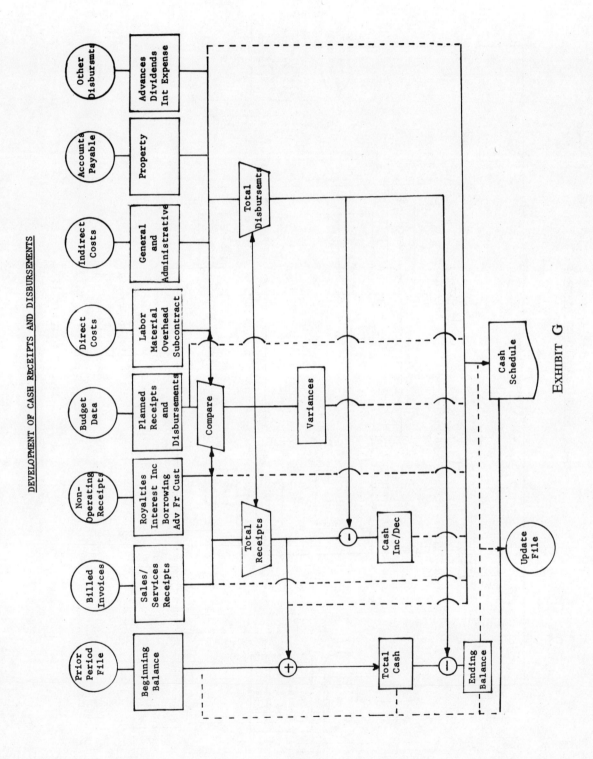

DEVELOPMENT OF CASH RECEIPTS AND DISBURSEMENTS

EXHIBIT G

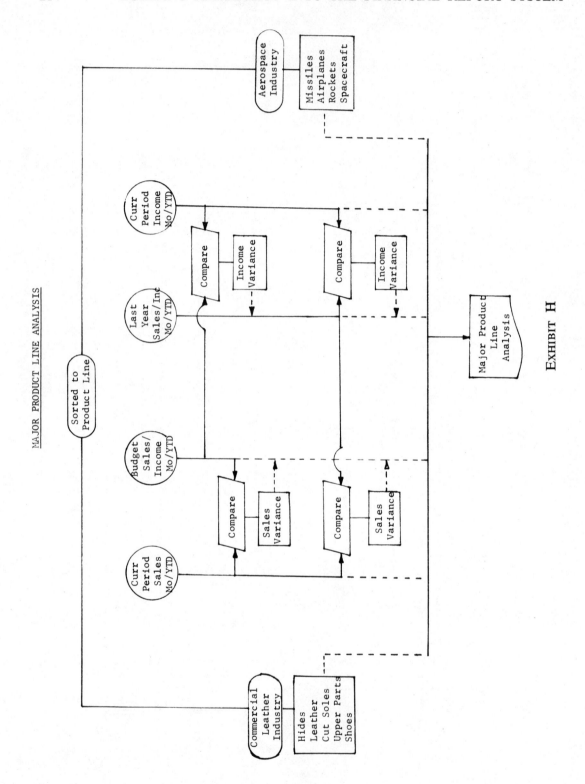

EXHIBIT H

OPERATING AND FINANCIAL ANALYSES DATA

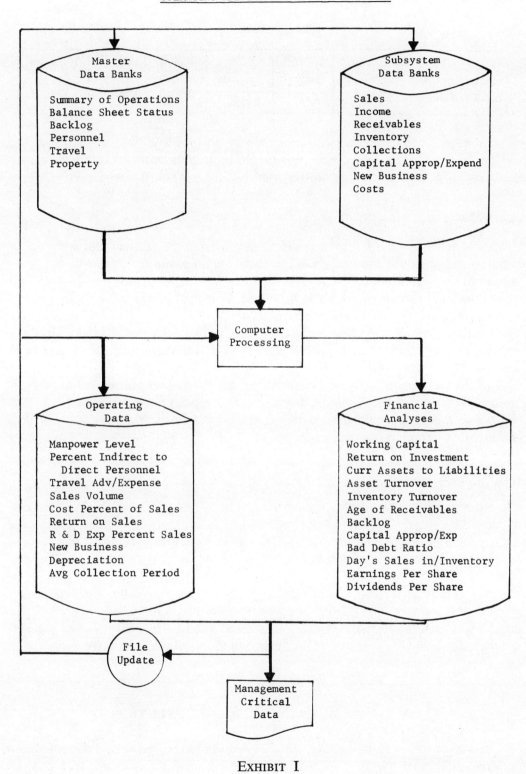

Master
Data Banks

Summary of Operations
Balance Sheet Status
Backlog
Personnel
Travel
Property

Subsystem
Data Banks

Sales
Income
Receivables
Inventory
Collections
Capital Approp/Expend
New Business
Costs

Computer
Processing

Operating
Data

Manpower Level
Percent Indirect to
  Direct Personnel
Travel Adv/Expense
Sales Volume
Cost Percent of Sales
Return on Sales
R & D Exp Percent Sales
New Business
Depreciation
Avg Collection Period

Financial
Analyses

Working Capital
Return on Investment
Curr Assets to Liabilities
Asset Turnover
Inventory Turnover
Age of Receivables
Backlog
Capital Approp/Exp
Bad Debt Ratio
Day's Sales in/Inventory
Earnings Per Share
Dividends Per Share

File
Update

Management
Critical
Data

EXHIBIT I

The format of the balance sheet columnar headings is as follows:

Balance Sheet Reporting

Account or Data Description	Current Period	Budget	Variance	End of Last Period	Begin Curr Year	This Date Last Year

The storage file for the balance sheet data is organized in the same format and therefore historical data is available to provide projection statistics based on experience correlation data. Variances are reported for analysis and investigation.

Cash Receipts and Disbursements

This schedule is a natural for the mechanized process if the detailed files are properly organized and identified for the processing cycle requirements.

Exhibit G indicates the flow of data from its source, the processing involved and the output schedule. The appropriate detail will be developed at the contract or product line level and summarized to the organization totals.

The "dash" lines on the chart represent the data that is reported in the schedule. The data in this schedule can be either detailed or in summary form depending upon need and the extent of the analysis to be performed.

All of the files shown at the top of the chart are mechanical and, therefore, the required data is extracted from each file into one computer processing program. The comparison of data and computations are computer-generated. Year-to-date as well as current period information is reported.

Major Product Line Summary

In order to critically evaluate your operations at the management level, it is necessary that this analysis be made at the product line level. In most organizations, some products are more profitable than others. The product evaluation in terms of sales and net income is an immediate indicator as to the problem areas for concentration and action.

Exhibit H displays the files and processing performed mechanically. As noted in this exhibit, the current period's month and year-to-date information is compared to the budget and the similar period last year. This comparison is necessary so that the performance can be readily measured to the plan and prior year's activity volume and income.

COMPUTER SUMMARY RECORDS/STATISTICS

There are a number of storage records required in order to generate the appropriate and varying financial schedules as well as to develop operating and financial analysis statistics. Exhibit I displays the files concerned and the data that resides therein.

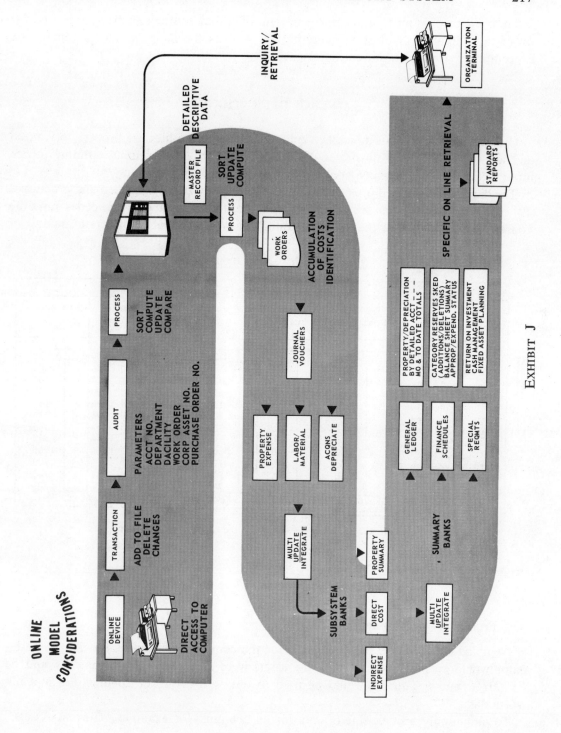

EXHIBIT J

These file records provide management with data that can be selectively retrieved for review and/or analysis of their operations as well as the capability to project future expectations based on historical experience.

ONLINE OPERATIONS

Online processing is not difficult to achieve providing the files are properly organized and identified. Exhibit J illustrates the flow of data from the remote terminal device input to the data banks which contain the various financial schedules.

The data can be entered directly onto magnetic tape or cards produced and processed. To gain access to the various schedules and specific information, line codes must be constructed for inquiry to the files. Illustrated below are typical identifiers to data:

<u>Balance Sheet Item Designations</u>

	Requirement	Designator	This Date Budget (1)	This Date Actual (2)	Last Month (3)	Begng Year (4)	This Date Last Year (5)
(1)	Complete Schedule	FS200000-or	FS200001	FS200002	FS200003	FS200004	FS200005
(2)	All Assets	100 "	101	102	103	104	105
(3)	Liab. & Net Worth	580 "	581	582	583	584	585
	Cash	050	051	052	053	054	055
	Accounts Receiv.	130	131	132	133	134	135
	Net Inventories	270	271	272	273	274	275
(4)	Current Assets	360	361	362	363	364	365
	Net Property	540	541	542	543	544	545
	Total Assets	560	561	562	563	564	565
	Total Curr. Liab.	720	721	722	723 (5)	724	725
	Long Term Liab.	740	741	742	743	744	745
	Capital	780	781	782	783	784	785
	Tot. Liab/Net W.	FS200840	FS200841	FS200842	FS200843	FS200844	FS200845

Financial Schedule Designation

Column location of data

Line number of data location

The Procedure for Online Inquiries

As noted above, if the requirement is for the complete schedule retrieval, the designator would be *FS200000*. If only the assets were required, the designator would be *FS200100* and *FS200580* would be used to obtain a listing of all liabilities and net worth data.

To obtain only a single line of data for all columns, for example, "Current Assets," the designator would be *FS100360*.

To obtain a particular and specified data, for example, "Total Current Liabilities for the Beginning of the Year," your designator would be *FS200724*.

Any combination of data can be obtained—total, column, line or single item.

The same organization of data and type of procedure applies for the profit and loss data. The proper assignment of designators is very important and provides capability and flexibility for making specific or total changes and/or retrieve the data required.

The results of the mechanical preparation of financial statements will minimize clerical operations and provide more time for analysis of data, timeliness of preparation, flexibility in making changes, and provide a means for simulating the effect of alternate courses of action.

14

The Effective Management Budget
and Forecasting Program

The dynamics of information technology and progress has provided advanced capabilities and accelerated the need for more effective planning if an organization is to survive successfully in the ever-increasing competitive environment. Intelligent decisions and responsible action by the guiding management results from a thorough understanding of the major factors involved in operating their business and the ensuing effects of their direction leadership.

BUDGET AND FORECAST OBJECTIVES

The tools that are necessary to accomplish the above are sound budget and long range forecasting techniques and practices. The tools provide a formalized plan of operating objectives in financial terms which represent a means for measuring actual results against the projected anticipations. An organization's growth or contraction, planned profits, return on investment, cash flow, sales and backlog are all necessary requirements for effective plan development.

A budget represents the overall establishment of projected operational and financial plans for generally a one-year time span and provides all of the detailed data relative to all aspects of an organization's operations. The forecast, on the other hand, is a longer range plan of projections—generally for five years or more. Its first year data is predicated on the annual budget premises and then beyond that point, it represents the most reasonable probabilities for the future.

Before a budget or forecast cycle is initiated, a series of studies are undertaken by the planners to determine the economic outlook as a whole and its anticipated effect on the organization's future business conditions. Management issues a basic assumption or premise letter which describes the projected environment in terms of business trends and assessment, courses of action, and relates this data in terms of the possible effect on the organization's activities. In addition to the economic evaluation, the other main considerations involve total manpower levels, profit anticipations or losses, sales/production volumes, research and development allocations, capital acquisitions, etc. The "groundrules" for making projections are only as good as past performance can be measured and assessed as to "what happened and why" and what are the likely probabilities for the future.

SYSTEM DESIGN AND INFORMATION FLOW

The manual process requires countless hours of effort to provide manpower projections which are translated into labor hours, priced and then establishing overhead rates for application to hours and/or dollars. Material requirements and other direct costs have to be determined. This data is further detailed by organization, project, contract, product, burden center and other possible organization needs. The above represents only the basic data which must be manipulated and summarized into financial statements and meaningful summary statistics for management review and approval. Computerization is the only answer to this type of task which involves hundreds of calculations, varying summaries, multi-reporting and flexibility for making timely changes.

System Development

To achieve the mechanical forecasting capability, each step of the manual procedure must be reviewed and flowcharted in minute detail. Source documentation must be analyzed in order to trace the information flow from its initial generation to the end usage.

As examples of the overall information flow to determine the major data needs and processing, three exhibits have been developed to illustrate cost plus fixed fee and fixed price contracts and the commercial business oriented enterprise.

Cost Plus Fixed Fee (CPFF)

This type of contract generally involves research and development type activity but also could include production. Sales are predicated on the allowed costs incurred plus the application of a negotiated fee rate. Some costs are disallowed if they do not contribute to the cost of contract requirement performance such as certain entertainment, advertising, travel, etc. The expense disallowances are a negotiable item with the customer.

Exhibit A presents an overview of the data requirements and information interface on this type of contract activity.

Based on current or anticipated contracts, a level of effort is established and costed, the associated overhead is applied, material and other direct purchases are projected and general and administrative expense determined.

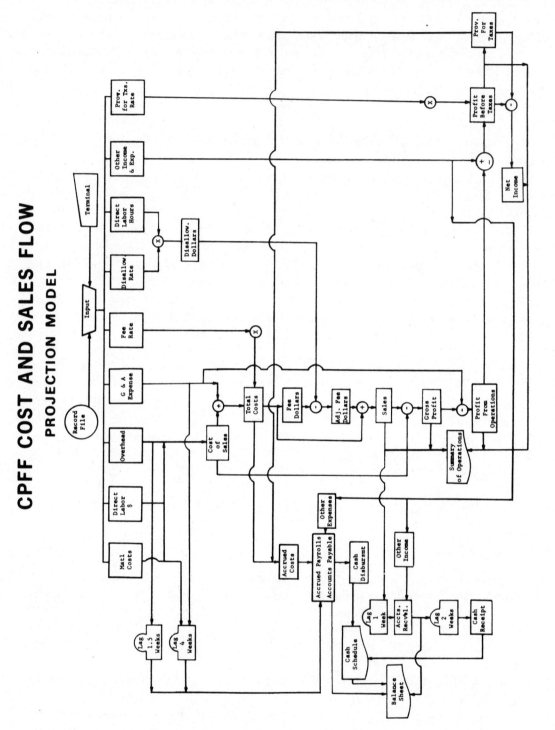

CPFF COST AND SALES FLOW
PROJECTION MODEL

Exhibit A

The costs are accumulated and a negotiated fee rate is applied to determine the amount of fee dollars. Based on historical experience, a disallowance rate is projected and applied to the direct labor hours in order to provide a contingency for anticipated disallowances. The disallowances are deducted from the total fees to obtain net fee dollars. Total costs plus fee dollars then represent CPFF sales.

There are three prime financial schedules that are affected by the development of the above data. The profit and loss statement (or Summary of Operations) as shown in Exhibit A reflects the sales and costs to determine profit from operations. Other income represents cash receipts for interest, royalty payments or sale of fixed assets. Other deductions include interest expense, land gifts and miscellaneous.

The sales are invoiced to the customer and set up as an account receivable until paid. The receivable is reported on the balance sheet. When paid, a cash receipt value is generated which is reported in the cash schedule.

As costs are generated, they represent an accrued liability which is reported in the balance sheet. These costs are segregated into pertinent accounts such as accrued salaries and wages, accrued taxes and accounts payables. Upon payment, the amounts are reflected as disbursements in the cash schedule.

Fixed Price (FP) Data Flow

Fixed price contracts are those which have been negotiated at a definite value which includes the fee margin in the total price. If the extent of the effort or cost of product exceeds the negotiated price, the result is an overrun and represents a loss on the contract. Good sound estimating of the price proposal and close control of performance and costs are very necessary in negotiating this type of contract. Exhibit B reflects the data flow and processing on this type of contract.

Projection of sales for this type of contract as well as others are generally segregated into four categorizations which are described as follows:

Firm Business represents approved commitments for purchase of a product or service in terms of specific requirement definition, quantity, if applicable, level of effort, price and other necessary and pertinent terms of the agreement with the buyer.

Follow On contracts represent predicted additional effort to the firm business contract. This is predicated on an understanding with the customer or based on knowledge that additional follow-on business can be normally achieved. In commercial firms, particularly, the supplier anticipates future orders for its product because of uniqueness, quality, buyer need, goodwill and technical capability.

New Product business is based on an anticipated need by the customer in the future. It represents a high probability of capture due to improvement over current product capability, possible customer commitments or plans and possibly the organization's competitive position.

Special Product or Service sales are based on the anticipated need for technical

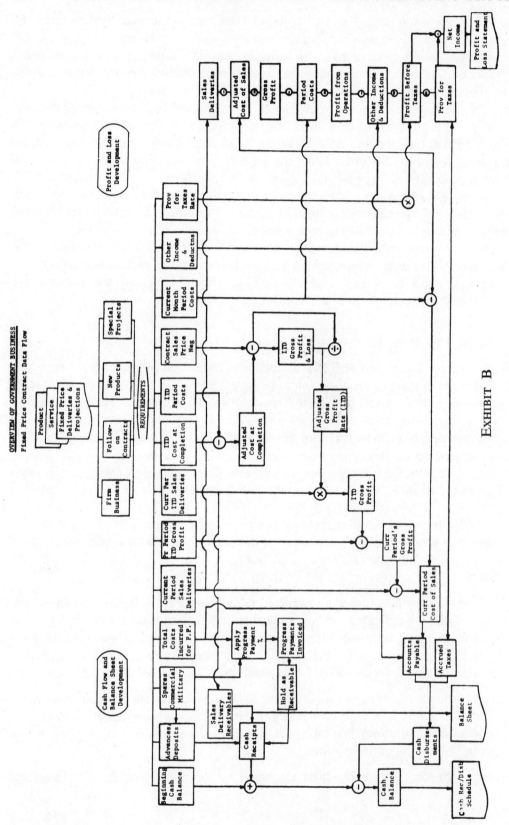

EXHIBIT B

consulting, research and development needs, problem investigation or a customer's verbal indication or inquiry. There is some evidence that the projected sales will materialize.

As noted in Exhibit B, when a delivery is made, the customer is invoiced for the quantity involved and at the sales price rate established in the contract. Level of effort invoicing is also possible on long lead completion items through negotiation with the customer.

In order to obtain cost of sales, however, and preclude possible profit margin losses because of the delivery schedule, a reassessment of the appropriate gross profit rate to be used is made each time a sale is booked. The procedure is as follows:

- The inception-to-date (ITD) current projected cost at completion represents the latest cost estimates by operating organizations and the project budget or planning groups.

- From this estimated cost at completion value, the inception-to-date period costs (G and A expense, for example) are deducted to arrive at an inception-to-date adjusted cost at completion.

- This amount is deducted from the contract sales price to arrive at an inception-to-date adjusted gross profit.

- The adjusted gross profit amount is divided by the contract sales price to derive an adjusted gross profit rate.

- The gross profit rate is applied to the ITD priced sales deliveries at the end of the current period to obtain an ITD adjusted gross profit. Prior month's ITD gross profit is deducted from the current period's developed gross profit to obtain the current period's adjusted gross profit.

- The adjusted gross profit is then deducted from the sales deliveries for the current period to obtain an adjusted cost of sales for the period.

- The cost of sales at this point includes the current period costs which are deducted in order to obtain the true gross profit value to be reflected in the income statement.

The balance of the profit and loss statement and the cash and balance sheet schedules' development is quite similar to that described for CPFF contracts above with the exception of the progress payment aspect. Through customer negotiation, a certain percentage of the costs incurred can be billed prior to the actual delivery of the product. This then involves "holdback and liquidation" criteria in the billing process.

Commercial Enterprises

This type of organization generally produces products or performs services of non-military nature although they can be and are purchased by miliary agencies. The information flow is reflected in Exhibit C.

The elements of cost are the same as those discussed in CPFF and FP contracts. The

OVERVIEW OF A COMMERCIAL BUSINESS
PRODUCT COST AND SALES DATA FLOW

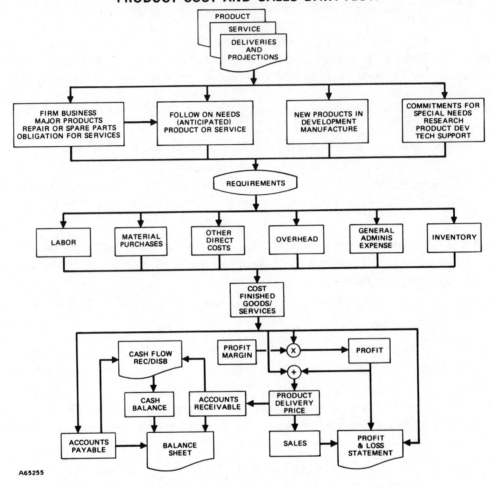

A65255

EXHIBIT C

costs must be known in order to determine the sales price of the product(s). The profit margin is included as part of the sales price. Costs are collected and allocated to specific item, lots, product line and other levels of activity associated with the needs and practices of an organization. Sales orders are a more common term in this type of business and represent documented buyer commitments for a product or service. The flow of data and reporting as shown in this exhibit is similar to that described for CPFF and FP contracts. The "shelf" inventory is characteristic of this type of business.

COMPUTER ORIENTED PROJECTION TECHNIQUES

Some of the more common, but effective, approaches to the projection process include correlations (direct, linear and multiple), statistical trends (arithmetic, geometric, Scurves), scattergrams (correlation between two statistical data series) and breakeven charts. Scattergram correlation projection is quite advantageous in that it is not influenced by values of extreme or unusual size. Breakeven charts are often used as a tool to express what happens to profits when costs and sales changes are made. An example of the chart usage is illustrated in Exhibit D using various formulae for indicating advisability of plant expansion, volume of sales that will be required to yield a given profit and the profits that result from projected sales volumes.

All of the techniques discussed above have their own uniqueness in projecting trends, values and providing analysis data. To be effective, however, in computer processing they must be translated into mathematical formulae.

DEVELOPMENT OF DETAIL REQUIRED

In order to develop the detailed projections required, a determination must be made as to the specific information that is necessary in order to meet the report objectives. Exhibits A, B and C indicate the overall needs. Sufficient detail must be projected in order to provide a capability for an analysis of the information if the actual results deviate from plan. It must be known what the component values are of the end-resulting numbers in terms of sales, costs, profit, cash balances, investment and liabilities.

For model flexibility, sales values should be derived from cost buildup plus fee and from sales values to costs, profit and manpower requirements. This technique thus provides the capability to test alternate courses of action from data changes at the top information level (sales) or at the detailed level (material, labor, overhead, etc.).

Labor Cost Development

The first requirement in a cost buildup to sales value is concerned with manpower projections. The headcount forecast is developed by the various concerned organizations for the projected periods based on current business "in house" and anticipated new business or requirements correlated to the business economic trends. The direct manpower is generally associated with specific contracts, product and product line. The organizational manning provides a means to also summarize the headcount to major product centers as identified through a computer "look-up" table record association. With the direct manning projection, there is also included an estimated percentage for overtime based on historical experience and projected contract or product delivery plan requirements.

An indirect to direct headcount ratio is forecast by organizations based on past experience factors and/or management edict. The above input data is entered into the computer along with hours per period and wage rate factors as shown in Exhibit E.

The following processing is performed by the computer:

The direct manpower is summarized by period, organization, contract, product and/or other levels of reporting required.

BREAK - EVEN POINT

CHART OF VOLUME — PROFIT RELATIONSHIP

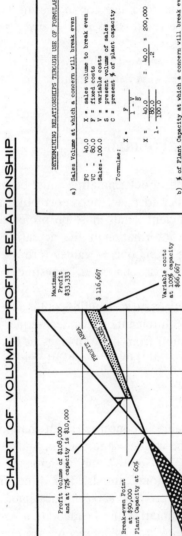

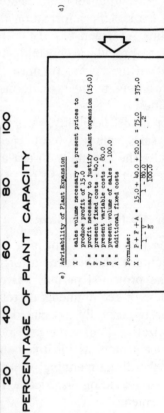

Exhibit D

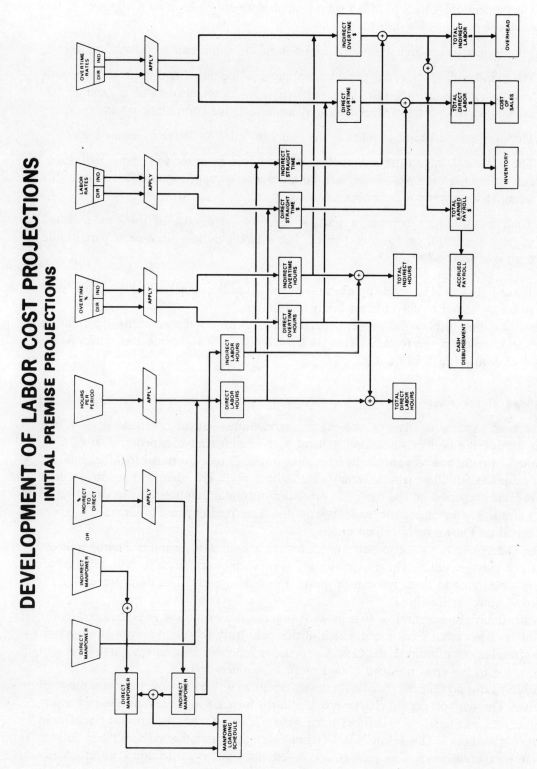

DEVELOPMENT OF LABOR COST PROJECTIONS
INITIAL PREMISE PROJECTIONS

EXHIBIT E

The percent of indirect to direct ratio is applied to obtain indirect manpower in the same categories as for direct above.

Summarizes direct and indirect manpower in the same categorizations as above.

The man-hours of effort per period are applied to the direct and indirect headcount to obtain the hours worked. It is noted that midpoint headcount is used in the calculation in order to reflect averaged headcount for computing hours.

The overtime percent is applied to the hours in order to derive overtime hours.

The projected wage rates are applied to the hours in order to obtain both direct and indirect labor costs giving consideration also to applying a different rate differential for overtime dollar calculations.

Total labor dollars become a part of inventory and cost of sales as reflected in payroll earned, accrued and paid. The indirect dollars become a part of the total overhead costs.

Exhibits F, G and H illustrate an example of the projection criteria and the procedures used in the computer to derive labor hours and dollars.

These exhibits display the input, program processes and the resulting information from the calculations performed. The "Loc" and "ID" files provide the retrieval addresses of each element in the file.

Overhead Development

Overhead expense consists of two major segregations—direct overhead costs which are a part of the cost of sales, and general and administrative expense. The G & A expense is a reduction to your profit from operations. Direct overhead includes indirect labor, supplies, utilities, travel, rentals, etc. These costs are identified to an account number and projected on the basis of correlation formulae relationships to direct labor hours, headcount or other independent variables. The fixed expense is separately generated based on known or historical criteria.

The G & A overhead is also based on direct labor hour association excluding indirect labor and fixed expenses. These expenses are general in nature such as selling, administration, research and development, proposal and bidding, etc. The data processing involved is noted in Exhibit I.

This exhibit also emphasizes that in some organizations the G & A is included in the cost of sales to obtain gross profit which in this case truly represents profit from operations. In other organizations, the G & A expense is reflected as a separate line item and a reduction to the gross profit to obtain profit from operations.

Exhibit J displays the overhead data development as well as its flow to obtain the total expense. The symbols on the chart were developed for ease in indicating the processing involved; for example, A1 (indirect manpower) X A2 (hours per period) results in indirect labor hours. This result X A3 (labor rate) generates the indirect labor dollars. Variable expense correlation factors are based upon an organization's historical ex-

BASIC STATISTICS FOR MECHANICAL PROJECTIONS
(Headcount and Labor Costs)

File						
Loc	ID	Data Description	Unit of Measure	Projection Criteria	Source of Data	Usage of Data
001	000	Labor Statistics				
	010	Total Hrs/Day	Hours	8.0	Projected	Obtain Total Hours/Day
	A	Prod. Hrs/Day	Hours	7.5 or .9375	Formula	Obtain Prod. Hours/Day
	B	Non-prod. Hrs/Day	Hours	.5 or .0625	Formula	Obtain Non-prod. Hours/Day
	C	Days Per Period	Days	20	Projected	Obtain Total Hours/Day
	01D	Hours Per Period	Hours	160	Projected	Obtain Total Hours/Period
	020	Overtime				
	A	Direct %	Percent	5%	Proj/Formula	Obtain Dir. O. T. Labor Hrs
	02B	Indirect %	Percent	3%	Proj/Formula	Obtain Ind. O. T. Labor Hrs
	030	Wage Rates				
	A	Direct/Hour	Rate	4.00	Proj/Formula	Obtain Dir. Labor Dollars
	B	Indirect/Hour	Rate	3.00	Proj/Formula	Obtain Ind. Labor Dollars
	C	Direct O. T./Hr	Rate	6.00	Proj/Formula	Obtain Dir. O. T. Labor Dollars
	03D	Indirect O. T./Hr	Rate	4.50	Proj/Formula	Obtain Ind. O. T. Labor Dollars
	040	Manpower				
	A	% Ind. to Dir.	%	50%	Proj/Formula	Obtain Ind. HC if Not Given
	B	Direct	Headcount	400	Projected	Obtain Direct Headcount
	C	Indirect	Headcount	200	Projected	Obtain Indirect Headcount
	04D	Total	Headcount	600	Calculation	Manning
001						

EXHIBIT F

DEVELOPMENT OF PROJECTED LABOR HOURS

Loc	ID	Data Description	Developed Projections	Calculation Procedure	Program File Ref. Calc.
001	050	Labor Hours/Period			
	A	Total Dir. S. T.	64,000	MP x Hrs/Day x Days/Period	010x04Bx01C
	B	Total Dir. O. T.	3,200	Hrs/Period x O. T. %	05Ax02A
	C	Total Dir. Hrs.	67,200	Sum of A and B	05A+05B
	D	Total Dir. Prod.	60,000	Total Dir. Hours x .9374	05Ax01A
	E	Total Dir. Prod. O.T.	3,000	Total O.T. Hours x .9375	05Bx01A
	F	Total Prod. Dir.	63,000	Sum of D and E	056+05E
	G	Total Dir. Non-prod.	4,000	A-D	05A-05D
	H	Total Dir. Non-prod. O.T.	200	B-E	05B-05E
	I	Total Non-prod. Dir.	4,200	Sum of G and H	05G+05H
	J	Total Ind. S. T.	32,000	MP x Hrs/DayxDays/Period	04Cx010x01C
	K	Total Ind. S. T. O. T.	960	Hrs/Period x O. T. %	05Jx02B
	L	Total Ind. Hrs	32,960	Sum of J and K	05J+05K
	M	Total Ind. Prod.	30,000	Total Ind. Hrs x .9375	05Jx01A
	N	Total Ind. Prod. O. T.	900	Total Ind. O. T. x .9375	05Kx01A
	O	Total Ind. Prod.	30,900	Sum of M+N	05M+05N
	P	Total Ind. Non-prod.	2,000	J-M	05J-05M
	Q	Total Ind. Non-prod O. T.	60	K-O	05K-050
	05R	Total Ind. Non-prod.	2,060	Sum of P+O	05P+050

EXHIBIT G

DEVELOPMENT OF PROJECTED LABOR DOLLARS

File Loc	ID	Data Description	Developed Projections	Calculation Procedure	Program File Ref. Calc.	Usage of Data
001	060	Labor Dollars/Period				
	A	Total Dir. S. T.	$256,000	Hrs/Period x Wage Rate	03AxO5A	Statistic Analysis
	B	Total Dir. O. T.	19,200	Hrs/Period x O. T. Wage Rate	03CxO5B	Statistic Analysis
	C	Total Direct	275,200	Sum of A & B	06A+06B	Statistic Analysis
	D	Prod. Dir. S. T.	240,000	Prod. Dir. x Wage Rate	03AxO5D	Statement of Income
	E	Prod. Dir. O. T.	18,000	Prod. Dir. x O. T. Wage Rate	03CxO5E	Statement of Income
	F	Total Prod. Dir.	258,000	Sum of D & E	06D+06E	Correlation Data
	G	Non-prod. Dir. S. T.	16,000	A-D	06A-06D	Overhead Budget
	H	Non-prod. Dir. O. T.	1,200	B-E	06B-06E	Overhead Budget (O.T.)
	I	Total Non-prod	17,200	Sum of G & H	06G+06H	Overhead Budget
	J	Total Ind. S. T.	96,000	Hrs/Period x Wage Rate	03BxO5J	Overhead Budget
	K	Total Ind. O. T.	4,320	Hrs/Period x O. T. Wage Rate	03DxO5K	Overhead Budget (O.T.)
	L	Total Ind.	100,320	Sum of J & K	06J+06K	Overhead Budget
	M	Prod. Ind. S. T.	90,000	Prod. Ind. x Wage Rate	03BxO5M	Statistic Analysis
	N	Prod. Ind. O. T.	4,050	Prod. Ind. x O. T. Wage Rate	03DxO5K	Statistic Analysis
	O	Total Prod.	94,050	Sum of M + N	06M+06N	Statistic Analysis
	P	Non-prod Ind. S. T.	6,000	J-M	06J-06M	Statistic Analysis
	Q	Non-prod Ind. O. T.	270	K-N	06K-06N	Statistic Analysis
	R	Total Non-prod. Ind.	6,270	Sum of P+Q	06P+06Q	Statistic Analysis
001	065 S	Total Labor Dollars	375,520	Sum of C+L	06C+06L	Statistic Analysis

EXHIBIT H

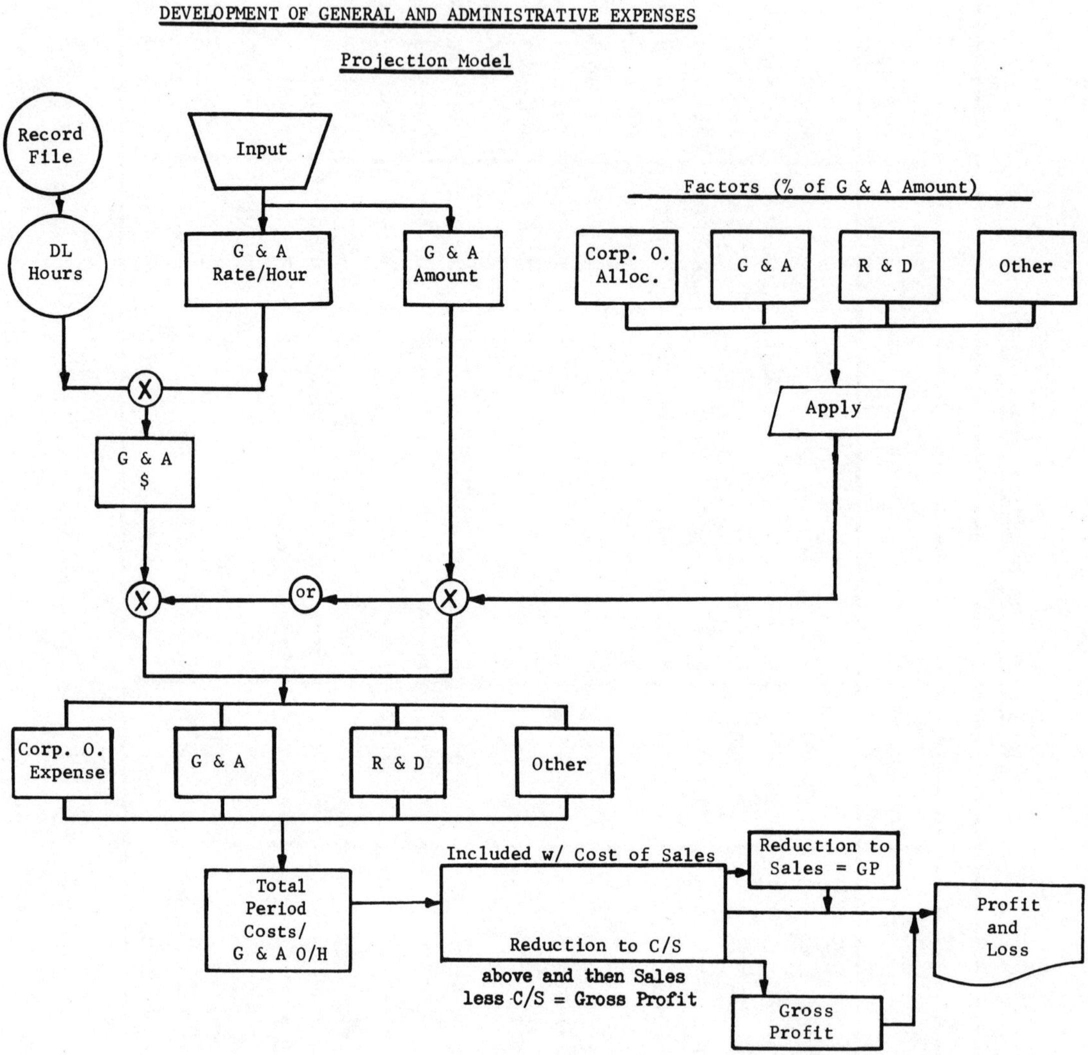

DEVELOPMENT OF GENERAL AND ADMINISTRATIVE EXPENSES
Projection Model
Record File
Input
Factors (% of G & A Amount)
DL Hours
G & A Rate/Hour
G & A Amount
Corp. O. Alloc.
G & A
R & D
Other
X
Apply
G & A $
X
or
X
Corp. O. Expense
G & A
R & D
Other
Total Period Costs/ G & A O/H
Included w/ Cost of Sales
Reduction to Sales = GP
Profit and Loss
Reduction to C/S
above and then Sales less C/S = Gross Profit
Gross Profit

EXHIBIT I

OVERHEAD FORECAST DEVELOPMENT
PROJECTION MODEL

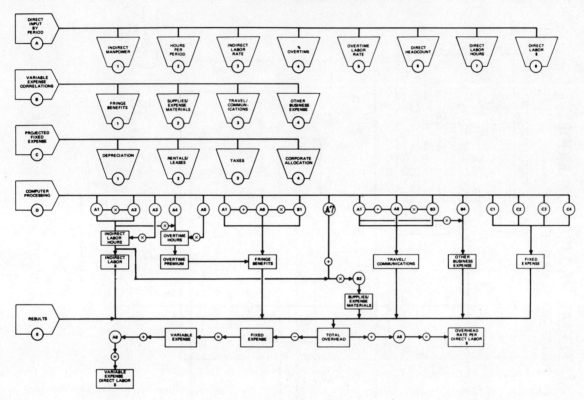

EXHIBIT J

perience. In another instance, indirect labor dollars plus the direct labor dollars (A8) are used with the formula to develop supplies and material expense—hours could have been used just as well, however.

Material and Other Costs

These direct costs represent purchases of material for production or experimentation, direct travel, subcontract effort, tool and test equipment purchases and other miscellaneous costs associated with a product cost. In cost type contracts, material costs are projected by a direct labor correlation and making allowances in the formula for anticipated price increases on future purchases. In production type contracts, material projections can be more easily predicted because of past history records on what is required

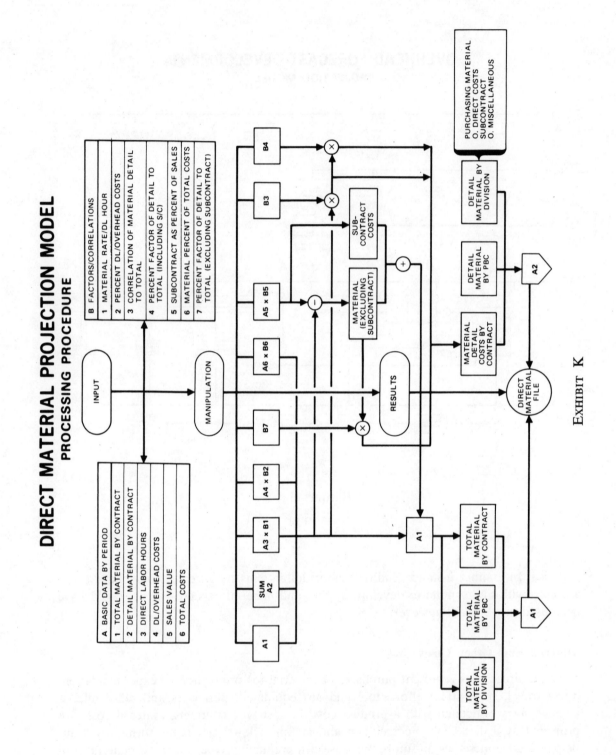

EXHIBIT K

and the associated costs of producing an item(s). The correlation is then based on production. Exhibit K displays the various means by which material costs can be projected.

The symbols shown on this chart are identifiers to the input and processing involved in developing both total material costs and/or its detail. Various formula combinations can be used depending upon an organization's most effective correlation.

Subcontractor Costs

As a prime contractor, these costs can be fairly significant and therefore should be highlighted in your reporting. Based on past experience or negotiation terms with the subcontractor, this cost can be accurately projected. In situations where this cost is nominal, it is best projected as a percent of total material costs.

Other Income and Deductions

Other income is not derived from operations but represents discounts earned, royalties, interest and dividends. Because of the variability of this account, it is a direct input based on known or anticipated future transactions.

Other deductions represent a reduction to the income from operations. It consists primarily of research costs, loss on sale of fixed assets, project abandonment expense, write-offs, etc. As in the case of other income above, the data for this account is a direct input.

Fee Rates

Cost type contracts are negotiated with costs and fees specified and therefore fee rates are readily determinable for projection on firm business. On potential business, however, the projection is predicated on historical experience.

On fixed price or commercial type contracts or sales orders, the profit margin has been included in the delivery price. Overrun and underrun of costs have a direct bearing on profits and therefore cost control is very important particularly on these type contracts—this is not to infer that cost control is unimportant on cost type contracts.

Sales and Profit Forecast

After the basic data described above has been developed by the computer and the direct input entered into the system, the data is processed to obtain the elements of costs, profit and sales as shown on Exhibit L. This display illustrates the cost type contract data flow.

This exhibit illustrates the step by step process in obtaining the end results in terms of sales and profit. It is noted that factory and engineering overhead is developed separately in order to obtain their individual rates. A definition of some of the lesser known abbreviations is noted as follows:

ID—Interdivision
CO—Corporate Office
ODC—Other Direct Costs

Cost and Manpower Development from Sales

With the tremendous capability of today's computers, the projection program can also include the means to start with projected sales and fee data and develop the details. Exhibit M displays this procedure.

As noted in this exhibit, the sales are divided by 100% plus the fee rate to obtain total costs. The costs reduced by the G & A expense yields the cost of sales. The elements of direct costs are developed by a correlation formula application to direct labor hours or as a percent of cost of sales. After developing the direct labor costs, the direct hours and manpower can be calculated as shown in the exhibit.

Advantages of "Up and Down" Projections

The advantage of projecting the profit and loss data both through detailed cost and fee development to sales or from sales and fee to costs is that this flexibility provides the capability to test your forecast both ways. It provides the opportunity of making changes in either direction and verifying results. Since the sales forecast is the most fundamental of all projections and because of its impact on most all other financial schedules, the success of the "whole plan" is contingent upon the soundness of the sales projections.

Manipulation of Sales, Costs and Fee Data

Upon development of the profit and loss data, the next step is to utilize this information in the preparation of other schedule projections. The following general procedure governs this process with respect to the major items and processes:

Direct costs are lagged (time element between accrual and disbursement) and set up as payable accounts in the balance sheet.

Upon payment to vendor, the transaction becomes a cash disbursement and a reduction is made to the concerned payable account.

Sales values are lagged (time element between invoicing the customer and receiving payment) and the amount is set up as a receivable in the balance sheet.

Upon receipt of payment from the customer, the transaction becomes a cash receipt and a reduction to the receivable accounts.

Indirect expenses are also lagged into payables until paid.

Cash Flow and Net Income

Exhibit N displays the development of cash receipts and disbursements as well as net income.

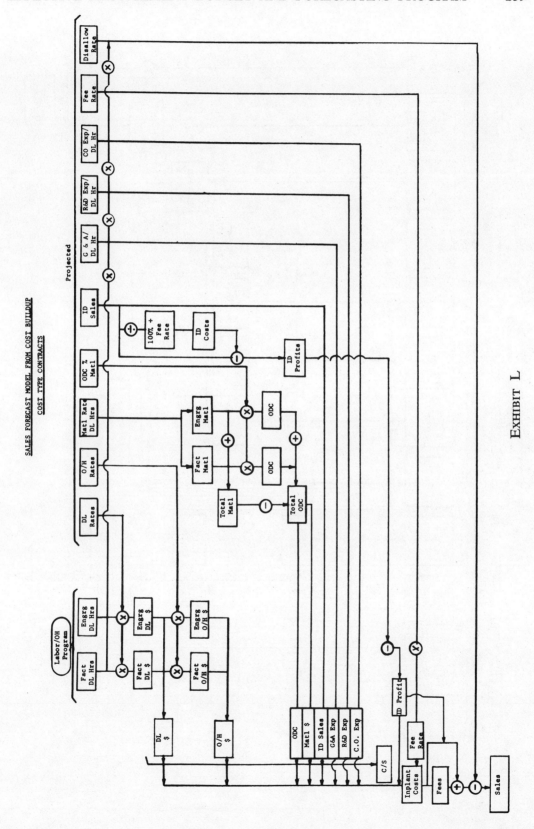

SALES FORECAST MODEL FROM COST BUILDUP

COST TYPE CONTRACTS

EXHIBIT L

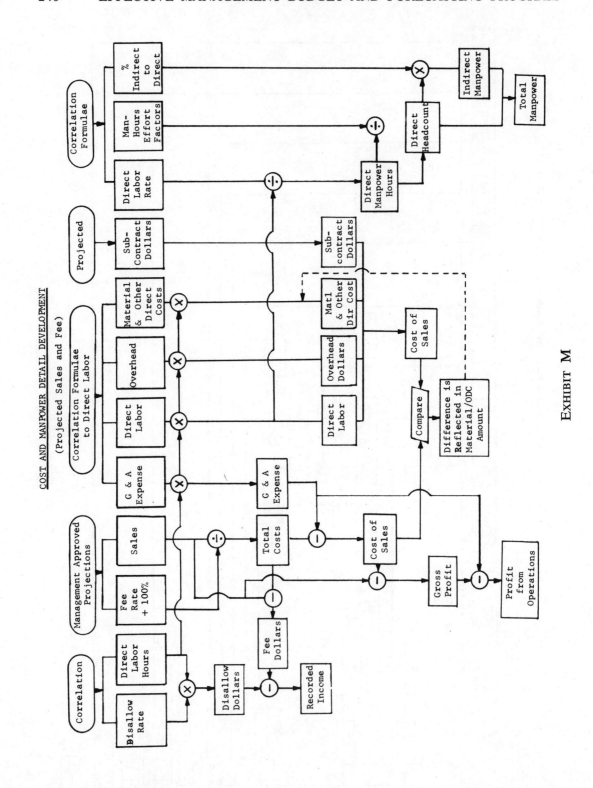

COST AND MANPOWER DETAIL DEVELOPMENT
(Projected Sales and Fee)

EXHIBIT M

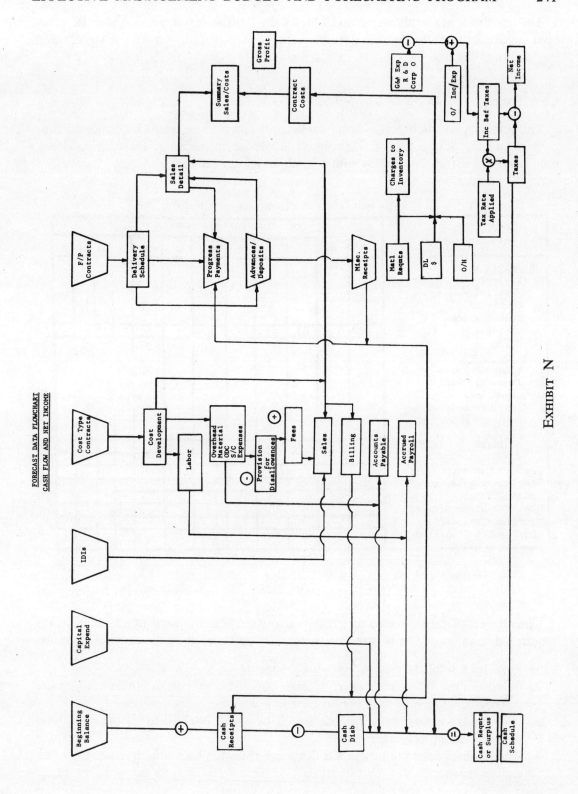

FORECAST DATA FLOWCHART
CASH FLOW AND NET INCOME

EXHIBIT N

This exhibit is self-explanatory and follows the pattern of the general manual processes involved in developing this data. It displays the interface between the profit and loss data and the cash flow to the cash schedule.

Cash Receipt and Disbursement Schedule

The summary cash schedule reflects the receipts and disbursements by projected time periods and the output format is displayed below. It encompasses the cash balances, requirements and/or cash surplus with a resultant ending balance.

Cash Receipts and Disbursement Schedule

Data Description	Projected Periods (Amounts in 000s)											
	J	F	M	A	M	J	J	A	S	O	N	D
Receipts												
Inplant												
Material												
Commercial												
Miscellaneous												
Total (1)	50	40	60	25	45	65						
Disbursements												
Accounts Payable							thru					
Gross Payroll							projected					
Fixed Assets							period					
Fed Income Taxes												
Property & O. Txs												
Dividends												
Total (1)	35	45	30	40	45	70						
Net Increase (Dec) (2)	15	(5)	30	(15)	--	(5)						
Beginning Balance (3)	20	20	20	20	20	20						
Ending Balance (4)	35	15	50	5	20	15						
Cash Requirements (5)	--	5	--	15	--	5						
Surplus Transfer (6)	15	--	30	--	--	--						
Ending Bal Projected (7)	20	20	20	20	20	20						

The above illustrates the type of schedule that would be produced to reflect all of the required data involved. As is noted, the computer performs the following calculations:

1. Provides a total for receipts and disbursements.
2. Calculates the difference between receipts and disbursements to obtain net increase or (decrease) in cash from period cash flow activities.
3. Uses an actual beginning balance which has been established as the cash level required during projected period.
4. Adds cash increases to or deducts decreases from the beginning balance to obtain ending balances.

5. Determines if cash is required—if the balance is below the (20) minimal established by policy or direction.

6. If cash balance exceeds the planned requirements, it is classified as surplus and a reduction to the balance on hand—generally released to the corporate office or used as loan "payoff."

7. Reports the established level of ending cash balance.

The above type of projection process is also a good control tool in that unusual cash requirements or surplus are highlighted and could be indicators to cash problems or the anticipated availability of cash for future needs.

Balance Sheet Development

The data used for projecting the balance sheet results from transactions that occurred in the cost, sales and cash development processes plus the beginning balances and unusual non-operational input. The following represents the major items and their source for this schedule development:

Cash—Ending balance from the cash schedule.

Accounts Receivable—Beginning balance plus customer invoicing less customer receipts (could also be employee or other type receivables but the principle of calculation is the same).

Inventory—Beginning balance plus purchases and less usage for work in process and advances to subcontractors.

Prepaid Expenses—Because of the variable nature of these accounts, the input is direct and based on past history records.

Gross Property—Derived from the prior period ending balance plus purchases from capital asset budget plan less planned sales or writeoff.

Depreciation—Derived from the prior period ending balance plus the expenses projected in the overhead budget. This amount is deducted from gross property to obtain net property or projected book value.

The total of the above represents the total assets although there can be others dependent upon an organization's operations and requirements.

Liabilities—Represent cost, loan or advance commitments plus beginning balance and less payments from the cash disbursement schedule.

Equity—Represents investment plus retained earnings.

As in the manual process, the computer totals liabilities and equity and compares this amount to the total assets and, if there is a variance, it is reported for correction. If the difference represents a certain established small tolerance due to the rounding process, then the computer makes an adjustment to the accounts payable balance for reconciling purposes.

ANALYSIS OF PROJECTED PLANS

Having generated the data discussed above, the following individual analyses are possible from the information projected:

Comparison of sales volumes and profits (project, contract, product line and total) to past actual performance and an analysis of variances.

Return on sales and investment comparisons.

Increase or decrease in cash flow representing cash requirements or surplus.

Borrowing and payback capability.

Cost performance improvement in operations or deficiencies.

Manpower growth or decline with its attendant requirement for facility expansion or contraction.

Need for new business in terms of current product sustenance or marketing new products and services.

Unusually high inventory and receivable balances that require attention.

The analysis of projected detail will reveal problem areas and this evaluation can be performed mechanically through a programmed exception comparison to past performance vs. the projected data and trends.

BUDGET AND ACTUAL DATA COMPARISONS

After the budget has been established as the plan of future operations, it will be stored in the computer files. As actuals become available, they will be compared mechanically to the plan and the variances will be reported on an exception report. Important comparisons that can highlight problem areas for further analysis or action would include the following:

Return on assets employed.

Sales volume, costs and profits.

Average collection period and debt payments.

Backlog status versus the plan and prior periods.

Certain meaningful ratios such as—annual net sales divided by inventory, investment and working capital; cost of sales divided by inventory and as a percent of sales; current assets divided by current liabilities; total debt to equity and number of days' sales in inventory.

The comparisons would be at any level of activity—contract, organization, product line, total operation, etc. It would be by period and year to date as well as a comparison to prior year, same period, statistics. Data comparison and evaluation is absolutely necessary in order to determine the operation status, problems, progress and efficiency. It also affords the concerned management to determine control requirements and provides them with the necessary data for their decision-making process.

CAPABILITY FOR INSTANT REVISION

The capability to make changes rapidly in the projection process is possible through the proper identification and organization of data in files and through the use of decision table techniques. Online access and data retrieval capability is highly recommended for revision processing. This will allow for obtaining immediate results due to changes, additions or deletions to the projected plan.

In organizing the file, each data set must be given its proper location and identification. The numbering must be sequential so that the computer program can recognize where the data is to be found for its manipulation process.

An example of the numbering identifications and sequential processing steps is displayed in Exhibits F, G and H which are concerned with the labor hour and dollar development as previously discussed. The procedures were also outlined for the overhead, material costs, etc. Revisions can be made to any data element and the results reflected throughout the entire budget or forecast based on revised premises.

As a preliminary step, however, to changing the actual forecast data, it would be advisable to initially do this on an online mode in order to determine the effects of the proposed changes. This is accomplished through the use of a "gaming" model or decision table technique wherein it is possible to test alternate courses of action with immediate results for evaluation. Exhibit 0 displays a profit and loss statement "gaming" model, the processing steps involved and the results.

This exhibit indicates four alternatives for financial statement development and its associated data. Provided with certain input designated by the "X" on the left-hand side of the exhibit, the projected results are shown on the right-hand side of the exhibit and in the sequential steps that the data is derived. There is no limit to the number of alternatives that can be utilized—it is dependent upon an organization's needs and complexity. A brief description of the model's operation is noted below:

Alternative 1—The primary objective is to obtain the sales and net income values having been provided with manpower, hours factor, wage rates, overhead rate, overtime %, material dollars, G & A, disallowance rate and fee %. This process typifies a cost type contract profit and loss development. The computer program

MANAGEMENT DECISION DATA DEVELOPMENT
PROJECTION "GAMING" MODEL

REPRESENTS INPUT AND/OR COMPUTER DEVELOPED DATA OUTPUT

ESTABLISHED INPUT AND/OR CHANGES

ID		I	II	III	IV
a	DIRECT MANPOWER (MP)	X	X		X
b	INDIRECT MANPOWER (MP)	X			X
c	% INDIRECT TO DIRECT		X	X	
d	MP HOUR FACTORS/PERIOD	X	X	X	X
e	OVERTIME % OF DIR LABOR HRS OR $	X	X	X	X
f	WAGE RATES (DIR/IND)	X	X	X	X
g	OVERTIME RATES (DIR/IND)	X	X	X	X
h	FEE % TO TOTAL COSTS	X	X		
i	DISALLOWANCE RATE/HOUR	X			
j	PROV. FOR TAX RATE	X	X	X	X
k	OVERHEAD RATE/DOLLAR	X	X		X
l	G & A RATE/DOLLAR	X	X		
m	DIRECT LABOR HOURS				
n	DIRECT LABOR DOLLARS				
o	DIRECT MATERIAL DOLLARS	X			X
p	OVERHEAD DOLLARS				
q	SALES DELIVERIES		X	X	X
r	G & A DOLLARS			X	X
s	OTHER INCOME & EXPENSE	X	X	X	X
t	NET INCOME % TO SALES			X	
u	CORRELATION FACTORS				
1	OVERHEAD TO DIR. LABOR $				
2	MATERIAL TO DIR LABOR HRS				
3	G & A TO DIR. LABOR $				
4	E.O.C. TO COST OF SALES			X	
5	G & A CATEGORIES TO TOTAL G & A			X	
6	MATERIAL CATEGORIES TO TOTAL MATL $				
v	SALES RATE/HEAD COUNT				
w	COST OF SALES % SALES				

NOTE:
Certain combinations of direct input or changes therto result in development of various data output in the sequential steps shown at the right of this exhibit. The "ID" represents data indentifiers.

ID		ALT. I SEQ STEP	ALT. I INPUT/CALCUL.	ALT. II SEQ STEP	ALT. II INPUT/CALCUL.	ALT. III SEQ STEP	ALT. III INPUT/CALCUL.	ALT. IV SEQ STEP	ALT. IV INPUT/CALCUL.
A	MANPOWER								
1	DIRECT	1	a	1	a	25	B1 ÷ d	1	a
2	INDIRECT	2	b	2	a x c	26	a x c	2	b
3	TOTAL	3	A1 + A2	3	A1 + A2	27	A1 + A2	3	A1 + A2
B	DIRECT LABOR HOURS								
1	STRAIGHT TIME	4	a x d	4	a x d	22	C1 ÷ f	4	a x d
2	OVERTIME	5	e x B1	5	e x B1	23	C2 ÷ g	5	e x B1
3	TOTAL	6	B1 + B2	6	B1 + B2	24	B1 + B2	6	B1 + B2
C	DIRECT LABOR DOLLARS								
1	STRAIGHT TIME	7	f x B1	7	f x B1	21	C3 – C2	7	f x B1
2	OVERTIME	8	g x B2	8	g x B2	20	e x C3	8	g x B2
3	TOTAL	9	C1 + C2	9	C1 + C2	19	E1	9	C1 + C2
D	SALES	23	H + K	10	q	1	q	10	q
E	COST OF SALES								
1	DIRECT LABOR $	10	C3	11	C3	18	E4 – E(2 + 3)	11	C3
2	OVERHEAD	11	k x C3	12	k x C3	17	u4 x E4	12	k x C3
3	MATERIAL	12	0	23	E4 – E(1+2)	16	u4 x E4	13	0
4	TOTAL	13	E (1+2+3)	22	H–G4	15	D – F	14	E (1+2+3)
F	GROSS PROFIT	24	D–E4	24	D–E4	14	K + G4	15	D – E4
G	GEN./ADMIN. EXPENSE								
1	G & A – MISC					13	G 4 – G(2+3)		
2	RES/DEV.					12	u5 x G4		
3	CORP. OFFICE					11	u5 x G4		
4	TOTAL	14	l x C3	13	l x C3	10		16	
H	TOTAL COSTS	15	E4 + G4	14	D ÷ 100% + h	9	D – I	17	E4 + G4
I	FEE DOLLARS	16	h x H	15	D – H	8	K	18	D – H
J	DISALLOWANCES	17	i x B1		–		–		–
K	ADJUSTED FEES OR PROFIT FR OPNS	18	I – J	16	I	7	M+/–L	19	I – J
L	OTHER INCOME (EXPENSE)	19	s (+/–)	17	s (+/–)	6	s (+/–)	20	s (+/–)
M	PROFIT BEFORE TAXES	20	K+/–L	18	K+/–L	4	0 ÷ 100% + j	21	K+/–L
N	PROV. FOR TAXES	21	j x M	19	j x M	5	O – M	22	j x M
O	NET INCOME	22	M – N	20	M – N	3	D x P	23	M – N
P	NET INCOME % SALES	25	O ÷ D	21	O ÷ D	2	t	24	O ÷ D
Q	OVERHEAD RATE/DL $	26	E2 ÷ E1	25	E2 ÷ E1	28	E2 ÷ E1	25	E2 ÷ E1
R	G & A RATE/DL$	27	G4 ÷ E1	26	G4 ÷ E1	29	G4 ÷ E1	26	G4 ÷ E1

B67021

EXHIBIT O

prices the manpower, generates the overhead and adds the material cost to obtain cost of sales. The G & A expense is calculated (application of the given rate to direct labor dollars) and added to the cost of sales in order to obtain total costs. The fee % is applied to the total costs to obtain fee dollars which are adjusted by the computed disallowances to obtain net fees. Total costs plus net fees (profit from operations) equals sales dollars. Profit from operations plus or minus other income/expense and less the tax provision results in net income. The specific program processing is reflected under the "Inp/Calc" column for each data element using the "ID" identifiers for simplicity rather than using the complete data descriptions. After the P & L has been developed, the appropriate information is reflected in the receivables, cash receipts, payables, cash disbursements, etc. The changes would be made to the projected cash schedule as well as the balance sheet and other relevant schedules.

Alternative 2—The primary objective in this alternative is to derive material dollars, cost of sales and net income having been provided with sales and fee projections plus other input parameters shown under the Alternative 2 column. As in the case of "Alt 2" above, the computer generates the balance of the data as shown.

Alternative 3—The primary objective is to obtain labor dollars, manpower and other costs having been provided with sales, net income % and other input under "Alt 3". The processing is shown, step by step, to accomplish this.

Alternative 4—The primary objective is to obtain net income and other values having been provided with sales and cost input. The processing steps involved are shown in the exhibit.

This type of gaming model affords flexibility in making various changes to the projections by testing alternate courses of action and deciding which is most representative of their anticipations.

EFFECT OF CHANGES TO PROJECTED DATA

Exhibit P displays the result of changes to sales volume for example.

As noted in this exhibit, revisions to sales can affect practically every financial data element—costs, profits, cash, receivables, payables, inventory, payroll, etc. The associated financial schedules and ratios would be influenced. This exhibit further indicates the necessity for data integration, proper file organization and linkage and data interface in order to reflect changes properly not only in the "actual" but also in the projection environment.

Mechanization of budgets and forecasts provides the capability to develop projections in detail and summary which can be readily adjusted to meet changing conditions and environment. Alternate courses of action can be preliminarily tested and thus provide

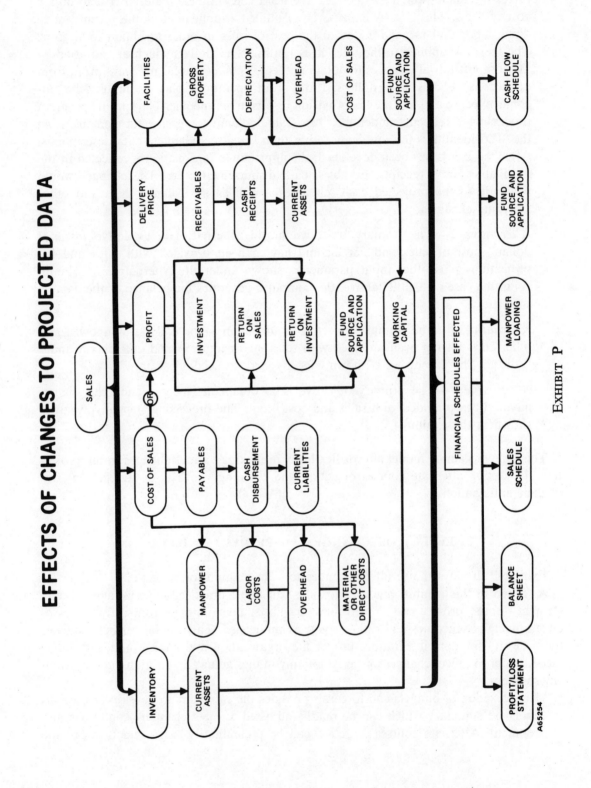

EFFECTS OF CHANGES TO PROJECTED DATA

EXHIBIT P

the means to select the final operation plan. Instant revisions and budget comparisons can easily be accomplished and evaluated. Clerical effort would be minimal and the greatest concentration of effort would be devoted to data and operation plan analysis and updating as required.

INFORMATION TECHNOLOGY
(SUMMARY)

- HERE TO STAY

- SCIENTIFIC TECHNOLOGY APPLICATION IS A MUST

- A MANAGEMENT TOOL FOR ASSISTANCE IN
        PLANNING
        CONTROLLING
        DECISION PROCESS

- MUST BE THOROUGHLY PLANNED

- MUST CONSIDER THE "TOTAL" INFORMATION ASPECT

- MORE EMPHASIS ON SYSTEMS TO REDUCE
  COSTS/DISAPPOINTMENTS ON COMPUTER END

- EVERY GOOD COMPUTERIZED INFORMATION PROCESS RESULTS
  FROM GOOD SYSTEMS' TECHNIQUES

- COMPUTERS ARE THE MEANS, SYSTEMS ARE THE WAY,
  MEANINGFUL INFORMATION IS THE NEED!

- MUST BE ORIENTED TO SPACE AGE PHILOSOPHY AND THINKING

A74418

Index